# THE
# INVITATION-
# ONLY
# ZONE

# THE INVITATION-ONLY ZONE

## The True Story of North Korea's Abduction Project

### ROBERT S. BOYNTON

ATLANTIC BOOKS
*London*

First published in the United States of America in 2016 by Farrar, Straus and Giroux,
an imprint of Macmillan Publishers, New York.

Published in hardback in Great Britain in 2016 by Atlantic Books,
an imprint of Atlantic Books Ltd.

10 9 8 7 6 5 4 3 2 1

A CIP catalogue record for this book is available from the British Library.

Hardback ISBN: 978 178 2398486
Export trade paperback ISBN: 978 178 2398509
E-book ISBN: 978 178 2398516

Printed and bound by CPI Group (UK) Ltd, Croydon, CR0 4YY

Atlantic Books
An Imprint of Atlantic Books Ltd
Ormond House
26–27 Boswell Street
London
WC1N 3JZ

www.atlantic-books.co.uk

*In memory of*

ALICE TYSON BOYNTON

*(1930–2013)*

# CONTENTS

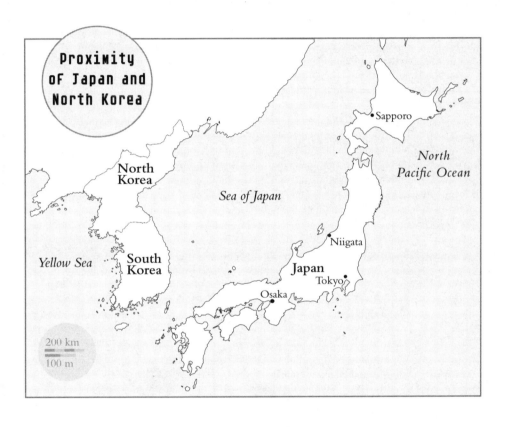

Proximity of Japan and North Korea

Sapporo

North Pacific Ocean

North Korea

Sea of Japan

Niigata

Yellow Sea

South Korea

Japan

Tokyo

Osaka

200 km

100 m

# KEY PEOPLE

Note: Japanese names are rendered first name/last name. Korean names are rendered last name/first name.

SHINZO ABE—Japanese prime minister from 2006 to 2007, 2012 to present

KAZUHIRO ARAKI—chairman of the Investigation Commission on Missing Japanese Probably Related to North Korea

KAYOKO ARIMOTO—mother of Keiko Arimoto

KEIKO ARIMOTO—abducted in 1983 while studying English in London

FUKIE (NÉE HAMAMOTO) CHIMURA—abducted from Obama, Japan, in 1978

YASUSHI CHIMURA—abducted from Obama, Japan, in 1978

CHOI EUN-HEE—South Korean actress and former wife of Shin Sang-ok, abducted from Hong Kong in 1978

KENJI FUJIMOTO—sushi chef who worked for Kim Jong-il, 1988–2001

TAKAKO FUKUI—girlfriend of Japanese Red Army Faction member Takahiro Konishi

TADAAKI HARA—chef abducted from Osaka, Japan, in 1980

KAORU HASUIKE—abducted from Kashiwazaki, Japan, in 1978

KATSUYA HASUIKE—daughter of Kaoru and Yukiko Hasuike

SHIGEYO HASUIKE—son of Kaoru and Yukiko Hasuike

TORU HASUIKE—older brother of Kaoru Hasuike

YUKIKO HASUIKE (NÉE OKUDO)—abducted from Kashiwazaki, Japan, in 1978

KENJI ISHIDAKA—TV Asahi producer, author of *Kim Jong-il's Abduction Command*

TORU ISHIOKA—Japanese student abducted from Barcelona in 1980

BRINDA JENKINS—daughter of Charles Robert Jenkins and Hitomi Soga

CHARLES ROBERT JENKINS—U.S. Army sergeant, defected to North Korea in 1965, married abductee Hitomi Soga in 1980

MIKA JENKINS—daughter of Charles Robert Jenkins and Hitomi Soga

KIM EUN-GYONG—daughter of Megumi Yokota and Kim Yong-nam

KIM HYON-HUI—North Korean agent who bombed Korean Air Flight 858 in 1987

KIM IL-SUNG—founder and leader of North Korea from 1948 to 1994

KIM JONG-IL—leader of North Korea from 1994 to 2011

KIM YOUNG-NAM—South Korean abducted in 1978, married Megumi Yokota in 1986

JUNICHIRO KOIZUMI—prime minister of Japan from 2001 to 2006

HARUNORI KOJIMA—abductee activist

TAKAHIRO KONISHI—Japanese Red Army Faction member

EDWARD S. MORSE—American zoologist (1838–1925)

HIROKO SAITO—emigrated from Japan to North Korea, 1963

KATSUMI SATO—director, Modern Korea Institute, abductee
    activist (1929–2013)

YASUHIRO SHIBATA—Japanese Red Army Faction member

SHIN KWANG-SOO—North Korean secret agent

SHIN SANG-OK—South Korean film director, ex-husband of
    Choi Eun-hee, abducted from Hong Kong in 1978

HITOMI SOGA—abducted from Sado Island, Japan, 1978

MIYOSHI SOGA—abducted with her daughter, Hitomi, from
    Sado Island, Japan, 1978

TAKAMARO TAMIYA—leader of the Red Army Faction
    (1943–1995)

HITOSHI TANAKA—senior Japanese diplomat

TAKESHI TERAKOSHI—abducted from Shikamachi in 1963;
    currently lives in Pyongyang, North Korea

TOMOE TERAKOSHI—mother of Takeshi Terakoshi

RYUZO TORII—professor of anthropology, Tokyo University
    (1870–1953)

SHOGORO TSUBOI—professor of anthropology, Tokyo
    University (1863–1913)

MEGUMI YAO—wife of Yasuhiro Shibata

MEGUMI YOKOTA—thirteen-year-old schoolgirl abducted from
    Niigata, Japan, in 1977

SAKIE YOKOTA—mother of Megumi Yokota

SHIGERU YOKOTA—father of Megumi Yokota

# THE
# INVITATION-ONLY ZONE

# PROLOGUE

People began disappearing from Japan's coastal towns and cities in the fall of 1977. A security guard vacationing at a seaside resort two hundred miles northwest of Tokyo vanished in mid-September. In November, a thirteen-year-old girl walking home from badminton practice in the port town of Niigata was last seen eight hundred feet from her family's front door. The next July two young couples, both on dates, though in different towns on Japan's northwest coast, disappeared. One couple left behind the car they'd driven to a local make-out spot; the other abandoned the bicycles they'd ridden to the beach.

What few knew at the time was that these people were abducted by an elite unit of North Korean commandos. Japanese were not the only victims, and dozens also disappeared from other parts of Asia, Eastern Europe, and the Middle East during the same period. In May 1978 a Thai woman living in Macau was grabbed on her way to a beauty salon. In July 1978 four Lebanese women were taken from Beirut; later that year, a Romanian artist disappeared, having been promised an exhibition in Asia. Some were lured onto airplanes by the prospect of jobs abroad; others were simply gagged, thrown into bags, and transported by boat to North Korea. Their families spent years searching for the missing, checking mortuaries, hiring private detectives and soothsayers. Only five were ever seen again.

Because the locations they were taken from were dispersed, and their numbers relatively small, almost nobody in Japan drew a connection among the incidents. A local paper slyly described one couple as having been "burned up" by their passion, the implication being that they had eloped after the woman became pregnant. Rumors about the disappearances surfaced periodically, but newspapers reported them as urban myths, akin to alien abductions. When the families of the missing went to the police, they were told that with no evidence of foul play, there was nothing to investigate. After all, thousands of people disappear from Japan every year, the police explained, dying lonely deaths or fleeing drugs, debts, or unhappy relationships. While some members of the Japanese government and police force became aware of the abductions, they avoided acknowledging them officially, which would have required them to take action. And what, after all, could be done? Japan had neither diplomatic relations with North Korea nor a military that could take unilateral action, and its mutual security treaty with the United States wouldn't be triggered by a handful of kidnappings. And what if a Japanese official raised the issue and North Korea hid the evidence by killing the abductees? "It can't be helped" (*Shikata ga nai*) is the phrase the Japanese commonly use to rationalize inaction. So, for the next quarter century, dozens of abductees were fated to languish in North Korea.

# 1

# WELCOME TO THE
# INVITATION-ONLY ZONE

On the evening of July 13, 1978, Kaoru Hasuike and his girlfriend, Yukiko Okudo, rode bikes to the summer fireworks festival at the Kashiwazaki town beach. The cool night air felt good against their skin as they whisked down the winding lanes of the coastal farming village 140 miles north of Tokyo. They parked their bikes by the public library and made their way past the crowd of spectators to a remote stretch of sand. It was a new moon, and the fireworks looked spectacular against the black sky. As the first plumes rose, Kaoru noticed four men nearby. Cigarette in hand, one of them approached the couple and asked for a light. As Kaoru reached into his pocket, the four attacked, gagging and blindfolding the couple and binding their hands and legs with rubber restraints. "Keep quiet and we won't hurt you," one of the assailants promised. Confined to separate canvas sacks, Kaoru and Yukiko were loaded onto an inflatable raft. Peering through the sack's netting, Kaoru caught a glimpse of the warm, bright lights of

Kashiwazaki City fading into the background. An hour later he was transferred to a larger ship idling offshore. The agents forced him to swallow several pills: antibiotics to prevent his injuries from becoming infected, a sedative to put him to sleep, and medicine to relieve seasickness. When he awoke the next evening, he was in Chongjin, North Korea. Yukiko was nowhere in sight, and his captors told Kaoru she had been left behind in Japan.[1]

Young Kaoru
(Jiji Press)

With his fashionably shaggy hair and ready smile, the twenty-year-old Kaoru Hasuike impressed those who met him as a young man who was going places. Like much of his generation in Japan, he wasn't interested in politics and knew almost nothing about Korea, North or South. Cocky and intelligent, he was at the top of his class at Tokyo's prestigious Chuo University. Yukiko, twenty-two, the daughter of a local rice farmer, was a beautician for Kanebo, one of Japan's leading cosmetics companies. She and Kaoru had been dating for a year, and he planned to propose once he finished his law degree. Japan's economy was surging ahead, and the future looked bright. He'd get a job at a corporation; they'd move from Kashiwazaki to Tokyo and build a life together. That was the plan, anyway.

The overnight train from Chongjin to Pyongyang was extremely bumpy, and by the time Kaoru arrived in the North Korean capital the next morning he was furious. "This is a violation of human rights and international law! You must return me to Japan *immediately*!" he shouted. His abductor watched calmly as Kaoru vented. When Kaoru saw that confrontation wasn't working, he tried evoking sympathy. "You have to understand that my parents are in ill health," he explained. Their condition would worsen if they worried about him. Surely his abductors could understand that?

The abductor listened to Kaoru's tirade in silence. "You know," he said, pausing for effect, "if you want to die, this is a good way to do it." He spoke in the flat, matter-of-fact way of one for whom such encounters were routine. He explained to Kaoru that the reason he had been abducted was to help reunify the Korean Peninsula, the sacred duty of every North Korean citizen. After all the pain his Japanese forefathers had inflicted on Korea, the man continued, it was the least that Kaoru, who had benefited from his country's rapacious colonial exploits, could do. Precisely how Kaoru would hasten reunification was left ambiguous, although the abductor hinted that he would train spies to pass as Japanese, and perhaps become a spy himself. The good news was that so long as Kaoru worked hard and obediently, he would eventually be returned to Japan.

The abductor saved his most astounding claim for last. Far from suffering from having been abducted, Kaoru would ultimately benefit. "You see, once the peninsula is unified under the command of General Kim Il-sung, a beautiful new era will begin," he explained. North Korean socialism would spread throughout Asia, including Japan. "And when that glorious day comes, we Koreans will live in peace. And you will return to Japan, where your experiences here will help you secure a position at the very *top* of the new Japanese regime!" Kaoru couldn't believe his ears. How could anyone make such preposterous statements?

While North Korea today is one of the poorest, most isolated nations on earth, when Kaoru was abducted in 1978, it was one of the most admired and prosperous Communist regimes in Asia. In 1960 the North's income per capita was twice that of the South's. Despite being nearly obliterated by American bombs during the

Korean War, the industrial North had enormous advantages over agrarian South Korea, having inherited 75 percent of the peninsula's coal, phosphate, and iron mines, and 90 percent of its electricity-generating capacity. So equipped, the North's economy grew by 25 percent per year in the decade following the Korean War.[2] In 1975 the North *exported* 328,000 tons of rice and corn.[3] The military dictatorship in South Korea, by comparison, was a basket case, its economy so far behind that its American backers feared it would never catch up. The bitter irony for Kaoru was that 1978 was precisely the year South and North Korea traded places, the former on its way to becoming a global economic powerhouse and the latter beginning its descent into destitution and even famine. In other words, it was the last point in history when the North's political and economic system was thought to be so self-evidently superior that its spies could snatch people off beaches, show them the glories of the North Korean revolution, and assume they would join the struggle.

Born in 1957, Kaoru Hasuike had a blissfully innocent childhood. Overlooking the Sea of Japan, Kashiwazaki was largely rural farmland at the time, and he and his older brother, Toru, would fish for carp, catfish, and snake heads in the Betsuyama River, which ran behind their house. The brothers were extremely close, and Toru's advanced knowledge of music and fashion helped Kaoru cultivate an aura of cool, worldly sophistication. An obedient, well-behaved child, Kaoru was captain of the baseball team and a student at the top of his class. Like so many creative, bright students of his generation, he grew more rebellious and bohemian, singing rock music and wearing hole-riddled jeans. In 1974, when Kaoru moved to Tokyo to attend university, the brothers shared an apartment. One day, Kaoru, ever careless, dropped a lit cigarette on a brand-new rug. Without pausing, he simply shifted a flowerpot to cover the smoldering hole. "He shot me that 'Aren't I clever?' look and lit up another cigarette," says Toru. "Kaoru had it all figured out."[4]

Now a captive and with no one to commiserate with, Kaoru was desperately lonely. Although he didn't have a religious background, he tried praying, placing his palms together and pressing them to his eyes. This display of piety elicited ridicule from his captors, because in North Korean movies the only characters who prayed were the cowardly Japanese prisoners begging for mercy. Not even sleep provided an escape, as Kaoru's dreams were filled with fantastical versions of his nightmarish days. "I had a recurring dream that some of my friends from back home in Kashiwazaki had been abducted and taken to North Korea, just like me," he says. "In the dream I'd see them and say, 'Oh no, they got you *too*?'"

A few months after arriving in Pyongyang, where he was kept in an apartment, Kaoru realized he was probably stuck there for the foreseeable future, the secretive regime not being in the habit of releasing witnesses to its espionage operations. He was certain that nobody in Japan knew what had happened to him, so he didn't expect any search parties or diplomatic missions to secure his release. Escape was impossible; three "minders" monitored him twenty-four hours a day, each taking an eight-hour shift. And even if he somehow managed to slip past them, where would he go? It wasn't as if he could count on receiving help from ordinary North Koreans, who would surely turn him in. The stories he heard about those who had tried to escape weren't encouraging. The regime had once assigned two military units, three thousand men in all, to capture an abductee who had managed to slip away. Kaoru wondered if he might be able to get help from one of the few Western embassies in Pyongyang. Then he heard about a female detainee who was forcibly removed from an embassy where she had sought asylum—a violation of international law. Kaoru took stock of his options. He was too young to give up on life, no matter how bizarre the circumstances. "As long as I didn't know the rea-son for my abduction, or what was going to happen to me, I felt that I couldn't just die like this," he says. But how could he sur-vive, cut off from everyone he loved and everything he knew?

Kaoru was given access to a restricted library that held a collec-tion of Japanese-language books about North Korea. Japan's post-war educational system dealt superficially with the period during which it colonized Korea and much of Asia, so most of what Kaoru was learning was news to him. He was surprised to find out that North Korea had a large following of international sympathizers, many of them in Japan. He read about the wartime exploits of Kim Il-sung's anti-Japanese insurgency, and the lengths to which ordinary Koreans had gone to resist the Japanese. "After some time, I had to admit that the people of this land had fought bravely against Japanese colonialism. I was able to rationally separate the troubled history of the Korean people from my forceful abduction," he says.

Over and over, Kaoru's captors told him he was in North Korea to help right the wrongs of his Japanese colonial forebears. His minders regaled him with accounts of how Japanese soldiers had raped Korean women, dragooned men into slave labor, and generally humiliated Korea's ancient civilization. "I was horrified by what they told me. I didn't doubt it was true, but I didn't know what it had to do with me," he says. Coming from the quiescent seventies generation of young Japanese, Kaoru had seldom heard history discussed with such vitriol. How had Japanese-Korean relations gotten to the point that, thirty years after the end of World War II, Koreans were so filled with hatred toward the Japanese that they talked about them as if they were a different species? How had the two cultures developed such a twisted relationship?

# 2

# THE MEIJI MOMENT:
# JAPAN BECOMES MODERN

The problems between Japan and Korea began long before 1910, when the former annexed the latter into its burgeoning empire. The Meiji Restoration of 1868 set Japan on the course to modernize its economy and culture in order to avoid being colonized by the West, and the two themes of modernization (renewing one-self) and colonization (ruling another) were thereafter intertwined. Forty years later, Japan imposed upon Korea the same practices it had adopted. It used the Western pseudoscience of racial classification to legitimize its actions, arguing that Japan and Korea's ancient racial kinship fated them to reconnect. As non-Western colonizers, the Japanese faced a dilemma: Could a classification scheme that white colonizers had deployed to distinguish themselves from the distant, darker colonized be applied to a nearby and similarly hued people? In other words, could a theory that bound Japan to Korea be construed to justify rule over it? Japan's answer—a brew of racial reasoning and military power—enabled it to build one of the largest empires of the twentieth century, and has poisoned relations between the two cultures to this day.

Japan had largely closed itself off to the outside world for two hundred years when U.S. Navy commodore Matthew Perry navigated the *Susquehanna*, a black-hulled steam frigate, into Edo Bay on July 8, 1853. He carried a simple message from President Millard Fillmore: if Japan didn't open its ports to U.S. merchant ships, Perry would return in a year, with more ships, and take Tokyo by force. In the decade before Perry appeared, the Japanese had watched with growing unease as their neighbors were subjugated by Western powers. With a modest navy and few modern weapons, it realized it had no choice but to accept Perry's terms. "It is best that we cast our lot with them. One should realize the futility of preventing the onslaught of Western civilization," argued the scholar Yukichi Fukuzawa in his essay "On Leaving Asia."

The Meiji era was proclaimed on October 23, 1868, when the fifteen-year-old emperor moved his residence from the Kyoto Imperial Palace to Tokyo ("eastern capital"). Charting a starkly different path from the previous government's policy of self-imposed isolation, the new imperial government decreed in the Charter Oath that "knowledge shall be sought throughout the world," and set Japan on the path of studying, emulating, and in many respects surpassing nations around the globe. The Japanese of the early Meiji years were fascinated by the "new," and would try anything as long as it was different from what came before. "Unless we totally discard everything old and adopt the new," the novelist Natsume Soseki wrote, "it will be difficult to attain equality with Western countries." Japan's first minister of education urged his countrymen to intermarry with Westerners in order to improve Japanese racial stock, and proposed adopting English as the national language.[1] Japan built railroads, public schools, and modern hospitals; it established a banking system, a postal network, and a modern military. With the end of the feudal system, people were for the first time free to choose their occupations, rather than follow in their fathers' footsteps; and new industrial inventions provided many new professions for them to pursue. Children attended free public schools; and as literacy rates soared, so did the number of books and newspapers.

Japan's fascination with the West was reciprocated. In 1876, eight million people visited the Philadelphia Centennial Exhibition to view thirty thousand exhibits from thirty-five nations. The United States showcased George H. Corliss's steam engine, Alexander Graham Bell's telephone, and the Singer sewing machine. Japan's investment in the exhibition was second only to that of the United States, and included an entire pavilion filled with elaborate bazaars and exquisitely tended gardens. Compared with Japan's, other countries' displays looked "commonplace, almost vulgar," noted *The Atlantic Monthly*. "The Japanese collection is the first stage for those who are moved chiefly by the love of beauty or novelty in their sight-seeing. The gorgeousness of their specimens is equaled only by their exquisite delicacy."[2] Visitors praised the clean lines and simple elegance of Japanese design. Following the Centennial Exhibition, America went Japan crazy. New Englanders, with their transcendentalist philosophy and love of nature, were particularly smitten. "How marvelously does this world resemble antique Greece—not merely in its legends and in the more joyous phases of its faith, but in all its graces of art and its senses of beauty," wrote the journalist and Japanophile Lafcadio Hearn.[3]

Among those attendees who became captivated by the exotic country was Edward Sylvester Morse. A zoologist who specialized

Edward Sylvester Morse (Wisconsin
Historical Society)

in the study of shell-like marine animals known as brachiopods,
Morse was spellbound by Commodore Perry's descriptions in his
*Journals* of the shells he had spotted along Japan's coastline. On paper, Morse wasn't the most academic character. Born in Portland,
Maine, in 1838, he was a restless boy with the kind of intellectual
curiosity and vivid imagination more suited to expeditions than to
the classroom.[4] When Morse was twelve, his oldest brother, Charles,
died of typhoid, and the minister who led the funeral decreed
that, not having been baptized, Charles would spend eternity in
hell. After his death, their father, a preacher, grew more rigidly
religious, denouncing Edward's passion for science as an affront
to God. Morse's mother, however, was so enraged by the minister's words that she vowed never again to set foot inside a church.
Edward, too, became a rebel, and by the time he was seventeen,

he had been expelled from four schools. Although eventually awarded several honorary degrees, he never earned one himself.

Morse escaped the confines of life in provincial Portland by searching for shells on the Maine coast. Portland had a rich history of trade with destinations all over the world, and sailors regularly returned with strange-looking shells, some of which were sold for vast sums. Morse amassed an enormous collection of native New England specimens, which drew the attention of scholars from around the country. At age seventeen he presented a paper to the Boston Society of Natural History, which named one of his discoveries, *Tympanis morsei*, after him. Word of Morse's collection spread to Harvard, where Louis Agassiz held the university's first chair in geology and zoology. The Swiss-born Agassiz was one of the most famous scientists in the world, having made his reputation by proving that much of the globe was once covered by glaciers. A superb promoter, he convinced New England's Brahmins to support science and, specifically, to fund the construction of the world's largest Museum of Comparative Zoology, where he intended to display his specimens. In Morse, Agassiz found a young man with the intelligence and energy to catalogue his vast holdings; in Agassiz, Morse found a father figure who, unlike his own father, encouraged his scientific work. "There is no better man in the world," Morse wrote of Agassiz in his journal. Paid twenty-five dollars per month, plus room and board, Morse became one of Agassiz's assistants, an elite group, destined to become some of America's foremost natural historians and museum directors. A classically educated European, Agassiz was as much their mentor as their employer, inducting them into the modern priesthood of science, while also urging them to study history, literature, and philosophy. Conscious that he was the only one in this group without a college degree, Morse became a diligent student, attending lectures on zoology, paleontology, ichthyology, embryology, and comparative anatomy, while also cataloguing thirty thousand specimens in his first year.

Morse arrived in Cambridge in November 1859, the month Charles Darwin published *On the Origin of Species*. A pastor's son, Agassiz couldn't bring himself to replace the biblical creation story with the theory of evolution, and became one of Darwin's foremost critics. Morse read Darwin's book with excitement but was careful not to antagonize his mentor while he considered the validity of Darwin's revolutionary ideas. By 1873, however, he had fully embraced Darwin. "My chief care must be to avoid that 'rigidity of mind' that prevents one from remodeling his opinions," he wrote. "There is nothing [more] glorious . . . than the graceful abandoning of one's position if it be false." He sent Darwin a paper in which he used his framework to reclassify brachiopods as worms rather than mollusks. "What a wonderful change it is to an old naturalist to have to look at these 'shells' as 'worms,'" Darwin replied.

Having broken with his mentor, Morse left Harvard and discovered he was such an entertaining speaker that he could earn five thousand dollars a year lecturing on popular science. He illustrated his lectures with detailed sketches, drawing with both hands simultaneously, a bit of chalk in each.[5] During a San Francisco lecture, he learned that the waters of Japan held dozens of species of brachiopods that were unknown in the United States. In the spring of 1877, Morse boarded the SS *City of Tokio*.

On the evening of June 18, Morse's ship moored two miles offshore from Yokohama, and the next day he took a rickety boat to the mainland, rowed by three "immensely strong Japanese" whose "only clothing consisted of a loin cloth," he wrote in *Japan Day by Day*. He was overwhelmed by the foreignness of the lively city. "About the only familiar features were the ground under our feet and the warm, bright sunshine," he wrote. Morse brought a letter of introduction to Dr. David Murray, a Rutgers College professor of mathematics who had been appointed the superintendent of educational affairs for the Japanese Ministry of Education and charged with creating an American-style public school system from grade school through university. Although private academies existed in pre-Meiji Japan, the Sino-centric curriculum was largely restricted to the teachings of Confucius. The Japanese wanted universities comparable to the great institutions that Europe had taken centuries to build, and they wanted them now. The Ministry of Education received a third of the government's total budget for the project, and Murray was given two years to get Tokyo University up and running.

Foreigners were forbidden from traveling outside Japan's designated treaty ports, so the only way for Morse to explore for brachiopods was to get special permission, which he hoped Murray would help him with. To reach Murray's office, he rode the recently completed train line eighteen miles to Tokyo University, which had welcomed its first students three weeks before. As the train approached the village of Omori, it traversed two mounds through which the tracks had been laid. A cockleshell dislodged by the digging caught Morse's eye. "I had studied too many shell heaps on the coast of Maine not to recognize its character at once," he wrote. It was a five-thousand-year-old *Arca granosa*.

Murray introduced Morse to several Japanese colleagues with whom he shared his passion for science. They found his excitement contagious, and made an astounding proposal. Would Morse establish a department of zoology and build a museum of natural history at Tokyo University? In return, they would provide him a biological laboratory, moving expenses, and a professor's salary of five thousand dollars per year. Darwinism had arrived in Japan during a period of drastic cultural change, and they wanted a

Western expert who could explain these foreign ideas.[6] Morse was asked to teach a class on modern scientific methods and give a series of public lectures on Darwin. Hundreds attended the lectures, and Morse was pleased both by the enormous size of the audience and by its openness to the idea of evolution. "It was delightful to explain the Darwinian theory without running up against theological prejudice, as I often did at home," he wrote. Not only were the Japanese not Christians, but the Meiji government was hostile to the creed, which it perceived as a threat to its authority. When Morse argued that "we should not make religion a criterion of investigating the truth of matter," he no doubt pleased Japan's bureaucrats and scientists alike.

With Murray's aid, Morse returned to Omori several weeks later with his students. "I was quite frantic with delight," he wrote. "We dug with our hands and examined the detritus that had rolled down and got a large collection of unique forms of pottery, three worked bones, and a curious baked-clay tablet." In order to cross-date the artifacts with ancient flora, fauna, and fossils, Morse and his students used the modern method of digging one layer at a time, a technique that had never been used before in Japan.[7] Morse's book *The Shell Mounds of Omori* (1879) was the first published by the university's press.

One of the most profound revolutions inspired by Darwin's *Origin of Species* was in the study of early human history, as the notion of "prehistory," the time before recorded history, led scholars to use physical remains to chart human development from "savagery" to "civilization," a hierarchy of cultural advancement Darwin later expanded upon in *The Descent of Man* (1871).[8] After Darwin, scholars who had searched far and wide for disparate clues to human development focused their research on chronicling the successive generations who had inhabited a single place, such as Omori. What Morse found at Omori puzzled him. Among the shells and pottery fragments were broken human bones mixed in with those of animals—not what one might find at a typical burial site. "Large fragments of the human femur, humerus, radius, ulna, lower jaw, and parietal bone, were found widely scattered in the heap. These were broken in precisely the same manner as the deer bones, either to get them into the cooking-vessel, or for the purpose of extracting the marrow," he wrote.[9] It was impossible to avoid the conclusion that the people who had once dwelled in Omori had been cannibals. Judging by the age of the bones, Morse didn't believe the cannibals were *direct* ancestors of either the Japanese (whom he praised as the "most tranquil and temperate race") or the indigenous Ainu (who were neither cannibals nor potters). Rather, he concluded, the artifacts had been produced by a pre-Japanese, pre-Ainu tribe of ancient indigenous people.

Morse's discovery gave birth not only to modern Japanese anthropology but also to the questions that would obsess the discipline for the next seventy-five years: Who were the Japanese people's original ancestors? Where did they come from? And how were they related to the fast-modernizing Meiji-era Japanese? Much as Western technology gave the Japanese control over their future, Darwin's theories provided the tools with which to understand their past. Like explorers embarking on an expedition to chart a new world, anthropologists were on a quest to create a modern map of Japanese origins.

Morse's best student was Shogoro Tsuboi, the twenty-two-year-old son of a prominent doctor. Tsuboi grasped the enormity of the revolution reshaping geology, biology, and the social sciences, and formed a study group that spent weekends excavating near Tokyo University and discussed their findings at evening salons. A cosmopolitan intellectual, Tsuboi studied in London for three years under the great anthropologist Edward Burnett Tylor, who used Darwin's system of classification to divide humanity into

Ryuzo Torii (second from right) and Shogoro Tsuboi (right)

racial groups.[10] When Tsuboi returned home, he introduced the new discipline to Japan by publishing in popular journals and lecturing widely on anthropology and evolutionary theory.

The Western, biological conception of race did not exist in Japan before this period,[11] and Morse's essay "Traces of an Early Race in Japan" was the first time it was applied to Japan. In pre-Meiji Japan, identity and class distinctions came from the customs, not the blood, one shared with a peer group. For millennia, Asian culture had been dominated by China, and it was believed that a country's level of civilization was determined by how far it was from the Chinese emperor. Indeed, Korea interpreted its own proximity to China as evidence that it was more civilized than Japan. In the hands of intellectuals such as Tsuboi, race took on a more biological and scientific significance than ever before.

Tsuboi was particularly eager to use historical anthropology to investigate the origins of the Japanese. Employing Darwin's schema, he reasoned that cultures, like species, develop unevenly, with the vigorous and adaptive jumping ahead and the isolated and recalcitrant lagging behind. He observed that European archaeologists of the day drew analogies between tools produced by Stone Age people and implements used by contemporary aborigines in New Guinea—the implication being that one could detect traces of ancient civilizations in the amber of surviving primitive cultures. If Western scholars could draw direct analogies of this sort, why couldn't Japanese scholars do so as well? It irked him that Morse, author of the much-resented cannibal hypothesis, was credited as the founder of Japanese anthropology, and going forward Tsuboi felt it should be a strictly Japanese affair. When he became the university's first full professor of anthropology, he removed Morse's Omori shell mounds from the museum to make room for "far more valuable specimens" collected by Japanese researchers. Tsuboi envisioned Japanese anthropology as a self-sufficient branch of social science, with Japanese scholars studying the history of the Japanese people in Japan. "Our research materials are placed in our immediate vicinity," he wrote. "We are living in an anthropological museum."

How were the Japanese different from other Asian peoples? Since they couldn't differentiate themselves by skin color, scholars argued that the difference had to do with the advanced level of "civilization" Japan had achieved. It was not an argument in favor of racial purity. In fact, Tsuboi championed racial pluralism, comparing Japan's diversity to Britain's mix of Irish, Scots, and English. "It is a mistake to believe that a race should be pure and that complexity is bad. Being a mixture is truly a blessing," he wrote. But the West's science came with nineteenth-century racial prejudices. Foremost among them was the privileged place that "whiteness" held in relation to darker races, and the way skin color was thought to correlate with one's level of civilization. The question facing the Japanese was whether it was possible for them to appropriate the Western concept of race without dooming themselves to an inferior place in the global hierarchy. Were they more closely related to the white West or to their darker Asian neighbors? The science of race proved to be a double-edged sword, and it is no wonder many Japanese scholars began to replace the Japanese word for biological "race" (*jinshu*) with the word for "ethnic group" (*minzoku*).[12] The vaguer concept of an ethnic group, one sharing a common history and culture, provided more room for the Japanese to maneuver as they reconceived their place in the world.

Ryuzo Torii (Tokushima Prefectural Torii
Ryuzo Memorial Museum)

As a boy, Ryuzo Torii spent long afternoons reading Commodore Matthew Perry's *Journals* (1854), imaging what Japan was like when it opened to the West. Born in 1870, two years into the Meiji era, Torii was raised on Shikoku, the most placid of Japan's four main islands, located in southwest Japan. He had a privileged childhood, growing up in a household full of servants, supported by his family's successful tobacco business. "If I wanted something, my parents bought it for me," he wrote succinctly in his memoir, *Notes of an Old Student* (1953).

Teachers in the Meiji era tended to be former samurai, noblemen who had been replaced by the emperor's new professional army. Disarmed, they traded their swords for books, although they kept their hair in the traditional style (pulled back) and wore kimonos over billowy silk pants and wooden sandals. Torii made a point of skipping their classes, interpreting their appearance as proof they were hopelessly out of touch with the exciting changes sweeping Japan. His favorite teacher wore modern, Western-style jackets and ties and had adopted a similarly forward-looking pedagogical style that favored empiricism and experience over rote memorization. On nice days, class would be held on nearby Mount Bizan, and the surrounding plants, trees, rivers, and hills were used to exhibit the lessons of botany and geography. Torii was thrilled to discover how much one could learn simply by exploring the natural world, and he yearned for adventures like those he heard about in the Saturday sessions when the teacher read aloud from books such as *Robinson Crusoe*.

Torii quit school when he turned nine. "One of my teachers told me I wouldn't be able to survive without an elementary school certificate. I told him I could do better at home by myself," he wrote. He found inspiration in Samuel Smiles's book *Self-Help* (1859), a Victorian paean to perseverance, which was a bestseller in Japan. "Every human being has a great mission to perform, noble faculties to cultivate, a vast destiny to accomplish," wrote Smiles. "He should have the means of education, and of exerting freely all the powers of his godlike nature." Torii's family supported his decision, buying him all the books he wanted, including the first Japanese-English dictionary. In the morning, a tutor would give him English lessons at home; in the afternoon, he'd scour nearby tombs for pottery and other artifacts; in the evening, he'd pore over scientific encyclopedias, history books, and archaeology studies, curating his growing collection.

One afternoon, Torii stumbled upon Yukichi Fukuzawa's *All the Countries of the World* (1869), an illustrated geography textbook with a color-coded portrait of humanity. The book's first sentences changed Torii's worldview forever. "There are five kinds of human races: Asians, Europeans, Americans, Africans and Malaysians. The Japanese are part of the Asian race," it read. Torii was familiar with "Westerners" and "Asians," but he was surprised by the additional diversity. "I had always thought that everyone else in the world was more or less the same," he wrote. What did it mean to belong to a race? he wondered. With this question, Torii was swept up in the Meiji-era effort to generate a Japanese national identity with which to navigate the modern world.

In September 1890, Torii, twenty, embarked on the three-hundred-mile journey from Shikoku to Tokyo. He had been following the development of Japanese anthropology from afar, reading the books and magazines in which the new scientific method was being applied to geology and archaeology. Torii had even submitted an essay on his fieldwork on Shikoku to the Tokyo Anthropological Society's journal, which Shogoro Tsuboi edited. Impressed with the young man's pluck, Tsuboi became Torii's mentor, invited him to study with him in Tokyo, and put him to work classifying specimens at the Anthropology Research Institute. Like many other young men in the Meiji era, Torii was gripped by "city fever" (*tokainetsu*) and mesmerized by Tokyo, spending his days exploring bohemian bookshops and teahouses, writing poetry, and studying German.[13] When not attending lectures, he pored over the precious English-language anthropology texts—E. B. Tylor's *Primitive Culture*, Sir John Evans's *The Ancient Stone Implements, Weapons, and Ornaments of Great Britain*—kept in the library's protective glass case.

In order to establish the journal's reputation as a center for modern research, Tsuboi included an English-language table of contents and discouraged breezy meditations from office-bound academics by stipulating that he would accept only articles based on "direct field observations."[14] Every issue included tales of expeditions from the northernmost reaches of Siberia to the distant islands of the South Pacific. Tsuboi needed a steady supply of intrepid explorers, and Torii was eager to oblige. Torii became the Japanese Indiana Jones, chronicling his adventures in bestselling books. Like Tsuboi, Torii was a true cosmopolitan. He studied the Incas in South America, and his books were translated into French and awarded the Ordre des Palmes Académiques. He was among the first anthropologists to use photography in his ethnography, often illustrating his pieces with photographs of "exotic natives," in which he himself occasionally appeared.

Studying with Tsuboi, Torii resurrected his fascination with race. "From the point of view of civilization and human solidarity, they are in an unhappy state that merits our pity," he wrote about Taiwan's indigenous people. "But for the anthropologist, they constitute a marvelous field of studies. To what race of the human species do these populations belong?" Torii never missed an opportunity to embark on field trips, usually accompanied by his wife, Kimiko, an anthropologist who studied Mongolian history. He supplemented his university salary with journalism assignments, which both paid well and made him famous. Both literally and metaphorically, Torii's career tracked the course of Japanese colonialism, with the explorer often arriving soon after

Ryuzo Torii, 1896 (© University Museum,
University of Tokyo)

Japan's troops. Japan had just won the Sino-Japanese War when he arrived in China in 1895. In 1905 he went to Manchuria and Mongolia, conducting research in the areas where Japan had only months before defeated the Russian army. He made his first trip to Korea in 1911, and to Siberia in 1919, shortly after both territories were occupied by the Japanese.

The argument about Japan's origins fell into two camps. The first held that the Japanese were a homogeneous people who had lived, relatively unchanged, in the same place for millennia. The other argued that the Japanese were a hybrid people whose ancestors drew from Korea, China, and other parts of Asia, synthesizing the most advantageous traits from each. The theories coexisted, each dominating different periods of Japanese history, depending on the political situation. When Meiji leaders were first fashioning an ideology to keep citizens obedient to the emperor, the notion of Japan as a homogeneous nation came to the fore. As the empire expanded across Asia, it made sense to characterize the Japanese as a collection of different Asian peoples.[15]

Torii's voice was the most influential in the hybrid camp. He argued that the Japanese synthesized the best characteristics of indigenous cultures from Manchuria, Korea, Indochina, and Indonesia. In addition to archaeological evidence, he cited the existence of contemporary Japanese people who possessed continental faces, southern features, and curly hair. Torii labeled the Stone Age group who synthesized this multicultural brew the "Japanese proper," a hybrid people who arrived in Japan after the Ainu, bringing sophisticated practices such as pottery, metallurgy, and monument building.[16] Korea played a large part in this project, as it did in Torii's career. "I have a particularly close relationship to Korea," he wrote. "Korea has become the center of economic, cultural and material trade between the Asian continent and Japan, which should be happily welcomed." Torii called Korea Japan's "mythical and beloved ancient motherland," which was why he favored uniting them in the modern era. "Korea is just like any other region of Japan such as the Kyoto-Osaka-Kobe region or Kyushu," he wrote in a 1920 essay. Even if the two are not quite as close as brother and sister, he adds, "Koreans and Japanese are equivalent to one's parent's cousins." Torii cited studies that found affinities between the two countries' language, material culture, religion, and customs. "Koreans are not racially different from Japanese. They are the same group and thus must be included in the same category. This is an anthropological and linguistic truth that cannot be changed."[17]

The dominant theory was that the Japanese were an amalgam

of races that had traveled to the archipelago and formed a nation whose cultural achievements towered over everyone else's. In other words, although Asians were racially similar, some nations, such as the Japanese, had advanced further than others. Whether this was because of their system of government or their cultural prowess wasn't certain. But as the Japanese Empire expanded and brought more races into the fold, the Japanese public turned to intellectuals such as Torii to explain how it was that the Japanese could colonize people with whom they shared so much.

# 3

# REUNITED IN NORTH KOREA

In May 1980, Kaoru Hasuike received the first good news since he'd arrived in North Korea twenty-two months earlier. He was summoned to his minder's office, where several of the officials who oversaw his education were waiting for him. The news? His girlfriend, Yukiko, with whom he had been abducted, was in North Korea after all. In fact, she was in the next room. Would he like to see her? "Yes!" Kaoru replied, so quickly that he was embarrassed.[1]

It turned out that the story about Yukiko being left behind in Japan had been a ruse designed to force Kaoru to cut all ties to Japan, leaving him with no choice but to accept his situation. In reality, she had been undergoing the same pedagogical routine: learning Korean, studying the regime's ideology, wondering whether she could survive in this strange country. Like much else in North Korea, their isolation had been staged. They had been living barely a mile apart and were overseen by the same minder, who shuttled back and forth between them. At the very least there was now *one* other person who could understand what the other was going through.

By the time of Kaoru and Yukiko's abduction, North Korea had perfected the process. All ships departing from North Korea in the 1970s were tracked by South Korean intelligence, so the spies would steer northeast to the Sea of Okhotsk, before doubling back toward Japan, where it would melt into the many fleets of Japanese fishing vessels to avoid being detected on radar. Once in international waters, it would release several smaller boats stowed in its rear. These vessels were disguised to look like Japanese fishing vessels; their users would conceal the presence of their high-speed engines by venting the exhaust underwater.

The strategy was to grab young Japanese couples from beaches and parks, and separate them before they arrived in North Korea. Isolation was the key variable. The regime found that it generally took a year and a half to break an individual down into a state of psychological helplessness, during which time they could teach him the Korean language and introduce him to *juche*, the regime's

Yukiko Hasuike
(Kyodo)

official ideology. If all went according to plan, they would begin to build him back up right before he descended into a state of absolute despair. Having experienced the total control of the North Korean state, he would become passive and compliant. The process had been tried with intact couples, but it was observed that the presence of a partner encouraged the abductees to resist, collaborate, and occasionally fight back. On the other hand, an abductee who was completely isolated for too long was *more* difficult to control; loneliness had a way of turning into depression and even, in some cases, led to suicide. But if the correct balance was maintained and the couple was separated, trained, and then reunited, the options were unlimited. They could serve the state together, whether as spies or language teachers, each functioning as a hostage with which to threaten and manipulate the other—a strategy the North routinely employed with Korean diplomats, athletes, and anyone else given permission to travel abroad.

Kaoru and Yukiko married three days after reuniting. "I would have done it that morning," says Kaoru. "I didn't want to wait." North Korean marriage ceremonies are straightforward affairs, with none of the opulence typical in the West. The groom received a haircut and was outfitted with a new white shirt and a necktie; the bride wore a simple flower-patterned dress. Six guests attended: Kaoru and Yukiko's minder (the man who guided their education and oversaw every aspect of their lives in North Korea), the two high party officials who oversaw their minder, their driver, the woman who cooked the food for the wedding party, and the barber who cut Kaoru's hair. Jewelry and adornments of any kind are frowned upon, so rings were not exchanged. The ceremony was officiated by the most senior official present, who opened by invoking the blessings of the Great Leader, Kim Il-sung. Kaoru and Yukiko then thanked their superiors for bringing them to the socialist paradise and allowing them to marry, and everyone bowed deeply before the photo of the Great Leader that hangs on the walls of every house and office in North Korea. Everyone raised his glass, shouted a hearty *Geon Bae!*, and sang a Workers' Party of Korea standard. It wasn't the wedding they'd dreamed of, of course, attended by family and friends, but it was the first time Kaoru and Yukiko had participated in a normal event since they'd been abducted, and it meant that, whatever their future held, they'd face it together.

The most important wedding gift a North Korean newlywed couple can receive is a home in which to start their new life. Because there is no private property, the gift is from the state and can be withdrawn at any time. The Hasuikes' first home was a traditional one-story cinder-block house an hour south of Pyongyang. Painted white, it had a wooden roof with ceramic tile shingles, and five rooms: a kitchen, two bedrooms, a living room, and a bathroom. In the back was a small garden where Kaoru learned to grow eggplant, cucumbers, lettuce, cabbage, and peppers. He got seed and fertilizer by trading cigarettes with a farmer from a nearby food cooperative, and arranged for a cow to till the field at the beginning of the growing season. The rest of the work he did himself. He had become fond of the spicy kimchi that had troubled his stomach when he first arrived, and now he made it for himself in the traditional manner, stuffing cabbage and hot red peppers into clay pots and burying them in the yard to ferment.

The smallest organized social unit in North Korea is the "people's group" (inminban), of anywhere between twenty and forty households, each with the duty of monitoring the others and providing labor for parades and state celebrations. The head of each group works with the resident police officer to make sure that everyone is properly registered and that all radios and television sets are rendered incapable of receiving signals other than those broadcast by the state. In addition, the Ministry of State Security has a network of informers, reputedly maintaining one for every fifty adults, for a total of three hundred thousand.[2] Even when there were no overt signs of surveillance, Kaoru and Yukiko knew they were always being observed.

Their house was located in one of the many mile-square, guarded Invitation-Only Zones that dotted suburban Pyongyang. The area served a dual function by limiting its inhabitants' freedom while warning nosy outsiders that only those "invited" to enter were welcome. All North Koreans develop a heightened sensitivity to coded language, and knew well enough to avoid anyplace that required an "invitation." Still, the area's euphemistic name did little to keep Kaoru from perceiving it as the gilded cage it was—a spacious, well-tended prison inside the secretive state. The Hasuikes' neighbors were an odd assortment: abductees, spies, and foreign-language experts—anyone whose access to outside information made him or her a threat to the regime's carefully crafted official narrative. Living in the area wasn't punishment, and in fact the housing and food supply were of a higher quality than that enjoyed by most North Koreans. As part of its attempt to control the flow of information into the country, the North grants few visas to foreign visitors, and rarely permits those allowed in to stay for more than a week. Therefore, the cluster of Japanese abductees provided a rare opportunity for the North's spies, many of whom would infiltrate Japan, to observe them in the way one might observe the habits of caged zoo animals.

With small clusters of houses fanning out from a central building, each separated from the others by densely wooded artificial hills, the Invitation-Only Zone was designed to discourage private contact among residents. At its center, the roads converged on a large guesthouse, which had spaces for meetings and classes. Monday was the designated study day, but when the New Year Editorials or Kim Il-sung's new policy declarations were published, work was suspended and everyone would retreat to the guesthouse and study for several days straight.

As much as Kaoru loathed the people who had abducted him, he was touched by the kindness and humanity of the ordinary Koreans he met. The cooks in the zone were usually women in their fifties whose husbands had been killed in the Korean War. The managers were unmarried young women in their twenties who prized the job because it came with membership in the Korean

Workers' Party, a credential that could help them marry someone of higher status. Kaoru was in a frail state of mind and was grateful for the kindness of "Granny Kim," a cook at the first of several Invitation-Only Zones he lived in during his time in North Korea. The combination of despair and an unfamiliar cuisine had caused him to lose weight, and the kindly cook prepared him blanched spinach and pickled cabbage in the milder Japanese style he was used to. Later, when his liver acted up and no suitable medicine was available, she prepared a traditional Korean remedy from roots and herbs. She treated him as a member of her family, confiding that she had lost her husband in an accident and had supported her three children by working in a munitions factory before becoming a cook. She raised his spirits with stories of her weekend visits to Pyongyang, when she brought her grandson snacks and candies. Kaoru was alone at first, so he sometimes ate with Granny Kim and the other workers. One night over dinner, his inhibitions lowered by a few glasses of beer, he told them the story of his being abducted from Japan. Using a combination of pantomime and primitive Korean, he described being beaten, put in a bag, and dragged to a boat. Kaoru had been instructed by his minder to keep the episode secret, but he hoped that Granny Kim and the others would show some sympathy for the ordeal he had been through. At first the women refused to believe it. How could their beloved country do such a thing? "But in their expressions, if not in their words, I knew that they felt empathy for me," Kaoru says.[3] It felt good to have bonded with a few other people. But a week later, his minder scolded him for divulging the state secret. Evidently, one woman's sense of duty had trumped her empathy, and she reported Kaoru's indiscretion. He was beginning to understand that in North Korea, loyalty to the state is the highest value.

As a married couple, Kaoru and Yukiko received the standard

allotments of food, delivered three times a week, even in the 1990s, when many North Koreans experienced hardship and famine. Food rationing is the regime's primary means of social control, and with the exception of small farmers' markets and home-grown produce, all staples (rice, vegetables, meat, poultry, and fish) are allocated through the public distribution system. In normal times, a working adult, depending on his occupation, receives 700–800 grams of grain a day. The elderly receive 300–600 grams, and children get 100–500 grams, depending on their age. White rice is the most prized staple, and any shortfall is filled with less desirable grains like wheat, corn, and barley. In addition, as "employees" of the state, Kaoru and Yukiko were each paid ten won per day, with which they could purchase additional food in private markets, usually at exorbitant prices. Chinese cabbage, cucumber, and eggplant were cheap, but apples, pears, and meat were expensive. If Kaoru was lucky enough to find a store selling pork, the meat was usually half fat. It wasn't anything like the abundance he had experienced in Japan, but he was grateful for what he got. One day an encounter with someone living outside the zone made him appreciate how well off he and Yukiko were, relative to ordinary people. "If the people could all eat as you do in the Invitation-Only Zone, then I guess we could say that the true Communist society had been realized," a man told him. "I sensed he was jealous, and in the future I was careful not to talk about how much food we had."

Kaoru did what he could to make the house feel more like a home. "In the same way that, as a child, I made up games without toys or playmates, I found ways to play by myself in the Invitation-Only Zone."[4] He carved a mahjong set out of wood and taught his wife to play. Although he hadn't played golf in Japan, he spent several weeks clearing a nearby area to create a five-hole golf course. He drew on his memories of watching the game on television to come up with something approximating the rules, and played obsessively, using balls made from glued-together cotton swabs. "As idiotic as it may seem, I was so starved for play that my golf course was a lot of fun." On occasion he'd dream he was back home. He'd stare out the living room window at a hill that resembled one in Kashiwazaki that he used to climb to look out over the ocean. "I'm going to climb to the top of that hill so I can see the water on the other side," he told himself, well aware that Pyongyang is a landlocked city and the quest for the ocean view was folly. Still, one day he sneaked out and scrambled up to the top of the steep hill just to see what was there. On the other side was a flat, dusty landscape. "The crazy thing is that even after I saw it with my own eyes, I still felt there should be an ocean behind that hill."[5]

The newlyweds fell into a routine. Every morning, after being woken up by the announcement coming from the loudspeaker that is installed in every North Korean house and workplace, Yukiko would prepare a traditional Korean breakfast of miso soup, rice, eggs, and kimchi. After breakfast Kaoru would go for a run, taking a route past identical small white cottages, down the paths that cut through the hills and trees. It wasn't a terribly long run, however, because after a few thousand yards, he would see the barbed-wire fence peeking above the trees.

Once a week, the theater on the second floor of the neighborhood center screened movies, usually educational films filled with revolutionary propaganda. Kaoru quickly realized that the first few movies screened were expressly directed at him: *Team 4/25* told the story of a North Korean soccer team touring Japan, the underdog beating the slick, arrogant Japanese—an unsubtle message about precisely who was in charge. Movies are one of the primary media through which the regime communicates with the people, and virtually every town in North Korea, no matter how small, has at least one theater. "There are no other tools in art and literature as powerful as cinema in educating people in a revolutionary manner," writes Kim Jong-il in his book *On the Art of the Cinema* (1973). "As an ideological weapon, it is crucial to produce a highly ideological artistic film for the education of the masses." Kim's first job had been running the Central Committee's Propaganda and Agitation Department, an organization responsible for stoking the people's revolutionary spirit via movies and other media. One of the most popular movie series at the time was *Unsung Heroes*, a multipart Cold War saga in which North Korean spies match wits with an evil American CIA agent, played by Charles Robert Jenkins, an American soldier who had defected to the North in the 1960s and later married a Japanese abductee. Another favorite was *Pulgasari*, the 1985 *Godzilla* remake directed by Shin Sang-ok, the South Korean film director whom Kim Jong-il abducted in 1978 along with Choi Eun-hee, Shin's glamorous actress ex-wife (known as the Elizabeth Taylor of South Korea). Kim kidnapped them in the hope they would revitalize the North Korean film industry. He treated them like (captive) royalty, hosting parties and dinners in their honor, in return for which they made seven films. Most nights, Kaoru and Yukiko stayed at home and watched the news on one of the two official television stations, Pyongyang Central Broadcasting and Kaesong Broadcasting, which were on air only from five until eleven each night. At eight o'clock, the news would end and a movie would begin. If they were lucky, the electricity would hold out long enough for them to see the whole thing. If not, they'd go to bed early.

During their captivity, the Hasuikes were moved ten times between and within various Invitation-Only Zones, occupying a house anywhere from one week to one decade. Sometimes it was simply a question of supply and demand; other times, the moves were designed to reduce the abductees' visibility by relocating them to ever-more-remote locations. Whenever news about the abductions surfaced in Japan, Kaoru and Yukiko had to pack up their belongings and move. The question of their needs or desires never arose. The power of the North Korean regime over its citizens is absolute. Much as Koreans were dictated to by Japan during the thirty-five years they lived under colonial rule as "children of the emperor," Kaoru and Yukiko, as citizens of North Korea, sublimated their own desires in order to serve the all-powerful Great Leader, Kim Il-sung.

# 4

# JAPAN AND KOREA'S
# "COMMON ORIGINS"

In their study of Western imperialism, Meiji intellectuals noted that the most successful world powers possessed colonies.[1] Having a colony was a status symbol, marking a nation as international and modern, and between 1876 and 1915, one-quarter of the globe's land surface was controlled by a half dozen Western states.[2] Nineteenth-century colonialism was condoned by international law, and Japan was careful to employ recognized legal procedures as it extended its borders.[3] It was also careful to distinguish itself from Western colonizers, whom it characterized as interlopers, driven solely by their desire for power and money. Japan, however, characterized itself as a unifier, not a conqueror, with a duty to *protect* Asia from the West. There had been few instances in world history of a nation subjugating an ethnically similar nation— England's amalgamation of Wales, Scotland, and Ireland was noted—so Japan's brand of colonialism was idiosyncratic from the start. The foundation of its pan-Asianist political rhetoric was the "common origins" (*Nissen dosoron*) theory that Japan and Korea shared an ancient ancestral lineage, a theory Japan augmented with the new sciences of archaeology and anthropology to argue that its expansion was rationally justified. How could any nation defend itself against an army that flew the flag of modernity itself? In particular, Ryuza Torii's historical analysis of the Japanese as simultaneously inviolable and protean—the core "Japanese proper" synthesizing the best of other Asian ethnic groups—gave the project a veneer of intellectual respectability, implying that Japan was superior precisely because it had been forged through natural selection. Japan's first conquest was China, which it defeated in 1895. The terms of the peace treaty gave Japan possession of Taiwan and forced China to release its grip on Korea. Japan further bolstered its reputation as a modern power in 1905 by defeating Russia, which possessed the largest army in Europe. It was the first triumph of a nonwhite nation over a white one, and was celebrated in Japan and throughout Asia as evidence of Darwin's theory of the "survival of the fittest."

Another lesson Japan learned from the West was that modern states "catalogue" their pasts, funding surveys and archaeological excavations and exhibiting historical artifacts in museums.[4] Beginning in 1895, the Meiji government dispatched dozens of anthropological and archaeological teams throughout Asia to record the history of the empire it was assembling. "It is most important for Japan to have, in place of general ethnology and ethnography, the ethnological and ethnographic studies specialized on Asia," Torii wrote. "Japan is no longer what it used to be, but has obtained those people of the colonies who are the most interesting from an academic point of view."[5] Japan literally wrote the first draft of Korean history in a thirty-eight-volume encyclopedia, which folded Korea's past into Japan's new narrative of Asian his-

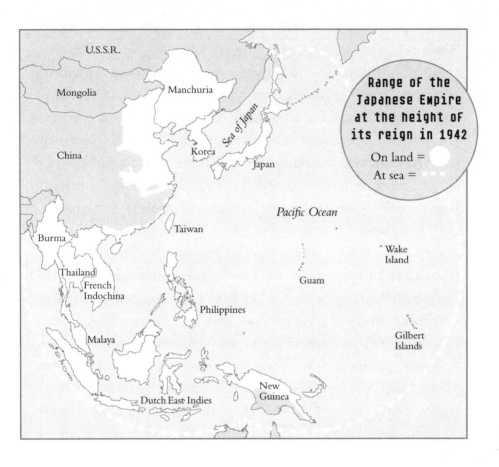

tory. The Korean Peninsula received the most extensive attention from anthropologists, whose studies served a dual role: first, to preserve the historical record. The second role was more practical: to document the culture and customs with which colonial administrators would have to contend. One of the main points of dispute between the two countries was that Korea had refused to acknowledge the recently "restored" emperor Meiji as the Chinese emperor's equal. Having taken its cues from China for hundreds of years, the Korean royal court couldn't conceive of a world with two emperors, so it snubbed a series of Japanese emissaries. The affront provided diplomatic cover for the Japanese takeover of Korea.

On September 20, 1875, the *Unyo*, a small Japanese gunboat, landed at Ganghwa Island, thirty miles west of Seoul. The Koreans shelled the intruder, an action that, according to international law, justified return fire. With its modern armaments, Japan won easily, and the resulting Japan–Korea Treaty of Amity imposed on Korea the same terms the United States had imposed on Japan nearly twenty years earlier. It opened the country to trade, reduced Chinese influence over it, and made it accept various internal reforms. Japanese troops were stationed in Korea, ostensibly to protect the Japanese merchants now permitted to work there, but in reality the troops were used to begin Japan's conquest of Asia, with Korea as the staging ground.

Japan's takeover was an act of slow-motion colonization. Korea was forced to sign the Japan–Korea Protectorate Treaty in 1905, after which Japan installed a "resident-general" to oversee Korea's international affairs. In 1906, Japan convinced the United States to place the country under the rubric of Japan on official maps, deleting all references to Korea. In 1907 it demobilized the Korean army and forced King Kojong to abdicate. Finally, on August 29, 1910, Japan officially annexed Korea. The major world powers accepted Japan's narrative of a dissipated Korea that had, through corruption and misgovernance, lost the capacity for self-rule and would benefit from Japanese oversight. The Japanese were careful to distinguish between Korean leaders (inept, corrupt) and the Korean people (proto-Japanese, full of potential), and predicted that Korea would thrive as part of the Japanese Empire. Japan classified Korea as a "new territory" and referred to the annexation as an "extension of the map," euphemisms designed to obscure the true nature of the relationship.[6]

The Japanese media portrayed Korea's capitulation as inevitable.

"The Annexation of Korea Is a Natural Course of Events," read the headline to an Osaka *Asahi Shimbun* editorial. "Judging from history, anthropology, and linguistics, there are no doubts that a close relationship existed between Japan and Korea," it explained.[7] And that relationship was embodied in even the highest level of Japanese society. A November 1910 editorial in *Taiyo* drew a biological link between ancient Korea and the Japanese royal family: "Korean blood runs in the veins of many Japanese noble families, even those of the Imperial family."[8] An article compared Koreans who resisted Japan to "Japanese who were hostile to Westerners when Japan's doors were opened" twenty years before. The notion that Japan was recapitulating its experience of modernization in order to save Korea was expressed succinctly by the historian Kunitake Kume. "This is not an Annexation, but a Restoration," he wrote.[9]

Annexation was embraced by Japan's Koreaphiles, who saw the peninsula as a prelapsarian paradise, an idealized version of what Japan had been like in a purer, simpler time.[10] Korea seemed like an antidote to the overly Western nation Japan had become. Tourists on nostalgic package tours visited ancient temples and archaeological sites discovered by explorers such as Ryuzo Torii. "I feel as though I were living three thousand years back," wrote the diplomat Inazo Nitobe of his 1906 visit. Korea was promoted as an ideal destination for summer retreats, its climate praised as "the most pleasant and agreeable in the empire."[11] By 1910, there was a proliferation of guidebooks and travel journalism about Korea, which became an essential stop for Japanese citizens trying to understand their growing multicultural empire. "Now anyone can travel in Korea and experience the same beauty and level of efficient and convenient service as we do in Japan proper (*naichi*), since there is now no difference between Korea and Japan," advised one guidebook.[12]

Japan's domination over Korea was cruel, exploitative, and ruthlessly efficient. But the gravest damage, both to Japanese-Korean relations and to Korean national identity, was inflicted by Japan's often-successful campaign to appropriate Korean culture. Many Koreans had watched enviously as Japan modernized itself during the Meiji era, and the synthesis of modern and colonial rhetoric made it difficult for even the most nationalist Koreans to reject all aspects of Japanese rule. "Aggression and exploitation also coincided with fairly remarkable development and a learning-by-doing experience of how education, military, polity, and economy can be modernized," writes historian Bruce Cumings. "Thus the Japanese set up a love-hate conflict that has gnawed at the Korean national identity ever since."[13]

For the first ten years, Japan ruled primarily through its military might—until March 1, 1919, when two million Koreans took part in a well-coordinated protest for national independence. The Japanese army put down the protest violently, but the passion behind the Koreans' actions made the government realize its policies were ineffective.

Between 1920 and the late 1930s, Japanese rule relaxed somewhat, granting Koreans limited freedom of expression in a strictly regulated environment, treating them more like an ethnic subculture—Korean was called a "dialect" of Japanese—than a subjugated people. Rather than depend solely on the threat of violence (although that was always an option), the Japanese co-opted Korean pride instead of trying to eliminate it.[14] They exploited the ambiguity between ethnic and national identity to create an intellectual space where Koreans could experience simultaneously Korean ethnic pride and Japanese nationalism.[15]

The most brutal, and best remembered, period of colonialism was from the late 1930s through 1945, when Japan accelerated the pace of assimilation, forcing Koreans to speak Japanese, take

Japanese names, and worship at Shinto shrines. Korean men labored in Japanese factories and mines, and Korean women were dragooned into sexual slavery as "comfort women" for the Japanese military.

No manipulation or coercion was required, however, for Koreans to see that, under the Japanese, their economy had leapfrogged from late feudalism to twentieth-century capitalism. Railroads, mines, and factories were built as Korea became more urbanized and less rural. Modern agricultural techniques and new chemical fertilizers increased rice output. Mortality rates declined and literacy rates increased.[16] Colonial subjects were awarded citizenship, with the same (limited) privileges of native-born Japanese.[17] Starting in 1920, Koreans who lived in the Japanese isles had the right to vote.[18] Intermarriage between Japanese and Koreans was encouraged, the most famous example being the royal marriage of Korean crown prince Uimin and Japanese princess Masako.

The reforms gave birth to a new class of assimilated Koreans, a small group of educated urbanites who provided evidence that it was possible (though not easy) to better oneself under Japanese rule. Those opportunities only increased as Japan mobilized for war and more Koreans than ever joined the Japanese establishment at every level.[19] The police force and military were particularly popular routes for upward mobility, and by 1943 one-third of Korea's colonial police force was composed of Korean officers.[20] Two hundred twenty thousand Koreans fought in the Japanese Imperial Army and Navy, where they developed reputations as some of the fiercest combatants. Unlike the segregated U.S. Army, the Japanese armed forces integrated Koreans, promoting seven to the rank of general and others to positions where they commanded Japanese soldiers.[21] Kim Il-sung's brother was an interpreter for Japanese troops in China,[22] and Park Chung-hee, South Korea's future president, served in the Imperial Army, swearing he was "both physically and spiritually ready to be a Japanese subject and . . . willing to give my life for the emperor."[23] The Japanese colonizers set the terms for acceptable civic, political, and cultural activities, and Koreans throughout the peninsula "collaborated" through the simple act of living their lives. As in other authoritarian systems, such as North Korea today, one had few other choices.

By the end of the Second World War, four million Koreans were living outside their homeland, and one million Japanese civilians and troops were living inside Korea.[24] Imperial Japan had become a hybrid Asian nation at precisely the moment when the entire project collapsed. With the loss of the Japanese Empire came a need for a new theory of Japanese identity. If one role of the "common origins" theory had been to tie Japan to its colonies, it became irrelevant to a postwar Japan that had been stripped of them. Although the outlines of the theory were still supported by the historical and archaeological record, the politics of the era called for a new story for Japan, in which it played a less aggressive, less ambitious role. It didn't take long for Japanese intellectuals to fill the space left by Torii's now-unpopular ideas.

In 1948, Kotondo Hasebe, head of the Anthropology Department at Tokyo University and soon to be the president of the Anthropological Society of Nippon, published a paper on a human pelvic bone that had been discovered near the city of Akashi.[25] In "On the Primitive Nature of the Human Pelvis (Plaster Model) Discovered in the Old Pleistocene Stratum of Nishi-yagi, Near the City of Akashi," Hasebe classified what he called Akashi Man, along with other early examples of *Homo erectus*, such as Java and Peking Man.[26] For Hasebe, Akashi Man was evidence of the

Japanese archipelago's uninterrupted line of inhabitants, from the Paleolithic period to the present. The discovery of Akashi Man was the first step that Japan's postwar social scientists took to replace the bankrupt narrative of the militaristic, multinational empire. Hasebe expanded his thesis in his 1949 book, *The Formation of the Japanese People*, which was part of a series, The New History of Japan.

The image of Japan as a tranquil, homogeneous nation was attractive to a people who had tired of war and empire, and it quickly became the dominant paradigm, inspiring a popular intellectual genre (*Nihonjinron*) in which philosophers, historians, and psychologists parsed the causes of Japan's unique cultural identity. The default assumption was that Japan was a nation of peace-loving farmers and fishermen on an isolated island lacking any significant exposure to alien peoples. Those who, following Torii, had championed the mixed-race, common origins theories that dominated pre-1945 Japan were shunted aside and given teaching positions at minor universities.[27]

In postwar Korea, the notion that the peninsula had been continuously inhabited by a pure Korean race may have been the only thing the North and South agreed upon. The rhetoric of racial purity thrived in part because it fed the nationalist politics that each Korea used against the other as they competed over which better embodied pure "Koreanness," the common goal being to distance themselves from Japan's assimilationist policies.[28]

The quest to root out the traces of Japanese influence that pollute Korean purity continues to this day. South Korea banned the import of Japanese CDs and DVDs until 2004, and in 2005, it established the Truth and Reconciliation Commission, part of whose charge was to create the definitive list of Koreans who had collaborated with the Japanese almost a century before. As the scholar B. R. Myers argues, "Having been ushered by the Japanese into the world's purest race, the Koreans in 1945 simply kicked the Japanese out of it."[29]

In December 2001 the Japanese emperor Akihito used part of his annual message to the nation to acknowledge his Korean ancestors. "I, on my part, feel a certain kinship with Korea, given the fact that it is recorded in the *Chronicles of Japan* that the mother of Emperor Kammu was of the line of King Muryong of Paekche," he said. Confucian and Buddhist philosophy, court music, and much else in Japanese culture had arrived via the peninsula, he explained, adding, "I believe it was fortunate to see such culture and skills transmitted from Korea to Japan." The emperor ranged widely over the state of Japan at the press conference, whose contents the reporters present duly summarized. His comments about the royal family's Korean roots, however, did not appear in any of the accounts, other than a brief mention in the *Asahi*. The common origins theory was so tied up with imperial Japan's erstwhile ambitions, that neither the political left nor the political right wanted to think about it. The emperor's attempt to make common cause with Korea, and foster a better relationship with Japan's neighbor, was ignored.

# 5

# ADAPTING TO NORTH KOREA

When he was first abducted, Kaoru Hasuike realized that if he was to survive, he had to learn Korean. He had always been a good student and now threw himself into his studies, memorizing the Hangul alphabet, in which the Korean language is written. It was a solitary task, without language labs, conversation partners, or other pedagogical aids. One of his minders doubled as a language tutor, but Kaoru was generally left to fend for himself, using textbooks designed for the few foreign exchange students from Russia and Eastern Bloc or socialist countries at Kim Il-sung University. Study took his mind off his plight, and he was surprised to discover the structural and linguistic similarities between Japanese and Korean. Within nine months, he could read the official newspaper, *Rodong Sinmun*, with the aid of a dictionary. The articles were unlike anything he'd ever encountered in newspapers back home, with pages of praise for Kim Il-sung interspersed with denunciations of South Korea, Japan, and the United States. With the exception of the positive light shone on the heads of Communist countries who offered a steady stream of compliments, the world outside North Korea was portrayed as hostile and dangerous, obsessed with bringing the good, pure people of the nation to their knees through embargoes and military threats.[1]

Kaoru's minder instructed him to keep a journal, which the minder would read and correct. It quickly became apparent that the goal of the exercise was less to improve Kaoru's language skills than to give the minder access to his thoughts. The minder encouraged him to write "freely" about any subject he liked. Kaoru winced at the word. Indeed, in North Korea the word *freedom* usually carried negative connotations, as did phrases like *liberal democracy* and *democratic values*, which were used as euphemisms for the hostile ideology behind U.S. militarism. Under constant surveillance, Kaoru valued what little freedom he retained, such as the freedom to think, and vowed never to give his captors access to his innermost feelings. He was careful not to write about his family or his longing to return home to Japan. He found that the only way to keep from lapsing into depression was to push his desire to see his family as far down as possible. "I made sure that there was no way that my words could be misconstrued," he says. As a result, his journal entries read like the work of a bored elementary school student ("I woke up at six to exercise, ate breakfast, and studied from nine until . . .").[2]

"Isn't there anything *else* you would like to write about?" his minder inquired. "But every day here is the same," Kaoru responded, mustering as much good-tempered provocation as he dared. Surprised by his charge's honesty, the minder nodded in agreement, a small, conciliatory gesture that revealed a trace of compassion. Afterward, Kaoru wrote more politically correct entries, praising public works projects ("The new dam was very impressive . . .") and other developments he knew North Koreans were proud of. Reviewing these pages, the minder nodded with relief, as he now could present them to his superiors as evidence of Kaoru's successful reeducation. Kaoru realized that the minder was only a cog in a larger machine, and feared the consequences of failing as much as anyone else in North Korea did. While Kaoru at first assumed all the officials he met were villains, he gradually learned to distinguish those with genuine humanity from the petty tyrants who took revenge on him for the pain inflicted on Korea by Kaoru's forebears.

His original minder had learned Japanese during the colonial era and lived abroad afterward, so was familiar with the world beyond North Korea. He went to some lengths to understand who Kaoru actually was, drawing on his knowledge of the culture that had produced him. His replacement, however, was much younger and had clearly never left North Korea. He seemed to have been raised on a strict diet of Communist dogma, and spoke exclusively in the clotted language of theory and principles. "Being abducted is a very embarrassing thing, you know. You must not speak one word of it to anyone," he lectured Kaoru at their first meeting.[3] Kaoru was so enraged that it was all he could do to resist hitting the man. "If being kidnapped is something I should be embarrassed about, then what about the people who *kidnapped me*?" he thought to himself. But he held his tongue. As months passed and his political education continued, it struck Kaoru that his new minder was not just ignorant but also mean-spirited and arrogant. "I will clean and wash away your old thoughts and remake you into a *juche* revolutionary," the minder promised.

Kaoru grew inured to such ideological blather, but he couldn't contain himself when things turned personal. "Tell me, how many times did you steal when you lived in Japan?" the minder asked him one day.

"How dare you! I've never robbed anyone," Kaoru replied.

"Is that so? I understood that everyone commits robbery in capitalist societies," the minder responded. His cartoonish image of the world outside North Korea was most likely derived from the propaganda-infused textbooks he'd read in school.

"So there isn't a *single* robber in all of North Korea?" Kaoru retorted sarcastically.

"Of course not," his minder replied primly.

Kaoru was enraged, but his weak Korean made it impossible to express his thoughts effectively. However, he had one weapon. The next day, he described the encounter at length in his journal, noting that working with such a biased instructor was making it difficult for him to like or respect North Korea. Kaoru watched his minder's face turn white with fear as he read the entry. He begged Kaoru to delete the section, which he did. After that, the minder never uttered another disparaging comment about Kaoru or the Japanese people.

Inhabitants of the Invitation-Only Zone maintained their ideological health through weekly "lifestyle reviews," during which each member of the community reflected publicly on his shortcomings. The ability to articulate one's weaknesses is perceived as a virtue in North Korea, and each session would start with a confession, followed by critical responses from the group. As with his journal, Kaoru had trouble finding suitable subjects to discuss, but he learned to rotate through a few topics—camaraderie, study, work—appending minor criticisms about each. But the dynamic of the public lifestyle review was different from the semiprivate journal, and after months of superficial self-criticism, people often felt the urge to speak more honestly, in the hope that their candor would be recognized and perhaps rewarded. Kaoru, too, yearned for something authentic in his bizarre life, in addition to his love for his wife. If he couldn't have it in Japan, then perhaps it was possible in North Korea? By care-fully removing almost everything he held dear, the regime was trying to draw Kaoru to its way of thinking. "All they had to do was create a vacuum in my heart," he says. He began bringing up slightly more personal failings, until one day he was approached by one of the more humane minders. "Only bring up mundane issues and nothing that the Party might object to. There is no use wringing your own neck," the minder advised him.

Kaoru had arrived in North Korea without a strong politi-cal perspective. In Japan, the study of law is a largely techno-cratic pursuit, so when his captors engaged him in ideological or philosophical discussions, he wasn't prepared to martial strong counterarguments. Kaoru was intelligent but not particularly con-templative, so he didn't really understand what philosophy *was*. "They told me that a philosophy was something you needed in order to observe the world, and that made sense to me. I came to understand that it was useful to have a philosophy. I was a stu-dent, so I was curious about North Korea's philosophy of *juche*. Besides, it wasn't as if they were offering anything else," he says.[4]

Commonly translated as "self-reliance," *juche* is a protean group of ideas whose meaning has changed throughout North Korean history depending on the ideological needs of the regime. The word first appeared as *shutai* in the late nineteenth century as a Sino-Japanese compound meaning "subject." It grew popular in the first decades of the twentieth century when Korean national-ists employed it in their quest for self-rule and independence from Japan. Kim had studied the Western notion of self-determination in Chinese translation. Kim Il-sung didn't use the term *juche* until his 1955 speech "On Eliminating Dogmatism and Formalism and Establishing *Juche* in Ideological Work." In it he described *juche* as a creative application of Stalin's ideas, which offered the most up-to-date version of Marxism. "What we are doing now is not a revolution in some foreign country but our Korean revolution," he said. In the early seventies, North Korean children competed for medals and prizes by memorizing Kim Il-sung's writing on *juche*.[5] In 1972 the North Korean constitution was expunged of all references to other systems, and *juche* was enshrined as the state's official "guiding ideology." It wasn't long before *juche* became so closely identified with Kim Il-sung that his son, Kim Jong-il, described it in *On the Juche Idea* (1982) as "the previous fruit of the leader's profound, widespread ideological and theoretical activities. Its creation is the most brilliant of his revolutionary achievements."

Having grown up in the peaceful Japan of the 1970s, Kaoru was shocked by how common talk of war was in North Korea. War had always been an abstraction to him. As a young boy, he'd watched televised coverage of the Vietnam War and feared the fighting might spread to Japan. While his parents had experienced war, and the students in the sixties protested against it, Kaoru's generation shunned the topic altogether. Largely apolitical and apathetic, they adhered to what was known as the "Three Nos" (*san mu shugi*): no vigor, no interest, no responsibility. Passivity and pacifism dominated the day. "Our lives were growing wealthier day by day, and I became a person who took an interest only in things like music and fashion," he says.[6]

In North Korea, however, the assumption was that war was inevitable. Every spring, during the United States and South Korea's joint military drills, a sense of crisis descended over the country, with nightly blackouts and daily evacuation drills. Kaoru could have handled these periods if they'd been isolated, but they merely accentuated the everyday military culture that permeated the North. Even today war metaphors are everywhere: in factories, workers "battle" to meet production goals; students solve math problems framed in military terms ("If the brave uncles of Korean People's Army killed 265 American Imperial bastards in the first battle . . ."); the famine that killed more than a million people in the 1990s is referred to as the Arduous March.[7] War dominates North Korean popular culture, too, in popular movies such as *Sea of Blood, Flames Spreading over the Land,* and *Righteous War.* Every evening, the state-run television screens movies about the Korean War and Kim Il-sung's anti-Japanese campaigns. Those with family ties to the Korean War, no matter how tenuous, held an elevated social rank. All North Korean men served up to a decade in the military, so Kaoru was surrounded by people eager to hold forth on the topic. A Korean War veteran described his friend's internal organs splattered into a tree by an exploding shell. Another told him of a U.S. pilot who parachuted to safety when his plane was shot down. Although prisoners of war were supposed to be taken into custody, the North Korean soldiers executed him on the spot. The sounds of military drills, planes, tanks, and gunshots became familiar to Kaoru. It was a question not of whether war would come, but when. "We will definitely have to fight the U.S. one more time," a female guide at the Victorious Fatherland Liberation War Museum told Kaoru. "Let's get ready for that day!"

The story of North Korea is, essentially, a military story—the story of a never-ending battle waged by General Kim Il-sung, its founder, protector, and "eternal president." It has deep roots. According to the state's hagiography, in 1866 Kim's great-grandfather helped burn the *General Sherman,* the armed side-wheeled steamer that attempted to open Korea to trade; and Kim's father and grandfather are reputed to have been brave anti-Japanese fighters. Born southwest of Pyongyang on April 15, 1912, Kim Il-sung was the eldest of three sons in a tight-knit Christian family. Pyongyang

Kim Il-sung and Kim Jong-suk, 1935 (Associated Press)

was known as the Jerusalem of the East for its concentration of churches, and its Christian community fought the Japanese colonizers fiercely, their resistance fueled by faith. Kim's uncle, a preacher, was arrested for anti-Japanese activities and died in prison. In 1919, when Kim was seven, the family immigrated to Manchuria, where he spent most of the next twenty-one years. In 1929,

Kim, then seventeen, was arrested for taking part in a Communist youth protest and expelled from school, serving a short prison sentence. In 1935, he joined the Northeast Anti-Japanese United Army, a partisan group under the auspices of the Communist Party of China, fighting the Japanese in their puppet state Manchuria. Having lived much of his life there, Kim's Chinese fluency accelerated his rise. He is said to have fought with distinction, and was eventually given command over a unit of three hundred Korean soldiers.

Bound together by their love of Korea and hatred of the Japanese, the guerrillas became Kim's new family, a cadre of insiders who later helped him consolidate, and maintain, power in North Korea. Their small numbers made direct engagement with the larger and better-equipped Japanese military suicidal, so Kim's group ran hit-and-run operations, "liberating" money and supplies from villages, and forcing young men to join its ranks. Kim would regale new recruits with stories about the grandeur of communism, and he vowed one day to liberate all of Korea.[8] The Japanese used a two-pronged strategy against the insurgents, hunting down the leaders with single-minded intensity, while giving amnesty to soldiers in exchange for intelligence. The resulting paranoia and suspicion nearly tore the guerrillas apart, and Kim became known for his ruthlessness with alleged collaborators.[9]

The group's most famous exploit was the June 4, 1937, attack on a Japanese police station in the Korean town of Pochonbo, which killed seven officers, including the chief, and left the station in flames. Kim had become enough of a nuisance that the Japanese put a ten-thousand-yen bounty on his head, and in August 1940 he and his compatriots fled to the Soviet Union, where he married Kim Jong-suk, a cook in the guerrilla force, who gave birth to Kim Jong-il in 1941. Kim Il-sung received his first formal military training while serving as an officer of the Red Army. He also used the time to study Stalin's leadership methods: purging enemies, developing a cult of personality, and building a modern industrial nation. North Korean children are taught that Kim's Korean guerrillas single-handedly defeated the Japanese—neither Hiroshima nor Nagasaki is mentioned. In reality, Kim arrived in Pyongyang, resplendent in a Soviet officer's uniform, on September 19, 1945, a month after the Japanese surrendered to the United States. Stalin appointed Kim, then thirty-three, the country's "supreme leader," a position he held for fifty years. The cult of personality began immediately, with the *Pyongyang Times* describing Kim as "the incomparable patriot, national hero, the ever victorious, brilliant field commander with a will of iron . . . the greatest leader that our people have known for the last several thousand years."[10]

The dynamics of Kim Il-sung's guerrilla campaign—concentrated military leadership, tight internal security, a political system based on personal loyalty—set the terms for the North Korean state.[11] By the mid-sixties, anyone who wasn't part of Kim's guerrilla army had been purged from leadership positions. Kim's regime maintained a permanent state of high alert, its million-man army waging a hot war from 1950 to 1953, and a cold one that continues to this day. Kim modeled the structure of his new state on the Soviet Union, but his cult of personality was inspired by the figure who dominated the consciousness of every Japanese and Korean citizen between 1910 and 1945: In many respects, the role Kim fashioned for himself was essentially a Korean version of the Japanese emperor.[12] Both were godlike figures, with a pure racial lineage, who maintained a direct relationship with every one of their subjects. Like that of the emperor, Kim's cult was both political and spiritual,[13] and to this day it permeates every aspect of life in North Korea. Its citizens swear allegiance to Kim, not to the state. An official portrait of the "Dear Leader" hangs in every house and office. All citizens over age sixteen must wear a

Kim badge over their heart. It is estimated that there are thirty-four thousand statues of Kim throughout North Korea, the largest of which stands seventy-two feet high and was originally clad in gold. When Kim's name appears in print it is boldfaced, much like Jesus's words in some editions of the Bible.

The scenario for the final war against the United States, familiar to all North Koreans, is cast in apocalyptic terms. It will begin with a surprise attack by the United States at the Thirty-Eighth Parallel. The North will repel the invaders and inundate Seoul with rockets, before dispatching its special forces to meet up with the thousands of North Korean "sleeper" spies in the South, and destroy its infrastructure. With the Americans on the run, the North will take Seoul in days, and unify the peninsula in weeks.

Kaoru suspected that this scenario was a fantasy, but it was the North's contingency plans that terrified him. If the North was overrun, every citizen was supposed to repair to the system of underground tunnels and mountains to continue the fight in a Kim Il-sung–style guerrilla campaign. In preparation for evacuation, Kaoru kept a backpack filled with candles, matches, and food. Once in the mountains, he'd face a choice. Desert, and risk being shot by the North Koreans. Or try surrendering to the invading U.S. forces, but likely be mistaken for a guerrilla and shot. "As if being abducted weren't bad enough, now I'm going to be dragged into a war?" he thought to himself. To prepare for his encounter with the U.S. military, he memorized one English phrase: "We are abducted Japanese. Please help us!"[14]

# 6

# ABDUCTION AS STATECRAFT

Why did North Korea go to the trouble of snatching ordinary Japanese people from beaches and small towns? The question obsessed me for years, and I was hardly alone. Speculating about North Korea's inner workings has become something of a parlor game among Pyongyang watchers in Tokyo, Seoul, and Washington, DC. Probably no other country has been as thoroughly surveilled and parsed. However, none of the explanations for the abductions I heard from scholars, journalists, or spies was entirely convincing. I concluded that, ultimately, there was no single motivation. The most plausible explanation is that the abductions were a small part of a larger plan to unify the two Koreas, spread Kim Il-sung's ideology throughout Asia, and humiliate Japan. "The apparently senseless campaign of kidnappings becomes slightly more comprehensible if it is seen, not so much as a bizarre method for obtaining language teachers, but rather as linked to dreams of destabilizing Japan (and possibly other Asian countries) via revolutionary cells, composed either of kidnap victims themselves or of North Korean agents," writes the historian Tessa Morris-Suzuki. "The idea that Japanese society could be propelled into chaos through the actions of North Korean trained revolutionaries may have seemed marginally less far-fetched than it does today."[1]

On the evening of August 15, 1974, South Korean president Park Chung-hee took the dais at Seoul's National Theater to address an audience of government dignitaries and foreign diplomats on the twenty-ninth anniversary of the end of Japanese rule. It is a measure of the psychological and linguistic distance separating Japan and Korea that the former refers to August 15, 1945, the day it surrendered, as "The Day to Commemorate the End of the War" (*Shusen kinenbi*), while that date is known in Korea as "Restoration of Light Day" (*Gwangbokjeol*). Soon after Park began to speak, a young man bounded down the aisle firing a gun. The six men sitting beside Park leaped from their seats, while others subdued the attacker. In the midst of the commotion, Park's wife tilted over in her chair, a bullet having hit her head. Once the assassin was apprehended, and Park's wife was taken to the hospital, Park insisted on finishing the speech. His wife died later that night.

A twenty-two-year-old Japan-born ethnic Korean, the assassin was a member of the Chosen Soren, an organization that acts as North Korea's de facto embassy in Japan. He had entered the South legally, carrying a revolver he stole from a police station in Osaka, his hometown. The attack, the North's second attempt on Park's life, was the last straw. The South upgraded its already formidable security apparatus and conducted more thorough background checks on ethnic Koreans from Japan. The incident strained Japan's relations with South Korea, which accused it of neglecting the Communist threat posed by Chosen Soren.

The South had already cracked down on North Korean spies

posing as South Koreans, so the new focus on Japan-born ethnic Koreans presented a serious problem for the North. If its agents could no longer use South Korean identities or Japanese Korean proxies, how could it infiltrate and undermine its southern foe? The idea of using Japanese nationals to infiltrate South Korea had a kind of cockeyed brilliance to it. Japan circa 1977 looked more favorably on Kim Il-sung's regime than on Park Chung-hee's oppressive military dictatorship. And still atoning for the pain Japan had inflicted on Korea in colonial times, its left-leaning media, intellectuals, and politicians were loath to criticize anything Korea-related. As a result, when rumors about the abductions occasionally arose, they were dismissed as products of anti-Korean prejudice. Any newspaper reporter with the temerity to write critically about North Korea received angry phone calls and letters. "It simply wasn't worth the hassle, so it became a taboo to write about the North," a reporter told me.

Until the late seventies, the abduction project was an all-Korean affair. North Korean troops had occupied and retreated from Seoul twice during the Korean War, each time taking thousands of southerners with them. As Kim Il-sung explained in his 1946 decree "On Transporting Intellectuals from South Korea," the goal was to bring five hundred thousand people to the North to compensate for the exodus of professionals—bureaucrats, policemen, engineers—who fled in the years leading up to the war. There was nothing random about the operation. "North Korean soldiers with long lists of names went from house to house looking for specific men to take with them," remembers Choi Kwang-suk of the Korean War Abductees' Family Union.[2] Choi's father, a high-ranking policeman, was on one list, and the ten-year-old never saw him again. It is estimated that the North took eighty-four thousand South Koreans in all, sixty thousand of whom were inducted into its army. Although the number of abductions decreased dramatically after the Korean War, they never entirely stopped. The Korean Institute for National Unification reports that four thousand South Koreans, mostly fishermen, have been abducted since 1953. This includes five high school students abducted in 1977 and 1978 and a teacher snatched while on vacation in Norway in 1979.

The majority of those taken in the twenty-five years after the Korean War were fishermen. In the days before GPS technology, ships often drifted over the "Northern Limit Line," a waterborne demilitarized zone whose precise location the two Koreas have never agreed upon. Hundreds of fishing vessels were boarded by the North Korean navy and towed back to port. The abductees were welcomed to the socialist paradise and treated with the kind of respect that illiterate laborers seldom received in the South. Lee Jae-geun, a fisherman who was abducted in 1970, told me about the hero's welcome he received.[3] Upon disembarking from his ship, he was greeted by six women loaded down with flowers. "Don't go back to the South! Come live with us in the earthly paradise of the North," they begged him. Most of the abducted fishermen were returned after a few weeks or months, with the hope that they would talk about how well they had been treated, and spread the word about the higher living standards then enjoyed in the North. A few chose to stay in the North voluntarily, convinced (perhaps correctly) that poor fishermen would lead a better life in a socialist than in a capitalist country. And the North Koreans were always on the lookout for exceptional men who, despite their lack of formal education, had the kind of raw intelligence that might be of use. Many, including Lee Jae-geun, were recruited and trained to spy on the North's behalf. Most were returned to South Korea, and a few, like Lee Jae-geun, escaped. Five hundred South Korean abductees remain in the North today.

The abduction project matured during the period when Kim Jong-il was rising to power. In February 1974, Kim Jong-il was elected to the Central Committee of the Workers' Party of Korea, an event that marked his ascension to his father's position. Proving his worth was not as easy as many assume. Kim would often arrive to Politburo meetings late or hungover, only to be berated by his father in front of the senior leadership.[4] As part of his new portfolio, he ran the regime's intelligence service, and it didn't take long for him to conclude that it needed upgrading. Kim was particularly bothered that several North Korean spies had confessed after being captured, instead of committing suicide as instructed. Others had betrayed the regime by accepting bribes from foreign intelligence agencies. It was time to clean house. One by one, he recalled spies from around the world, putting them through drills and weeding out those he deemed unfit. Dozens were either executed or sent to the regime's far-reaching gulag. To replace them, Kim recruited an army of elite spies, handpicked from the best schools and universities, loyal to him alone.

The world in 1974 was a more complex place than the one his father had faced in 1948. Kim diversified and expanded intelligence operations, abducting native teachers to train North Korean spies to navigate the languages and cultures of Malaysia, Thailand, Romania, Lebanon, France, and Holland. Among the reasons Japanese nationals were abducted was to steal identities with which to create fake passports. The targets tended to be unmarried low-status men who lived far from their families and wouldn't be missed. Japan's traditional family registration system (*koseki*) had yet to be fully centralized in the late seventies, so there was no reliable national database against which a forged passport could be compared. And a Japanese passport granted the holder access to virtually any country on earth.

"Thank you for coming, Madame Choi. I am Kim Jong Il."[5] Choi Eun-hee, South Korea's most famous actress, felt a sense of

Kim Jong-il with camera (Associated Press)

terror the moment she heard his name. It was January 28, 1978, when Choi's boat entered the port of Nampo, on North Korea's western coast. A week earlier she had flown from Seoul to Hong Kong to discuss a project with an acting school she had been running since the closing of Shin Films, the studio she ran with her husband, the director Shin Sang-ok. The meeting, it turned out, was a ruse to lure Choi into the hands of her North Korean captors. Kim Jong-il reached out to greet her. "I didn't want to shake hands with the man who had engineered my kidnapping, but I had no choice," she writes in her memoir. At the moment they shook hands, a cameraman popped up to take their photo. "I didn't want any record of that moment. Nor did I want any long-lasting proof of my unkempt and ugly state."

Three weeks after Choi disappeared from Hong Kong, Shin went looking for her. Although they had divorced two years earlier, they were still extremely close. He had warned her that the invitation to Hong Kong seemed suspicious, and he was now determined to rescue her. Often called the Orson Welles of South Korea, Shin had made three hundred movies at Shin Films, the country's largest studio, before running afoul of President Park Chung-hee. At the time of his ex-wife's abduction, Shin was considering moving to Hollywood to continue his career. After a few days in Hong Kong, he, too, was taken to Pyongyang.

Shin was a less compliant "guest" than his former wife (whom Kim Jong-il had put up in one of his finest palaces) and made several escape attempts. As punishment, he was sentenced to four years in prison. Once he promised to stop trying to escape, he was released. On March 6, 1983, Kim Jong-il staged a party to reunite the couple. "Well, go ahead and hug each other. Why are you just standing there?" he said. The room erupted into applause as the two embraced. The Dear Leader hushed the crowd. "Comrades. From now on, Mr. Shin is my film adviser." The attraction of Shin was considerable. He was the most creative and influential director in South Korea, so his "defection" would be perceived as a criticism of its system. Shin was Kim's ideal director: trained in Japan and China, he had made films in the United States and was familiar with the most recent Western film techniques. Yet he was Korean (born in prewar *North* Korea, no less), so Kim couldn't be accused of bowing to the imperialist West.

Movies have played an important role in North Korea since 1948, when Kim Il-sung lured South Korean filmmakers north with promises of unlimited funding and artistic freedom. Kim believed film was the perfect medium for raising national consciousness. Dozens of duplicates of every North Korean film were circulated throughout the country, with color copies going to the big cities and black-and-white to rural areas. Movies about Kim Il-sung himself were always distributed in color, and only on the highest-quality film stock from the United States (Kodak) or Japan (Fuji).

Before entering politics proper, Kim Jong-il ran the Movie and Arts Division of the Workers' Party Organization and Guidance Department. Kim was a huge film buff who watched movies every night. Enlisting the aid of North Korea's embassies, he had thousands of foreign films shipped back to him via diplomatic pouch.[6] His favorite movies were reported to be *Friday the 13th*, *Rambo*, and *Godzilla*. Soon after releasing Shin from prison, Kim took him to his twenty-thousand-film archive, a three-story humidity- and temperature-controlled, guarded building in central Pyongyang. The archive had 250 employees: translators, subtitle specialists, and projectionists. But no individual was more important than the director in helping the people develop into true Communists. "This historic task requires, above all, a revolutionary transformation of the practice of directing," Kim wrote in his 1973 treatise, *On the Art of the Cinema*. Kim wanted Shin to improve the North's film industry so it could produce movies worthy of the international festival circuit. North Korea would press the cause of world communism by getting films into Cannes.

The combination of political and financial pressure had driven Shin's South Korean film company out of business, and rumors were circulating that he had defected to the North voluntarily in order to advance his career. If Shin wanted the South Korean authorities to believe he had been abducted, he needed evidence. On the evening of October 19, 1983, Choi and Shin met with Kim Jong-il in his office. Choi had purchased a small tape recorder, which she carried in her handbag. The three sat around a glass-topped table drinking. Choi pretended to reach into her bag for a tissue and quietly turned the recorder on. She and Shin took turns asking Kim leading questions: Why did you bring us here? How did you organize our kidnappings? Clearly enjoying the repartee, Kim talked a blue streak. "I'll confess the truth only to you two," he said. "But I would appreciate it if you keep this a secret just between ourselves.

"Frankly speaking, we still lag behind the Western countries in motion pictures," Kim explained. "Our filmmakers do perfunctory work. They don't have any new ideas. Their works use the same expression, the same old plots. All our movies are filled with crying and sobbing." He was in a difficult situation. How could he open the country to outside influences without jeopardizing his control? He had sent directors to study in East Germany, Czechoslovakia, and the Soviet Union, but he couldn't allow them to go to Japan or the West. That was why Kim needed Shin so urgently. Shin said he was flattered, but wondered exactly why Kim had gone to the lengths of *kidnapping* them. "I absolutely needed you," Kim answered. "So I began to covet you, but there was nothing I could do. So I told my comrades, if we want to get Director Shin here, we have to plan a covert operation."

Toward the end of the conversation, Kim offered a weak apology. "I've also conducted my own self-criticism," he said. "That's because I never told my subordinates in detail what my plans were. I never told them just how we would use you and my intentions. I just said I need those two people, so bring them here. As a result, there have been a lot of mutual misunderstandings."[7] The tape ran out after forty-five minutes, and Choi was too frightened to change it. It didn't matter. She and Shin had the proof they needed.

Shin continued to make films for the next three years, directing seven and producing eleven more. As Kim grew to trust the couple, they were allowed to travel more, first in the Eastern Bloc and eventually beyond, although always accompanied by minders. On March 13, 1986, they escaped during a film festival in Vienna, evading their minders' car and asking for asylum at the U.S. embassy.

On hearing about their escape, Kim Jong-il assumed they had been kidnapped by the United States. The possibility that artists with whom he had been so generous would abandon him was too much for Kim to imagine. He sent a message offering to help them return to Pyongyang. They never replied.

Kenji Fujimoto (Associated Press)

Oddly, Kim Jong-il's most famous Japanese employee was hired, not abducted.

In 1982, Kenji Fujimoto[8] answered a classified ad for a job as a sushi chef. The name and location of the restaurant weren't listed, but the salary was twice what he was making as a freelance chef in Tokyo. Fujimoto didn't know much about North Korea, so he wasn't deterred when he learned that the job was at a new

Pyongyang restaurant that wanted a Japanese chef both to prepare sushi and to train a corps of North Korean chefs.

Fujimoto had received his training through the rigorous and lengthy system that dominates Japan's sushi industry even today. It typically takes ten years to go from being an apprentice, who cleans the restaurant and accompanies the chef to the fish market, to an assistant (a *wakiita*, Japanese for "near the cutting board"), who makes rice and prepares ingredients. The highest position is the chef (*itamae*). Fujimoto began at a restaurant in the exclusive Ginza area of Tokyo, where the smallest piece of sushi cost $30 (as opposed to $1.50 at most restaurants), and rose to chef in five years. "Starting at one of the best restaurants in Tokyo helped me rise quickly because the fundamentals I learned were also of the highest quality," he tells me.[9]

Fujimoto encountered Kim Jong-il a year after he arrived in Pyongyang. One evening, Kim and his entourage took over the whole restaurant, consuming a staggering amount of sushi and sake. With such important guests, Fujimoto pushed himself and his staff so that everything would be perfect. When it came time to pay the bill, Kim pulled out a white envelope bursting with money and tossed it casually at the chef's feet. Fujimoto just stared at the envelope. "I thought to myself, 'Here I just finished doing a good job for you. So why aren't you man enough to thank me and pay for it politely?'" Kim's entourage watched in horror, fearing, no doubt, the effect that Fujimoto's insolence might have on the unpredictable leader. Kim's interpreter picked up the envelope and handed it to Fujimoto, who accepted it with a bow but no smile.

Fujimoto was surprised when Kim returned to the restaurant the next week. "Fujimoto," Kim said, "I apologize for my conduct last week. Please forgive me." Fujimoto says, "Here is the second in command of the whole country, and I've made *him* feel he has to apologize to *me!*" Fujimoto felt ashamed. He also felt affection for Kim. "That was the day I fell in love with him," he says.

They became friends, shooting, horseback riding, and water skiing together. Kim gave him two Mercedes-Benzes. Fujimoto was permitted to marry a North Korean woman (a dancer), and became something of an "uncle" to Kim Jong-un, the country's current leader. But like so many love affairs, theirs ended badly. Fujimoto served as Kim's chef until 2001, when he was placed under house arrest for a perceived infraction against the regime. (While on a shopping trip in Japan, the chef was detained by Japanese immigration authorities, to whom he spoke a bit too freely about his employer.) Although eventually reinstated, he was shaken, and soon fled to Japan, where he went into hiding. He has since published four books about Kim—*I Was Kim Jong Il's Chef*, the first, was a bestseller—and supports himself by appearing as a North Korea "expert" on Japanese television. His emotional reunion with Kim Jong-un in 2012 was front-page news all across Asia.

When I meet Fujimoto at a smoky Tokyo café, I can see why he appealed to Kim. His strong hands are adorned with a diamond pinky ring and a gold Rolex. He favors jeans and skintight black T-shirts that show off his stocky, muscular physique. A black bandana is wrapped around his forehead, atop a pair of oversize mirrored sunglasses. A square gray goatee clings to his chin. He grooms himself in a manner designed to display as much as it hides, as if to say, "Look at me! I'm in disguise!" Fujimoto cultivates the appearance of a thug, though one who knows how to select the best wine at a fine restaurant.

The banquets Fujimoto prepared for Kim were elaborate, even orgiastic affairs. Kim insisted the sashimi be so fresh that the mouth of the fish was still moving. When drunk, he would command his guests to strip and dance nude. Kim thought nothing of spending fifty thousand dollars for ordinary occasions. And when there *was* something to celebrate, the parties cost several times that. U.S. secretary of state Madeleine Albright's 2000 visit was one such occasion. "He was absolutely thrilled to meet her because it meant that Clinton was reaching out to him. He was drinking a lot and was at the top of his game. He laid out between one hundred and two hundred thousand per party, and they went on for three days. He gave everyone presents and served the finest cognac. It was really *something*," Fujimoto recalls.

But the parties also served a serious political purpose. "By inviting his trusted subordinates to a party, he can observe their personalities at close range," reported Kim's erstwhile adviser Hwang Jang-yop, who defected to the South in 1997.[10] Members of the North Korean elite lucky enough to be invited became "vassals" to the king. Kim regularly dispatched Fujimoto on shopping trips to scour the globe for delicacies. Other than trips to Russia and China, usually in his private, bulletproof train, Kim never traveled abroad. Still, he knew where to find the best of everything. He sent Fujimoto to Denmark for pork, Iran for caviar, France for wine, Czechoslovakia for beer, and Japan for seafood and appliances. "However, Kim insisted his refrigerators must come from the U.S., since they made the best ones. He gave me one as a present. It was enormous, created ice quickly, and held tons of food at all different temperatures," Fujimoto says.

He acknowledges that Kim valued him not only as a friend but also as a status symbol—proof that despite living in an isolated, impoverished country, Kim was a citizen of the world. "I think it was important to him that the chef who fed him Japanese food was himself Japanese," he says. "He is a man who values the best of everything, and that includes me." Kim would often pull Fujimoto aside and boast to his guests, "Isn't Fujimoto splendid? I hired him. He's in *my* club, and I get to keep him!"

# 7

# FROM EMPEROR HIROHITO
# TO KIM IL-SUNG

While North Korea remained mysterious to most post–Second World War Japanese, some viewed the young Communist nation as an antidote both to the emperor system that had driven Japan to war and to the Cold War capitalism that America had imposed on Japan after it. For members of the fast-growing Japanese Communist Party, the success of North Korea and, later, the Chinese Revolution were evidence that communism was the new modernism. When the dark side of North Korean communism revealed itself in the 1960s and '70s, some of its most fervent admirers became the most severe critics.

On a brilliant May morning in 1946, the freighter *Liberty* edged down the California coast, toward San Francisco. The ship reduced speed at the mouth of San Francisco Bay and veered toward the harbor. Katsumi Sato gasped at the enormous rust-red suspension bridge that loomed before him. Behind it was the most beautiful city he had ever seen. As the *Liberty* eased beneath the Golden Gate Bridge, he gazed up at the bright pink houses atop Russian Hill and the phalanx of office buildings peeking out from behind them. Compared to the devastated Japanese cities he had left behind, San Francisco was radiant, a magical city on a hill.

"What were we *thinking*?" The question played through Sato's mind as if on a tape loop. "There was no way we could win against a nation that can build bridges and cities like this! Japan is a country of peasants who live in buildings made of wood. We never had a chance. The emperor and the generals must have been out of their minds!"[1] Thinking back to all the times he'd nearly died during the war, Sato felt sick to his stomach. It was as if he were awaking from a dream, or, more accurately, a nightmare. Still recovering from the loss—of the war, of his friends—he hadn't until this moment fully understood the war's futility.

It was a miracle Sato had made it this far. Most of the other young men he'd served with were dead. Like many other Japanese boys in the final days of the war, Sato had dropped out of high school at age sixteen and enlisted in the military. Every man was needed, and some of his fellow volunteers were even younger. They were driven by a combination of patriotism and anxiety: What would happen if Japan won the war—and *everyone* was certain of a Japanese victory—before they'd had a chance to test themselves in combat? What if they missed their generation's defining experience?

At its peak, the Japanese Empire spanned three million square miles, including Korea, Burma, Singapore, Taiwan, the Philippines, Indonesia, and parts of China. The logistical challenge of dismembering the empire nearly eclipsed the war effort in its complexity. Millions of Japanese colonists and soldiers returned to Japan, and two million of the colonial subjects who had aided Japan returned to their homes. Forty billion dollars of military and industrial equipment was confiscated, dismantled, and shipped to Japan's former territories.

With 80 percent of Japan's merchant fleet destroyed, the Japanese had borrowed ships such as the *Liberty* from the Americans. Sato had spent the year after the war ended ferrying people back and forth among Japan, Manchuria, and Taiwan. The work was dull, but it gave him time to contemplate both his wartime experience and his uncertain future. The third of nine children, Katsumi Sato was born in 1929 in the mountains just north of Niigata. He came from a long line of rice farmers who had lived in the same spot since the seventeenth century. His father was a tenant who leased the land, giving the landlord 60 percent of his rice crop as rent. Sato had an active, curious mind, and the one thing he knew for certain was that he wanted no part of a farmer's life. When a recruiter visited Sato's high school class, every child, no matter his age, health, or size, volunteered. An older boy whom Sato admired served in the navy, so he decided to go to sea as well. He transferred to the naval academy in Kobe, but the need for sailors was so dire that his training lasted barely six months. It was useless anyway, "brainwashing, basically," he says. The instructors assured the recruits that the war was going well—no matter that a shortage of guns reduced them to drilling with bamboo spears.

In December 1943, Sato was assigned to a six-thousand-ton freighter delivering provisions and ammunition to troops fighting in Southeast Asia. One night the ship, fully loaded with ammunition, was attacked by American bombers while docked in Manila Harbor. The explosions shattered windows all across the city. Most of the crew was on port leave at the time of the attack and therefore survived. A few days later, Sato joined another ship en route to pick up supplies in Taiwan. After the attack on Pearl Harbor, President Roosevelt had implemented a policy of unrestricted warfare, and the waters around the Philippines were crawling with American submarines. Sato was standing on deck when he spotted a ripple of bubbles rushing through the water, directly at him. He recognized the telltale sign of an incoming torpedo and tried to run, only to find that he was paralyzed with fear. Fortunately, having unloaded its cargo in Manila, the ship was sitting high in the water and the torpedo slid beneath it. The next two torpedoes, however, hit the ship, sinking it. Sato and three others were left floating in the water.

The final four months of the war inflicted terrible hardship on the Japanese people. Cities burned to the ground, killing hundreds of thousands of civilians. Those who survived were starving. American B-52s were dropping floating mines to disrupt the shipping routes. In May 1945, Sato's ship, carrying much-needed rice from Thailand to Tokyo, hit one, exploded, and sank. By August 15, 1945, the day Japan surrendered, only one-quarter of the four hundred men Sato had enlisted with were alive.

The main goal of the Allied occupation of Japan (1945–52) was to transform it into a Western-style democracy. All legislation passed by the Japanese legislature was subject to approval by General MacArthur, the Supreme Commander for the Allied Powers. Japan's prewar government had been hijacked by politicians and generals, with virtually no input by its people. Therefore, the thinking went, the Americans would write a new constitution to foster the kinds of democratic institutions through which the Japanese could take control of their nation. The new constitution demoted the emperor to a figurehead and forbade Japan from waging war again.

Japan circa 1945 was in many respects a feudal state. While

farmers such as Sato's father comprised half the labor force, two-thirds of the land they tilled was owned by landlords, who took the bulk of the profits. Little more than indentured servants, the farmers passed debts from generation to generation. Under MacArthur's land-reform program, the government purchased 40 percent of Japan's cultivated land from the landlords and resold it at a discount to the farmers who worked it. The idea was that, as landowners, farm families would become economically independent participants in Japan's new democratic institutions. MacArthur also supported labor unions in the hope that they would provide democratic opposition to the old imperial system. The number of union members grew from five thousand in 1945 to over five million in 1947.[2]

On October 4, 1945, Order No. 93 directed the release of all persons imprisoned on other than criminal charges. Entitled "Removal of Restrictions on Political, Civil and Religious Liberties" directive, it guaranteed civil rights, such as the right to organize and strike, and released labor leaders and Communists who had spent decades in jail.[3] Illegal since 1925, the Japanese Communist Party was one of the few organizations that had opposed the emperor's militarism on pacifist grounds. The relationship between MacArthur and the Japanese left seemed promising. The Communists welcomed the Americans as liberators, thanking them, in the first postwar issue of the newspaper, *Akahata*, for initiating Japan's "democratic revolution." Membership grew quickly, and in 1949 the Communists won 10 percent of the popular vote, sending thirty-five members to the legislature.

Its influence growing, the Communist Party soon dominated the labor unions, which took a more militant pose. In January 1947 the National Congress of Industrial Unions, Japan's largest labor federation, announced its plans for a nationwide general strike. The honeymoon between the United States and the Communists was over. This was more democracy than MacArthur had antici-pated, and he reversed course, banning the strike the day before it was to begin. Whereas the Communists had once been wooed, they were now lumped in with the militarists and fascists as op-ponents of Japan's new democracy. In 1950, MacArthur accused the party of having "cast off the mantle of pretended legitimacy and assumed instead the role of an avowed satellite of an interna-tional predatory force." Twenty thousand Communists were fired from their jobs, and by 1952 the party had lost all thirty-five of its seats in the legislature.

After Sato delivered his ship to San Francisco, he returned to Niigata to work for Kawasaki Kisen, one of Japan's largest shipping companies. He had become active in the union movement and was stunned by the Americans' about-face. "Why did MacArthur stop us from striking? We thought it was the highest expression of our faith in democracy," he says. Sato, too, was fired, which shat-tered any belief he had in America's democratic ideals. MacAr-thur, he concluded, was no more trustworthy than the emperor.

The day he learned he'd been let go, Sato had just checked in to the Uchino hospital, a facility for tuberculosis patients. Diseases that had been widespread during the war had reached epidemic proportions in the postwar chaos and poverty. With food and water in short supply, tens of thousands of cases of cholera, dys-entery, smallpox, and polio broke out across Japan. In 1946 there were 20,000 reported cases of typhus. In 1947 more than 146,000 died from tuberculosis alone, with another million infected. The Red Cross found that 70 percent of Japanese under age thirty tested positive for the disease. Sato's case appeared mild, so he was treated and released within three months. With no job, he re-solved to complete his education and enrolled at a high school with students nearly a decade younger than he was. Despite the rev-olution the nation had undergone, he was struck by how little had changed. The teachers who years before had taught him to "hail the emperor" now displayed the same uncritical devotion to an abstraction called "democracy," and Sato was disgusted by the ease with which they had traded one set of beliefs for another. "This wasn't thinking for yourself," he says. "These people were simply obeying the ruling system, whatever it was. If the emperor had been reinstated the next week, they'd have followed him again."[4]

Tuberculosis is a devious disease whose symptoms wax and wane without warning. The month before Sato was to receive his high school diploma, his breathing problems returned. The bacillus had in fact never left his body and was now stronger and more resilient. Streptomycin, the first antibiotic capable of curing tuberculosis, was isolated in 1943 at Rutgers University but wasn't widely available in Japan until the early 1950s. Sato spent a good portion of the next five years in the hospital, getting discharged when his doctors thought they had rid his body of tuberculosis and then being readmitted when it returned.

Despite his condition, he continued to agitate, this time on behalf of his fellow patients. With the postwar economy in shambles, the hospital had furloughed a portion of the nursing staff, and Sato was outraged. "These men and women had sacrificed their health for the sake of their country, and now Japan was turning its back on them," he says. He formed a patients' association and went from ward to ward lecturing. He discovered he had a talent for public speaking, holding forth on subjects large and small without losing the audience's interest. His performances made an impression on a particularly beautiful girl named Tamiko Sakamoto, a doctor's daughter whose illness had confined her to the hospital for two years. While Sato wasn't as handsome as the boys who usually pursued her, he spoke with a passion she had never before heard. Tamiko's case was less severe than Sato's, so she was released after a small part of one of her lungs was removed.

Sato got to know her by sight—how could he not?—but was too shy to introduce himself. And anyway, what kind of suitor could he be stuck in the hospital?[5]

The war had destroyed Sato's faith in the emperor and the military, and the American occupiers had let him down by undercutting the very democratic institutions they had claimed to value. The only positive experience he'd had during the past few years was with his union brothers. They'd all worked together, for one another—not for the emperor, not for the military, and certainly not for the Americans. It was a sense of solidarity and friendship he'd never felt before.

Given the communicable nature of tuberculosis, a hospital visit from someone other than a family member was rare. The only people who visited Sato were union brothers from the shipyards. Sato was familiar with the basic ideas of communism, but he now delved into them deeply, reading Marx and Lenin from morning to night. He wasn't the only patient undergoing an ideological conversion. In fact, the Communist Party sent tutors with a selection of leftist books and magazines to the hospital. Sato also received a real-life lesson in dialectical materialism. Although streptomycin was now available in Japan, it was so expensive— thirty thousand yen, or eighty dollars back then, for twelve ampules—that it was out of the reach of most patients. "Those who could afford the medicine were cured, and those who couldn't afford it died," Sato says. "I saw one or two people die every day. It couldn't have been a more concrete lesson: in the capitalist society, those with money live, and those without money die."

Sato's parents somehow came up with the money, and he was cured—once again beating the odds. Never having held a steady job, he didn't have a lot of options and settled for working in a bookstore that rented titles to people who couldn't afford to buy them. Now that he was out of the hospital and supporting himself, his mind turned toward Tamiko. He found her address and wrote her a note, inviting her to visit him at the bookstore. She was intrigued and began visiting him regularly. The final note she received contained a marriage proposal, which laid out the reasons they should be together. Sato and Tamiko married one year after they met, and he left the bookstore and helped her run her family's cosmetics shop. Next to their shop was a Communist bookstore run by a young man named Harunori Kojima, whose life story was nearly identical to Sato's. Sons of poor Niigata rice farmers, both had joined the military in the final days of the war. The two became best friends and spent hours discussing the fine points of Marxist theory, and it wasn't long before Sato joined the Communist Party himself. The two men had witnessed a world turned upside down. Perhaps communism could set it right again.

# 8

# DEVELOPING A COVER STORY

North Korea is a country where everyone knows his place. In 1957 the central government created a caste system that classified every citizen according to his family's political reliability, dividing the country into three groups: the trustworthy "core" class (descendants of anti-Japanese guerrillas, Korean War heroes, laborers, and farmers), a suspect "wavering" class (merchants, professionals, and families originally from the South), and a "hostile" class (Christians, landowners, prostitutes, and wealthy businessmen). Individuals in these three groups were further classified into fifty-one subcategories, and the life prospects of every North Korean are still determined largely by one's caste. While the core class and their children comprise the country's hereditary elite, the hostile class and their progeny are essentially "untouchables," forbidden from living in major cities, attending the best schools, or serving in the military. As a member of the Japanese bourgeoisie, Kaoru

Hasuike didn't fit neatly into any of these categories, which made his prospect of successfully passing as North Korean unlikely.

With all the limitations of his situation came a few odd advantages, and Kaoru learned to make the most of his liminal status by gaming the system whenever he had the chance. North Korea is one of the few parts of the globe that remains untouched by multiculturalism of any kind, and one consequence of its homogeneity and rigid social hierarchy is that its citizens receive no training in how to deal with the unexpected or foreign. The Invitation-Only Zone's rules were designed to minimize the possibility that its residents—who had access to privileged information or, in Kaoru's case, were themselves state secrets—would come into contact with ordinary people living outside its confines. One rule was that the abductees were not supposed to leave the zone unless accompanied by a minder. However, Kaoru noticed that the more he and Yukiko settled into their lives in the zone, the less their minder checked up on them. When their minder started taking most Saturdays and Sundays off, Kaoru began making unauthorized trips outside the zone, nodding confidently to the guards as he left, if only to experience the thrill of breaking the rules. For someone with no freedom, even the smallest taste of liberty was intoxicating. His short trips got longer, and soon Kaoru would take his fishing rods an hour or so from the zone to a pond that he'd heard brimmed with carp and perch. Once there, he'd set his bait and spend hours enjoying nature, fishing by moonlight on warm summer evenings. Owned by a nearby school, the pond was officially off-limits, which made the transgression all the more satisfying.[1]

One Saturday morning, Kaoru made the pilgrimage accompanied by an acquaintance from the zone. As the two men arrived at the pond, they nodded to the fishermen already there, dropped their lines, and waited for a nibble. Just then, several security officers appeared. "What are you doing here? Don't you know that fishing is prohibited in this pond!" they shouted. North Korea is filled with petty officials either looking for bribes or rousting intruders to make a point, but their tone struck Kaoru as unnecessarily aggressive. An officer whose armband identified him as a second lieutenant grabbed at Kaoru's rod. "How dare you steal fish from the Department of Safety and Security!" he screamed.

Growing up in Japan, where indirection and understatement were the rule, Kaoru knew how to keep his thoughts to himself. And if North Korea had taught him nothing else, it was the wisdom of this practice. For all its bellicosity, there was very little crime here, and Kaoru had not been an object of violence since the night he and Yukiko were abducted. Yet now he felt the resentment that had been burning inside him for years suddenly burst forth. Turning to his companion, Kaoru began shouting in Japanese. "Who is this man? Why is he behaving so violently?" he asked. The officer fell silent, bewildered by the foreign language coming from Kaoru's mouth. Sensing a shift in the balance of power, Kaoru seized his own lapel, dramatizing the encounter while pointing to the officer. "He grabbed my jacket like this!" he said in Japanese. "What is going on?" At this, the officer was completely flummoxed. "I did no such thing!" he protested, pleading his innocence. Kaoru's companion caught on to the ruse and quickly assumed the role of the voice of reason. "You see, this man is a guest from a foreign country," he told the officer in Korean. "He came here to take a break and do some fishing. If you confiscate his gear, it will cause a lot of trouble for *everyone*." In North Korea, getting mixed up in the affairs of foreigners, regardless of the circumstances, is dangerous, and the officer dropped Kaoru's rod and gestured for them to leave. Kaoru hadn't won the argument, but he took satisfaction in having rattled the official.

Kaoru and Yukiko were allowed to take a long trip every two years or so—far more frequently than a typical North Korean, who would feel blessed if allowed to visit Pyongyang or Mount Kumgang even once in his life. Like all "leisure" activities in the North, travel had a revolutionary purpose, and a typical trip consisted of stops at historical sites such as Kim Il-sung's birthplace; the holy Mount Paektu, where it is alleged that Kim Jong-il was born; and the various battlefields where Kim Il-sung and his guerrilla army were said to have vanquished the Japanese. But for Kaoru, these trips stirred feelings other than North Korean patriotism, reminding him that he would never fit in.

In the summer of 1981, Kaoru and Yukiko drove 125 miles to the port city of Wonsan. It was the first time Kaoru had seen the Sea of Japan since being abducted, and he could barely contain his emotions. The ocean's aroma made him long for home. It was all he could do to stop himself from leaping into the waves. "If I just swam and swam, maybe I could make it back," he thought to himself. During a trip to Mount Paektu, Kaoru's minder took him and Yukiko to the banks of the Tumen River to view the Chinese towns on the other side. The border was open there, with no fences or guards. On the Korean side, women washed their clothes on stones, while their children frolicked naked in the water. On the Chinese side, a billboard read "Time Is Money," a slogan for the economic reforms spreading through the Communist country. Kaoru wondered if he and Yukiko could dash across and make their way to a Japanese consulate.

The only trip Kaoru enjoyed was to Mount Myohyang, known as the "Mysterious Fragrant Mountain"; its deep ravines, pristine waterfalls, and densely wooded forests soothed him. According to ancient legend, it was the home of Tangun, the mythical forefather of the Korean people. The area around the mountain is dotted with abandoned temples, but the modern attraction is the enormous museum exhibiting the gifts that foreign dignitaries gave Kim Il-sung and Kim Jong-il. While Kaoru came for the nature, his minders looked forward to the banquet at which they would drink copious amounts of *soju* (Korean vodka) and sing. Every night, his minders would press Kaoru to get drunk and sing with them. He would sip *soju*, and when his minders were inebriated, he would sneak out and explore the paths and bathe in the ravines. By tradition, one was allowed to wash only one's hands in the water, so Kaoru positioned himself behind a rock, away from the path.

"What are you doing? Don't you know that entering the water is *prohibited!*" shouted a hard-faced middle-aged man with an armband that identified him as the manager of the area. The sound shook Kaoru out of his state of calm. With a moment's hesitation, he put on his best penitent face. "I'm sorry, but the streams of my fatherland are so beautiful that I entered the water. I didn't know that doing so was forbidden," he said, modulating his Korean slightly to give it a foreign sound. "I live in the U.S. and this is the first time I've been able to visit the northern part of the Republic," he added, choosing his words carefully. The phrase "northern part of the Republic" was the locution international supporters of the regime used to describe North Korea, and the reference to the United States made Kaoru seem like an "important" visitor.

Hearing these words, the manager's face softened. "Oh, I see. You have made a long journey. The mountains and streams of our fatherland are splendid, aren't they? Please bathe yourself unobtrusively," he said with a big smile, and walked away.

When Kaoru and Yukiko had been reunited in 1980, they were told to come up with a plausible cover story that would hide their Japanese identities and help them blend into North Korean society.

Concocting a suitable cover would be easy in a pluralistic society where immigration and cultural differences were common, but the narratives Kaoru and Yukiko had to choose from to explain away their accents and their ignorance of all things North Korean were limited.[2]

There was one story, however, that seemed to fit the bill; it was about a group of Japanese-born immigrants who'd previously had trouble fitting into the North. These were the ninety-three thousand ethnic-Korean "repatriates" who had come to the North in the sixties and seventies to escape the discrimination and economic hardship of postwar Japan. Having relatives in Japan who could send them gifts, they were both envied and despised. Those whose Japanese relatives were too poor to support them were relocated to the cold, mountainous north of the country, far from Pyongyang. A disproportionate number ended up in the gulag, never to be heard from again. The fact that Kaoru and Yukiko had in reality grown up in Niigata prefecture, where the repatriation movement was based, bolstered their account. So Kaoru and Yukiko assumed the names Park Soon-chul and Kim Kum-sil, and manufactured elaborate stories of trading their lives in Japan for the adventure of moving to their sacred "homeland."

# 9

# THE REPATRIATION PROJECT:
# FROM JAPAN TO NORTH KOREA

At the conclusion of the Second World War, Japan was home to an estimated two million Koreans. One million had immigrated to Japan for economic reasons since the late nineteenth century, with roughly 80,000, many brought by force, coming every year from 1932 to 1940. During the war, 350,000 Koreans fought with the Japanese armed forces and 500,000 more worked in Japan's mines and factories.

The United States knew little about Korea when, on August 10, 1945, two young officers, future secretary of state Dean Rusk and Charles Bonesteel, drew a line across a *National Geographic* map dividing the Soviet and the American occupation zones at the Thirty-Eighth Parallel. The U.S. strategy was to refashion Japan into a bulwark against the Communist threat in China and the USSR, and the Koreans were perceived as an unstable and potentially disruptive leftist element. "As long as there is a sizeable Korean minority in Japan it will be a menace to law and order," concluded a British Commonwealth Occupation Force intelligence report. The United States was dimly aware of Japan's Korean minority and hoped they would simply return to Korea. And during the first three months of the occupation, from August through November 1945, eight hundred thousand of them did. The remaining six hundred thousand Koreans, many whose families had lived there for generations, became Japan's largest minority.

One reason they remained in Japan was the instability awaiting them on the divided Korean Peninsula. In the North, Soviet-style people's committees nationalized industry and redistributed land. On the brink of economic collapse, the South was ravaged by political infighting. Considering their options, many Koreans judged it safer to remain in Japan, where, as colonial subjects, they had been granted Japanese nationality. However, unlike other Japanese citizens, Koreans considered themselves victims of Japan, who, having been liberated by the Allies, deserved reparations. Against these sentiments, the United States weighed the fact that three hundred fifty thousand Koreans had fought *for* the Japanese.[1] So how should Koreans be treated under the occupation? As a liberated people who were victims *of* the Japanese, or as potential subversives who had fought *with* the Japanese? The compromise pleased no one: Koreans would be considered "liberated" nationals in ordinary circumstances and "enemy" nationals when military security was involved.

The 1951 San Francisco Peace Treaty formally ended the Allied occupation of Japan. The treaty stipulated that Japan relinquish the colonies it had acquired, which had the consequence of stripping Koreans and other ethnic minorities of Japanese citizenship, leaving them in legal limbo. Their fate was not resolved until 1965, when those Koreans who had been living in Japan before August 15, 1945, were allowed to apply for "permanent resident" status. They could remain in Japan indefinitely, but under the Alien Registration

Law they were barred from becoming lawyers, teachers, nurses, bank officers, or public servants (postal workers, firemen); in addition, they were ineligible for bank loans, scholarships, and welfare benefits. With Japanese unemployment soaring, most private-sector jobs were denied to them. As a result of these restrictions, a disproportionate number of Koreans in postwar Japan, much like blacks in Jim Crow America, pursued careers outside the mainstream, whether in sports, the arts, or organized crime. Others assimilated, using the Japanese names forced upon them in colonial times, and blended in so thoroughly that they unwittingly confirmed Japan's new self-image as an ethnically homogeneous nation.

Lacking citizenship and civil rights, Koreans in Japan saw their lives change little in the postwar era, and in many cases actually get worse. In 1952, 79 percent were unemployed. Excluded from the mainstream, Koreans committed crimes at six times the rate of the Japanese, and drug and alcohol abuse were problems. To improve their lot, Koreans sought help from two groups: Mindan, which served those who identified with capitalist South Korea, and Chosen Soren, which supported the Communist North. The Japanese Communist Party had cultivated a large Korean following after the war, and the number of Chosen Soren members vastly outnumbered Mindan's. Chosen Soren—its full name is the General Association of Korean Residents in Japan—became North Korea's de facto representative in Japan, issuing passports and performing basic diplomatic functions. It was also a social service provider, helping Koreans with jobs, housing, and education; facilitating travel to the peninsula; and maintaining the connection between Japan and North Korea.

In June 1956, Kim Il-sung issued Cabinet Order 53, in which he invited Japan's Korean population to return "home."[2] It was an enticing prospect, offering cash stipends in addition to free housing,

Repatriation ship in Niigata (Kyodo)

education, and health care. The Japanese government had been considering plans to get rid of the poorest, most left-leaning Koreans for several years, so it didn't take long for Prime Minister Kishi Nobusuke to give his consent.[3] Repatriation offered something for everyone. "In an era when Japanese politics were deeply polarized between right and left, repatriation brought both sides together. This issue was a vote winner, popular with media and the public alike," writes historian Tessa Morris-Suzuki in her study of the repatriation, *Exodus to North Korea*.[4] Japanese newspapers echoed Chosen Soren's promise of "Paradise on Earth," with headlines proclaiming, "Return of Compatriots from Japan Welcomed: Livelihood to Be Completely Guaranteed," and "No Unemployment for Returnees: Housing Ready to Receive 50,000 People." Under the auspices of the International Red Cross, the first of 187 ships, carrying 93,000 people, departed from Niigata on December 14, 1959.

The event was big news throughout Japan; the local *Niigata Nippo* assigned twenty reporters to cover it. Reporter Kimiya Nakajima recalls the sense of euphoria in the air.[5] "The repatriates looked radiant. They were emitting a kind of aura. They believed in North Korea and were excited to be contributing to its success," he tells me. "One man told me the North Koreans had developed a device fueled by atomic power that emitted a ray that could heal any disease. Japan didn't have one, but he swore that it was available to all North Koreans for free." Nakajima paid special attention to the eighteen hundred Japanese wives who accompanied the Korean repatriates. "It was never an issue of whether the wives believed in the stories about North Korea. Their husbands were going, and their nobility was believing in their husbands."

Born in Sabae City, in central Japan, in 1941, Hiroko Saito was barely eighteen when she met her husband.[6] Sabae is famous for the quality of its eyeglasses, and he worked in one of the factories. Born in Korea in 1936, he was three years old when his parents moved to Japan in search of employment. He understood a bit of Korean, but didn't speak it, and had assimilated so thoroughly that Hiroko wasn't aware he was Korean when they met. Once she learned of his origins, she panicked because she knew her parents would object. But in a gesture equal parts romance and rebellion, she defied them. "I told my mother I didn't care if he was Korean. I wanted to marry him," she says. She was tough, and confident that she could hold her own against any discrimination her decision brought her way. "As long as we were in Japan it didn't make any difference whether I married a Japanese or Korean," she says. They wed in 1959, and she gave birth to a girl the next year. Chosen Soren members began making the rounds of Sabae's Korean households in 1959, proselytizing about the wonders of North Korea. Hiroko's extended family—ten people in all—were extremely poor, and decided to make the journey.

Her sister-in-law was also Japanese, and the two women spent days agonizing over what to do. They wanted to remain in Japan, and suspected that the promises of a good life in North Korea were too good to be true. Also they felt it would be difficult to be separated from their families now that they had children. Yet, having defied their families and married men of Korean extraction, they couldn't move back in with those families. Still, the two women made the decision to stay in Japan, although they couldn't tell their families. Hiroko recalls the chaotic scene in Niigata. "There was a process in which they would ask us whether we were going to North Korea willingly. We thought the interview would be private, and that we'd each go into the room separately and say that we didn't want to go," she says.

Moving so many people from Japan to North Korea was a complex logistical affair. The two countries didn't have diplomatic relations and were still reeling from the destruction left behind by two wars. While the move was officially sponsored by the International Committee of the Red Cross, the governments of Japan, the United States, the Soviet Union, and North Korea were involved at every stage. The most contentious dispute was more philosophical than logistical. With ninety-three thousand émigrés—half of them women and children, many destitute—how could the Red Cross be certain they were moving to North Korea of their own free will? The organization insisted that it interview returnees one by one in private, to ensure that no one was being coerced and that each understood the step he or she was taking. But in such uncertain circumstances, what constituted a "properly informed choice"?

North Korea was enraged by the stipulation, and brought the whole process to a halt in protest. For the next few weeks, the hundreds of Koreans who arrived in Niigata by train were forced to live in tents. With their numbers growing and their living conditions worsening, a deal was struck. The Red Cross would be allowed to conduct its interviews, but the repatriates would be questioned as family units. And, as if to ensure a lack of privacy, it was specified that the interview rooms have no doors.

"Contrary to our expectations, we were interviewed all together, as a family," Hiroko recalls. She and her sister-in-law watched in pained silence as a Red Cross official asked her father-in-law, the patriarch of the family, if they were moving to North Korea of their own free will. "Yes," he replied.

Their boat departed Niigata on June 18, 1963, carrying thirteen hundred people, the largest number in the repatriation project so far. There were several other Japanese wives on board, and Hiroko remembers that they, too, looked nervous.

Precisely why Kim Il-sung invited Japan's Koreans to move to North Korea is still the subject of active debate. With all the challenges it faced in the wake of the Korean War, why would North Korea want such an enormous infusion of people? Was it a humanitarian act toward fellow Koreans? A pragmatic bid to alleviate a domestic labor shortage? Scholars have cast doubt on these explanations. North Korea's Five-Year Plan, released three months before the repatriation began, stated clearly that no increase in immigration was planned. "People who went to North Korea thinking they would work and contribute found that they didn't have much to do," says Park Jung-jin, a Seoul National University historian.[7] He argues that North Korea used the flow of people as a diplomatic tool. "The repatriation took place at precisely the moment when Japan and South Korea were making great advances in their normalization negotiations," he tells me. The spectacle of thousands of ethnic Koreans rejecting capitalist Japan and heading to the socialist North would throw a wrench into the process.

Judging by the fact that Japan–South Korea normalization talks didn't come to fruition until 1965, Kim Il-sung's intervention may have been successful. Since the majority of the Koreans in Japan originally came from the southern part of the peninsula, the repatriation was no small embarrassment for South Korea. In fact, South Korea was so incensed that it threatened to sink the ships sailing to North Korea from Japan.

In the end, North Korea probably had a variety of motivations for receiving the repatriates. But whether the ninety-three thousand returnees were victims of Japanese prejudice, beneficiaries of North Korean ethnic solidarity, or some combination of the two, they were surely also pawns in a tragic Cold War skirmish they knew nothing about.

Like Katsumi Sato, Harunori Kojima descended from a long line of poor Niigata rice farmers.[8] Born in 1931, Kojima, the second of nine children, grew up in Kameda, a village on the outskirts of Niigata. As a child he longed to take part in Japan's glorious war, and at thirteen his dream came true. In 1944, with U.S. forces advancing toward the home islands, Japan's fighter planes were outpaced by the improved U.S. models. If they couldn't hold their own in combat, perhaps they would be more effective as manually guided missiles? *Kamikaze* ("divine wind") is a historical reference to the gales that destroyed the Mongols when they tried to invade Japan in 1274. As the winds protected Japan then, the new kamikaze would protect it now. The first kamikaze attack occurred in October 1944, and it was a successful strategy at first. More than 2,000 planes made such attacks in the months that followed, but the death of 2,530 pilots had little impact on the course of the war.

Kojima arrived at training camp in July 1945, thrilled by the opportunity to take on the Americans, even though he knew it would cost him his life. With few functional planes available, the students were trained on ancient aircraft, some twenty years old. Because it was too dangerous to use real explosives, the planes were fitted with dirt-filled rice barrels to simulate the deadly pay-load. Miraculously, one month into Kojima's training, Japan sur-rendered. Although devastated by the loss, he was relieved to be alive. But what had all the young men of his generation died for? he wondered. He passed through Tokyo on the long slog back to Niigata and was shocked to discover that the city had been de-stroyed, block after block burned to the ground by incendiary bombs. This was what came from a nation geared toward war, he thought. "I understood then that Japan couldn't be rebuilt by mil-itarists. For that we needed an egalitarian, socialist state," he says.

It seemed to Kojima that everyone he knew in Niigata had come to a similar conclusion. He was impressed by the principled pacifism of the Communists who were released after long jail sentences, and he noted their growing presence in the legislature. Even his uneducated, rice-farming family had joined a leftist agricultural union. Kojima joined the Communist Party in 1950 and was assigned to the publishing division. He marched in Niigata's raucous May Day parade and applauded when Khru-shchev denounced capitalism on his 1959 trip to America. And it wasn't only the Japanese who were awakening to the miracle of socialism. "It seemed like all of Asia was taking up this philoso-phy," he says. "Why should we wait a day longer than we had to in order to reduce the terrible inequality of wealth in Japan?" One day, he stumbled on a copy of Edgar Snow's *Red Star over China* (1937), an admiring account of the author's time with Mao and his Red Army guerrillas. Kojima was intoxicated. "I saw the beauty and majesty of the Chinese experiment," he says. "We watched the flames of revolution spread across Asia and create the nation of North Korea."

Such was the ideological tenor of the Japanese who participated in the repatriation project. China seemed well on its way to success, but North Korea, devastated by the Korean War, needed help from its comrades. To support himself, Kojima ran a leftist bookstore two doors down from the cosmetics shop that Katsumi Sato and his wife ran. Sons of rice farmers and now fellow members of the Communist Party, Sato and Kojima met in 1955. "I trusted him deeply. We understood each other completely," says Kojima. From 1960 to 1964 they worked in the same downtown office building, Kojima for the Repatriation Cooperative Association, and Sato as secretary-general of Niigata's Japan–North Korea Friendship Association. Sato's job was to nurture the relationship between North Korea and the Japanese Communist Party, which he did so well that he was twice awarded North Korea's Medal of Honor. He had never known many Koreans, and he loved their passion and directness. "Their simplicity was magnificent. They didn't hide themselves: whatever they are, they'll show you," he says. While Sato cultivated the political alliance, Kojima took care of the repatriation project's day-to-day business. Families typically stayed in Niigata for three days before embarking, and he made sure their paperwork was in order. He noticed that Chosen Soren officials were always on hand to help the repatriates unburden themselves of possessions that were too large to take along.

The first of the Koreans to go were the poorest of the poor, the destitute who had nothing to keep them in Japan. Sato was surprised by how many of the men were missing fingers and limbs. It turned out that the Chosen Soren had, in good egalitarian fashion, given priority to those who'd worked dangerous wartime jobs in mines and factories. He was pleased that these unlucky souls were finally being treated like human beings. "This is what communism is all about!" he thought to himself. There were times when it felt like a big party. "I had never seen anyone so happy," says Kojima.[9] "They were smiling so much it looked like their faces were about to rip apart." Every night, the Korean repatriates and Japanese Communists would dance, and sing Korean folk songs.

Sato became particularly close to the head of Niigata's Chosen Soren branch and still gets emotional when he describes their last encounter, before the latter left for North Korea. "I said, 'Send me a letter when you get there so I know you are all right,'" says Sato. A few months passed, then a year, but Sato heard nothing. He asked colleagues if they had heard any news of his friend, but they had not. Finally, two years later, a letter arrived. The stock used for international letters was typically very thin, but the paper Sato's friend had used practically fell apart in his hands. "You wouldn't have used it for toilet paper, and all he had written on this miserable scrap of paper were praises for the Dear Leader, Kim Il-sung." The letter concluded with a request: "Please send me some pepper, seasonings, pens, writing paper, and a warm jacket."

More letters from repatriates arrived. The news was uniformly positive: life was wonderful, education and health care were free— all due to the generosity of Kim Il-sung. But they inevitably included requests for the most basic clothing, medicine, and food items, the kinds of things that even the poorest in Japan took for granted. Around 1961 the repatriates began using code to communicate their true feelings. The Japanese language, exquisitely sensitive to class distinctions, stipulates different grammatical constructions depending on the recipient. A letter from a close relative written in a style reserved for official communications sent a clear message: "Don't come." Other codes were based on the use of pencil or pen; if a letter was written in pen, it meant "You can believe what I have written," but if it was in pencil, that would indicate the opposite.[10] Other letters were more circumspect. As an addendum to the good news and praise for Kim Il-sung, they'd suggest their relatives join them—or so it seemed. In one, an uncle advised his nephew not to come until his twentieth birthday. The boy in question was a newborn, says Sato. In other cases, messages describing the abysmal living conditions were hidden on the back of the stamp.

 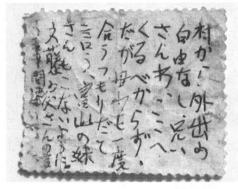

Stamp with secret messages sent from North Korea: "We cannot leave the village. Older brother, do not come. Mother says she wishes to see you. Tell our sister in Toyama also not to come. What Bunto's father said is correct."
(Courtesy of Kimikatsu Kinoshita)

The recipients were reluctant to discuss what they were learning, for fear that news of their discontent might reach North Korea, where it might endanger their families. Others held on to the chance that these were simply the complaints of a few ideologically suspect malcontents, as Chosen Soren officials assured them. Regardless of the veracity of the reports, nobody wanted to sully the reputation of the new socialist state.

In July 1964, Kojima was finally given permission to visit North Korea and see the promised land to which he had been sending people for the last five years. Despite the rumors, he was still a true believer in the Communist project and had made several requests to visit. Then, like now, North Korea was extremely secretive, and the only people who traveled back and forth between Japan and the North were government officials. Kojima visited all the important destinations: Pyongyang, Unsan, Kanko, Nampo, the demilitarized zone (DMZ) at the Thirty-Eighth Parallel. Conditions were more primitive than he had anticipated, but he chalked this up to the sanctions imposed by Western imperialists. More troubling was how closely his hosts monitored his group. Here they were, comrades in arms, watched over as if they were spies. They couldn't interact freely with North Koreans, and the people they did meet were too scared to say anything of substance. In fact, their responses felt rehearsed, invariably ending with some version of the phrase "due to the magnificent glory of Kim Il-sung." Kojima was especially eager to meet some of the repatriates he had helped emigrate, but he was told they were too busy working.

Like many other Japanese tourists at the time, Kojima was crazy about cameras and had brought two with him. One was a still camera, and the other was one of the new 8 mm video cameras whose sales were helping fuel Japan's postwar economic boom. Frustrated by how little he learned by talking to people, he vowed to take pictures of everything he saw. Kojima's enthusiasm made his government minders uneasy, and again and again they asked him to put his cameras away. At Unsan, he photographed a line of women walking down the road with baskets balanced on their heads in traditional fashion. His minder was aghast. "These are not the kind of photos you should take of North Korea," he said. A shot of a group of shirtless boys playing soccer in a village square was judged similarly inappropriate. Finally, they instructed him not to include *any* people in his photographs. Security officials went through Kojima's photos before he boarded his plane to Beijing, destroying any they deemed offensive. Fortunately, the 8 mm video camera was new enough that the North Koreans didn't have the technology to examine his footage.

Kojima was upset when he returned to Niigata. A condition of the trip was that he make several presentations describing the wonders of the socialist paradise. This posed a dilemma. How to avoid mentioning the disturbing aspects of the visit? He decided simply to describe what he had seen: new hospitals, schools, apartments, roads, and other products of a bustling nation. About the things he hadn't encountered—freedom to speak, freedom to inquire, freedom in general—he kept silent. "I was still working in the offices of the repatriation project, so I tried to rationalize it. I'd spent so many years as a Communist that telling the whole truth would have required me to reject everything I believed," says Kojima. There was only one person with whom he could share his doubts. A week after he returned, Kojima invited Sato to his house one evening to view the videos he'd made. "We started watching at about ten o'clock in the evening, and kept going until the sun came up. We'd watch the film through, again and again, stopping to discuss what we'd seen. Analyzing, arguing, wondering what it all meant," says Sato.

Kojima unburdened himself to his old friend, confessing his doubts about the North Korean experiment, and perhaps about communism itself. He told Sato how carefully his every step in North Korea had been choreographed by his minders, and how even the most seemingly innocent scenes were deemed inappropriate. He described the photos he had been forbidden from taking, and those that the censors had destroyed before he boarded his flight home. Had anyone other than Kojima said these things, Sato would have doubted him. But while watching the video footage, Sato began to realize that most of what he knew about North Korea was a carefully curated lie. "From then on, every time I saw an official photograph or article, I sensed the level of fabrication that had produced it," he says. "There was no relation to reality in what they were trying to feed us." As the sun rose, the two men sat in silence. They thought about the thousands of people they had sent to North Korea. "Sure, you've read the word *tyranny*, but have you ever really stared at tyranny itself? Have you seen concrete evidence that it exists, and known that you helped facilitate it?" asks Sato.

It took four years for Kojima to break with the party. He opened a kimono shop in northern Niigata, avoided his political friends, and tried to forget about the repatriation project. Sato had a more visceral reaction. A month after the night that Kojima showed him the video footage of North Korea, he came down with a psychosomatic asthmatic illness that made breathing difficult, sometimes impossible. He'd awake in the middle of the night gasping for air. At first he feared his tuberculosis was back, but the doctors found no evidence of that.

In 1965, Sato and his family moved to Tokyo, where he found a job with the Korea Research Institute, a pro–North Korea think tank that published policy papers about the peninsula. Working in a large city gave him access to a wider range of people and information than before, and he made the most of it, devouring anything having to do with North Korea. With his energy, Sato was soon running the institute. What's more, his neurotic illness disappeared, and he was able to breathe freely. Though disillusioned with North Korea, he still believed in the ideals of equality and justice he associated with the global Communist movement, and he refocused the institute to lobby for the rights of ethnic Koreans in Japan.

Sato visited China in 1975, during the final days of the Cultural Revolution, when Mao's cult of personality thrived and all who opposed him were terrorized. Sato was startled to see evidence of authoritarian tendencies similar to North Korea's. Mao, like Stalin and Kim Il-sung, dominated every aspect of society. Here, finally, was proof that the problems with the North Korean experiment weren't an aberration, but part of the DNA of communism itself. Sato's loss of faith was comparable to the one he had experienced at the end of the war. "I had memorized the Marxist discourse so well that I could pull it out and apply it to any situation. But now I had to refute all the ideas I had held as true, breaking down every theory. And then I had to build up my own sensibility from scratch, piece by piece. For the next three years I was barely able to write a sentence," he says. Sato's evolving ideology no longer fit with the Korea Research Institute's pro-North Korea policies, and in 1984 he broke with it and founded the Modern Korea Institute, starting a journal that became an important outlet for anti-North Korea essays and research. "I helped send the Korean residents in Japan to hell," he wrote in a remorseful 1995 essay, "instead of to the paradise they were promised."[11]

# 10

# NEIGHBORS IN THE
# INVITATION-ONLY ZONE

For all the regime's security arrangements, information circulated within the Invitation-Only Zone via one of humankind's most durable cultural practices: gossip. Soon after Kaoru and Yukiko moved into their first house, the woman who looked after them stopped by to introduce herself. The Hasuikes had not yet assumed their new identities and simply told her where they were from. "Ah, so you're Japanese!" the woman exclaimed, after hearing their accented Korean. "Another Japanese couple arrived a while ago. You should meet them!"

Engaged to be married in the fall of 1978, Yasushi Chimura and Fukie Hamamoto, both twenty-two, lived with their parents in Obama, a small coastal town three hundred miles west of Tokyo. Fukie sold cosmetics, and Yasushi worked in construction, and when they wanted to be alone, they drove Yasushi's car up a steep, twisty single-lane road to a cliffside park where couples came to gaze out at the ocean and kiss. July 7 was a moonless night, and

Young Yasushi and Fukie Chimura (Kyodo)

Yasushi and Fukie were sitting on a bench, picking out the familiar lights from the blackness that had enveloped the town, when four men jumped out from behind nearby bushes. After restraining the couple and placing them in separate bags, the men slung them over their shoulders and carried them several hundred feet down the hill to a waiting dinghy. As the men crossed the road from the bluff to the beach, Yasushi peered through the bag's mesh material and caught a glimpse of a passing car's taillights.

Like the Hasuikes, the Chimuras were separated before they arrived, each assured that the other had been left behind in Japan. Each morning when she awoke, Fukie would at first think she had only dreamed about the abduction. She yearned for Yasushi, whom she had expected to marry that fall. As weeks turned into months, and the reality of her situation sank in, her mood shifted from absolute despair to a kind of grim determination. She had to survive her ordeal. "I can live here, if I have to. But please, God, don't let me *die* here," she thought to herself.[1]

Fukie's minder repeatedly inquired whether she had any interest in getting married, which she interpreted as a tease about being of a "marriageable age." Gradually she realized he was serious, and feared she'd be forced into an arranged marriage, perhaps with a North Korean spy. "I knew I didn't want to marry anyone from North Korea, so I just replied as if it were a big joke. I'd say 'Are you *kidding* me? I couldn't do anything like that.'" So she had good reason to be apprehensive on the day she was presented with a pretty new dress and ushered into a suite of rooms that had been decorated for a formal occasion. An arranged marriage was indeed on the agenda, but the groom was familiar to her. After eighteen months of study and despair, Yasushi and Fukie wed the same day they were reunited.

Given that everyone living in the Invitation-Only Zone had secrets to hide, neighbors tended to keep their distance. It turned out that Kaoru and Yasushi had actually met during their first few months in captivity, but each had avoided discussing his circumstances for fear that the other was a spy planted to test his loyalty. In the Invitation-Only Zone, the two couples lived a few houses from each other. In order to talk privately, Kaoru and Yasushi developed a schedule for secret get-togethers, usually meeting at a designated spot in the surrounding woods. At the end of each meeting, they'd set a time, date, and place for the next one. They grew close, almost like brothers, and looked forward to talking, if only for the opportunity to compare notes and commiserate. Yasushi, a high school dropout, was impressed by Kaoru's intelligence and often turned to him for advice. After the birth of their children—the Hasuikes had a son and a daughter; the Chimuras, two sons and a daughter—the families would get together regularly for birthdays and holidays. There were times when, amid the pleasant excitement of friends and food, Kaoru would look out over the two families and momentarily forget where he was.

By paying the abductees for their work, as it would any other citizen, the regime perpetuated the myth that they were in North

Korea under normal circumstances. Although heavily regulated, certain markets were allowed in the North, even though the regime occasionally issued currency reforms and took other measures to curtail the freedom that came from exercising economic power. Paying the abductees in North Korean won would have been risky because it would have given them too much freedom to shop wherever they liked. So, initially, abductees were paid in a kind of government-issued scrip that could be used at only one store, the better to keep track of them.

During the later part of their captivity, the abductees were paid in American dollars. The official dollar-won exchange rate was absurdly low, fixed at the symbolically significant ratio of 2.16 North Korean won per U.S. dollar. (February 16 was Kim Jong-il's birthday.) One day, one of the chauffeurs offered to change Kaoru's dollars into won on the black market. He received a better rate and could therefore frequent inexpensive local merchants rather than only the designated foreign currency stores, where prices were several times higher. In the upside-down world Kaoru and the others inhabited, Japanese abductees posing as North Korean citizens were now able to exchange American dollars for North Korean won in order to purchase European toiletries.

Traveling outside the Invitation-Only Zone was permitted but was regulated by procedure. Fukie tried to leave the zone as often as possible. It was a change of scenery, a chance to buy some of the items she, a professional cosmetologist, missed from Japan. She usually shopped at the duty-free shop in downtown Pyongyang, using her government per diem to buy sweaters, cotton underwear, and a particular brand of French shampoo she was fond of. For her minder, however, every foray outside the zone was a potential security breach. A routine developed. Fukie's minder would pick her up at her home in an unmarked sedan and drive forty-five minutes to downtown Pyongyang. As their car approached the duty-free store, he would scan the license plates of the cars parked out front. North Korean license plates are color-coded—the license plates of foreign diplomats are blue, military plates are black, and the few people wealthy enough to own private cars have orange plates—so that the provenance of every vehicle can be identified from a distance. If he spotted a foreigner's plate, Fukie's minder would circle the block until the suspicious car left.

Oddly, once inside the shop, Fukie's minder didn't pay much attention to the people she encountered there. In fact, she suspects there were times when he intentionally arranged for her to come into contact with foreigners, just to see how she behaved. In addition to Pyongyang's few tourists and diplomatic staffers, Fukie met a virtual United Nations of abductees—from Italy, Thailand, Romania, and Lebanon. Always cautious, she would glance at her minder before initiating contact. "As long as I didn't talk to any Japanese people, I don't think he cared whom I met. After all, what could any of us do?" she says. Conversations were always circumspect, and nobody said a word about *how* they'd come to be living in North Korea. The abductees would swap items among themselves, trading shampoo for cosmetics and other goods, before getting back into their respective cars and returning to their own Invitation-Only Zones.

Having children tied Kaoru and Yukiko more firmly to life in North Korea. The couple gave their son and daughter secret Japanese names, Shigeyo and Katsuya, when they were born in 1981 and 1985. Kaoru had lost interest in his own life, but with children he now felt a sense of hope for the future. "I lost my family bonds due to the abduction, but was now able to create new bonds," he says. "To ensure that our kids could eat, have their own families, and live a life worth living after we died—that became the goal of my life," he explains. "Dreaming about their future made our lives more bearable." North Korea was his children's home in a way that it had never been his, and he had to do whatever he could to help them survive.[2]

Kim Jong-il's first public appearance, in October 1980, gave Kaoru cause for hope. The aging Kim Il-sung had been making arrangements for his son to succeed him since the late 1960s, and while newspapers had mentioned Kim Jong-il before (as when he joined the Politburo in 1974), his image had never appeared in public. "He represented a brand-new hope for us. A strong, young man who would lead the country into a new era," Kaoru recalls. "There was a great deal of excitement throughout the country, and I shared it." In addition to introducing Kim Il-sung's successor, the Sixth Congress of the Workers' Party kicked off a new seven-year economic plan, at the end of which every citizen was promised a color television, new clothes, and improved housing. "We were promised a new era with a very specific description of what that would entail," Kaoru says.

If he and Yukiko were confined to a bubble, their children lived in a bubble within the bubble. Every day, a minder would ferry the Hasuikes' son and daughter back and forth to daycare facilities outside the Invitation-Only Zone. Like kids growing up anywhere, the children perceived their lives as normal. For native North Koreans, secrets and omnipresent surveillance were as common as air. To them, the Invitation-Only Zone was not a prison, but rather the North Korean version of a gated community.

The Hasuike and Chimura children led happy, even privileged lives. Both Kaoru and Yasushi's daughters danced in the mass games, the synchronized multimedia extravaganza performed in Kim Il-sung Stadium each fall. All was well until their eighth birthdays. Receiving an education so close to the Invitation-Only Zone posed a problem. Now that they were entering the kinds of friendships in which children compared the details of their family lives, the regime feared that information about the Invitation-Only Zones would spread, along with curiosity about these special communities. The coast of North Korea is peppered with dozens of islands, many of which are too small for proper schools. For the children of those who inhabit the islands, the state set up a system of public boarding schools. So it was decided that the abductees' children would attend a boarding school two hundred miles north of Pyongyang, where whatever they had gleaned about the zone would be less meaningful. If none of the students knew precisely where, or with whom, their fellow students lived, any information they learned about them was useless. The abductees' children would visit home for three months, during winter and summer holidays. There were no parents' day visits or phone calls, and care packages took a month to arrive, if they were delivered at all.

Like their parents, the children were passing as North Korean. Unlike their parents, however, they believed they *were* North Korean. As they got older, they began to question parts of their parents' cover story. Doing so sometimes led to tension. Although they spoke only Korean in public, Fukie and Yasushi occasionally lapsed into Japanese at home. Hearing the language he had learned to associate with colonial oppressors, their eight-year-old son turned on his mother. "You're Japanese!" he shouted. Fukie couldn't help herself. "Well, if I'm Japanese, then you're Japanese, too!" she replied. He was taken aback by her irrefutable logic. The thought that he might not be pure North Korean upset him. "But I'm different . . . I'm not like *that*," he stammered. "Maybe Dad is Korean."

Perhaps the oddest aspect of the abduction project is how little the regime benefited from it. At first Kaoru taught Japanese language and customs to spies, but this came to an end in 1987, when a captured North Korean spy confessed to having been trained by a female Japanese abductee. From then on, their main job was to translate articles from Japanese into Korean, a task that could have been performed by any one of the millions of North Koreans who had learned Japanese during the colonial era. At the start of every week, the Hasuikes and Chimuras would receive a huge stack of Japanese magazines and newspapers—*Asahi, Akahata, Yomiuri, Mainichi, Sankei*—with large sections blacked out by the censor and specific articles circled for translation. (The elite members of North Korean society were allowed limited access to the foreign press through a government publication that aggregated approved international news for circulation.) Kaoru and Yasushi would translate, and Yukiko and Fukie would type the finished product on enormous manual typewriters. "I was able to hear more about the outside world than average North Koreans. I read Japanese and South Korean magazines, and there was a period when I could listen to NHK and the Voice of America broadcasts on a shortwave radio. I had a general grasp of the major global developments, although I was always one beat behind," says Kaoru.[3] And like all North Koreans, the abductees learned to read between the lines. In the run-up to the 1988 Seoul Olympics, the North did everything it could to detract from its rival's success. As with Japan in the 1964 Olympics, the 1988 Olympics symbolized the South's arrival as a democratic world power. In a desperate attempt to upstage the South, the North blew up a Korean airliner the year before, killing everyone on board. Kaoru could tell from the vehemence and character of the denial that the North was guilty.

The newspapers were heavily redacted, but censors inevitably missed things; because they weren't aware of the top-secret abduction project, articles about the abductions weren't always blacked out. One morning in 1997, Fukie came upon an article in *Asahi* about a new association created by the families of alleged abductees.

At the top of the page was an old photograph of her. It wasn't the most flattering picture, but it meant that someone in Japan knew what had happened to them. She ran home to show Yasushi. She wanted to cut the article out and keep it, but he insisted she return it along with the other papers, so as not to arouse suspicion. All their friend Kaoru could think when he saw the photos was how much older his father looked. "I felt like I was suffocating," he says. "I knew that my disappearance was the reason my father had aged so much."[4]

Like consumers of news anywhere, the abductees followed each world event with one eye on its implications for their lives. The assassination of South Korean president Park Chung-hee (by the head of the South's own intelligence agency) in October 1979 was immediately trumpeted over North Korean radio. The South was on the verge of collapse! Reunification was imminent! Kaoru wondered what reunification would mean for him and the other abductees. Would they be freed? However, when nothing happened, the official media went silent on the subject.

The fall of the Soviet Union was the most difficult story to comprehend. Kaoru deduced that the North Korean regime was feeling threatened from the fact that the censors were blacking out more material than ever. In 1985 he had interpreted Gorbachev's policy of perestroika as portending socialism's rebirth. He was therefore shocked four years later when the Communist leaders of East Germany, Poland, Romania, and Hungary were ousted. And not only were North Korea's friends falling from power, but those who survived, such as Russia and China, were normalizing relations with South Korea. Reading between the lines, Kaoru felt it was clear that nothing was going to change and that, in the future, the North was going to be more isolated than ever.

# 11

## STOLEN CHILDHOODS:
## MEGUMI AND TAKESHI

The two-hour bullet train from Tokyo to Niigata traverses a seemingly endless patchwork of rice fields. Intersected by two rivers, and hard by the Sea of Japan, Niigata is known as the "city of water," receiving more than one hundred fifty days of rain a year, the source of its prized sweet rice and sake. There is another sense in which it owes its existence to its climate. One of five cities the United States considered for the 1945 atomic bombing, Niigata was judged too cloudy for an accurate shot, so Nagasaki was obliterated instead.

Through wars hot and cold, the city has linked Japan to the outside world. In 1869 its ports were opened for trade by the Japan-U.S. Treaty of Amity and Commerce. During colonial times, many of Japan's military incursions into Asia were launched from here. In the sixties and seventies it was the organizational hub for the ninety-three thousand ethnic Koreans who left Japan for North Korea. In the 1970s Niigata's proximity to the North made it a natural destination for Kim Jong-il's spies. As recently as 2006, it was the destination of a regular ferry route between Japan and North Korea. Kaoru and Yukiko Hasuike were taken from a beach forty-five miles south of here; and the most famous abductee, Megumi Yokota, was snatched off a residential Niigata street, barely a hundred yards from her home.

I make a pilgrimage to Niigata whenever I'm in Japan, and have come to think of the city as psychologically divided into two neighborhoods: "Abduction-land" and "Repatriation-ville," both tied to the Korean Peninsula. Hop a cab at the central railway station and head west toward the ocean on Route 7. When you come to the Shinano River, you have a choice, much like the choice facing modern Japan. Cross the river and you're in Abduction-land, the neighborhood where a thirteen-year-old girl named Megumi Yokota was abducted in 1977. But if you turn right at the river and drive down Route 113 to the port, you're in Repatriation-ville, the staging ground where ninety-three thousand Japanese-born Koreans and their spouses set out for new lives in North Korea.

Something between a heavy mist and a light drizzle falls as my cab navigates its way over the Shinano River and through the narrow streets of western Niigata. The driver is puzzled that I want to visit the beach on such a miserable day, but when I explain that I'm investigating the disappearance of Megumi Yokota, he tells me he had just started driving his cab in 1977 and remembers the events of that fall well. "People were searching for her everywhere, on the beaches, on the streets," he says. We arrive at the ocean and he gestures at the desolate seascape. "See how open it is here? There's no protection for us. Anyone could come here without being noticed." Using a map, I walk down Megumi's street, searching for her house. I spot a mother and daughter, huddled beneath umbrellas, and ask if they know which house is Megumi's. The mother doesn't, but her daughter—a vision in neon,

Megumi Yokota (Getty)

wearing a yellow raincoat and pink boots—perks up and tells me
brightly that she knows exactly where it is. We make an odd trio:
a little girl leading her mother leading a journalist. A few blocks
on, the girl stops and points proudly to a well-tended stucco house
behind an impressive latticed gate. Soon after I arrive, the next-
door neighbor emerges from his house. Once he confirms I'm not
a burglar, he introduces himself as Susumu Yamashita, an interior
designer born and bred in Niigata. The house I've been led to
isn't Megumi's, he tells me. Rather, it was used as the backdrop
for a television movie about her, which is why the little girl recognized it. For her, Megumi is a television character. "The Yokotas' house was torn down several years ago," he says as we walk
down the street, toward a cluster of smaller, more modern homes

where Megumi's once stood. "After the Yokotas moved, every-one in the neighborhood kept the house in pristine condition, not changing a thing, so that Megumi would recognize it if she came home. Even after the house came down, they took great care to preserve the gate in front of it. But they eventually took that down, too."

The interior designer offers to show me around Niigata, and we hop into his car to trace Megumi's last steps on Japanese soil. We pass by her elementary school, which he also attended. "The assumption is that she left through this gate and then made a right turn down the road. The dogs followed her steps until this point," he says, gesturing to the intersection at which it is believed she was forced into a car. Over a thousand police from all across Niigata prefecture were called in to search for Megumi in the days after her disappearance, setting up roadblocks and stopping every car. "When she vanished, nobody used the word *abduction*. Nobody imagined her disappearance had anything to do with North Korea. From what I heard, the family was worried that a pedo-phile in town had taken her. The whole city was seized by a kind of moral panic," he says.

At six o'clock on the evening of November 15, 1977, Megumi Yokota was walking home from badminton practice with two friends. They parted company three blocks from the Yorii Junior High School, and the friends' last glimpse of Megumi was of her pausing at a traffic light, her badminton racquet stuffed in a white bag, a black book bag in her hand. Megumi was never late, so at seven o'clock her mother, Sakie, panicked.[1] Shigeru, Megumi's father, called the police when he got home from his job at the Bank of Japan, and the parents and officers spent a good part of the night searching the neighborhood. The following morning, the police moved a special kidnapping unit to the Yokotas' house to trace any calls. For the next week, the police, lined up ten abreast, combed the shore, prodding the ground with metal sticks. A helicopter looked several miles to the north and south. Divers scoured the harbor, and coast guard boats crisscrossed the sea beyond.[2]

The Yokotas put their lives on hold, making sure that one of them was always at home in case Megumi returned. They stopped taking family trips with Megumi's younger twin brothers, and they replaced the light on the gate with a brighter model, which they kept on day and night. Every morning, Shigeru walked along the shore, examining the objects brought in by the tide. During the day, Sakie circled the town on her bicycle, checking train and bus stations. Whenever a car idled in front of the house, Sakie would look out to see if her daughter was in it. She watched the movies Megumi had seen during summer vacation, hoping to find a clue as to whether she might have run away. Sakie and Shigeru appeared on several morning television shows with segments during which the families of missing people publicize their plights. Most guests received at least a few calls with information, but the Yokotas' phone sat silent. For the next few months, if Sakie spotted a girl on the street with a round face and short, straight hair, she would rush over to her to see if it was her daughter. Once, when she saw a newspaper photo of a little girl who looked like Megumi, she contacted the newspaper, which sent her enlarged versions of the original. Over the years, Sakie took note of women who looked the way she imagined Megumi would appear at various points in her life, whether as a teenager in high school or a young professional in her twenties. Shigeru scolded Sakie for her obsession, but when they both saw a portrait of a young woman in an art gallery, even he was struck by the resemblance. Perhaps Megumi had amnesia and was working as an artist's model? They contacted the artist, but it turned out the model was a friend of hers.

The Bank of Japan's policy at the time of Megumi's disappearance was to transfer executives every five years, but it allowed

Shigeru to remain in Niigata and look for his daughter. Six years later, however, the bank wanted to relocate him to Tokyo. As much as they wanted to stay, the Yokotas decided that with Megumi's brothers about to start high school, it was as good a time as any to move. The strain of having lost Megumi was often unbearable, and perhaps the family would benefit from a change of scene. The Niigata police assured them that the investigation would continue, so in 1983 they sold the house, posted a note (wrapped in plastic) on the gate with their new address, and moved to Tokyo. For the next twenty years they received little attention from the government or the media as they looked for answers to their daughter's disappearance. In 1997, Megumi became the patron saint of the abductee movement, her portrait, with dark bangs and dimpled cheeks, on posters at every event. Megumi's story has been told in four documentaries, an animated movie, a two-volume comic book, a television drama, and two songs, one by Peter Frampton and another by Peter, Paul and Mary's Paul Stookey.

North Korea claims that Megumi struggled with depression and committed suicide in 1994. Her parents believe she would never kill herself and insist she is alive. What isn't in dispute is that while in North Korea, Megumi married a South Korean abductee and had a daughter, Kim Eun-gyong, who majored in computer science at Kim Il-sung University and now has a daughter of her own. There is no need for genetic testing or diplomatic negotiations in this case. Kim Eun-gyong is the spitting image of her mother.

In August 1978, Kim Young-nam, a sixteen-year-old high school student, was on a trip with his friends on Seonyu Beach in southwest South Korea. The boys slept in tents while the girls stayed in homes in a nearby village. Kim was small for his age, and the older boys tended to pick on him. Fed up, he retreated to a remote part of the beach and hid in a small rowboat, where he fell asleep. "When I woke up, I was in the middle of the ocean

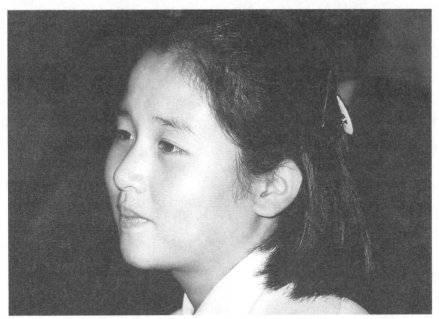

Megumi Yokota's daughter, Kim Eun-gyong (Associated Press)

and had no idea where I was. The shore was out of sight. I was so nervous that I thought I was going to die soon," he told a newspaper reporter many years later. After drifting a few hours, Kim says, he was picked up by a North Korean ship and taken to the port of Nampo. Choosing his words carefully, he describes the event as "neither an abduction nor a voluntary defection. It was simply a chance-happening in the era of confrontation."[3] The waters surrounding South Korea must have been particularly treacherous that August, because a week after Kim's rescue, another student had a similar experience. And a week after that, it happened again. All told, five South Korean teenagers disappeared within a few weeks of one another.

The South Korean National Security Service later learned that two of the students worked in a true-to-scale replica of downtown Seoul known as the Center for Revolutionizing South Korea. Buried deep beneath Kim Il-sung University in Pyongyang, it is a vast underground facility, reputed to be forty feet tall, one hundred feet wide, and five miles long. Though North Korean spies possessed the language skills with which to infiltrate the South, they lacked the cultural literacy required to navigate the vastly different society the South had become. In order to blend into daily life, spies had to be familiar with the chaotic marketplace culture that dominates everyday life in the capitalist South. The center contained mock-ups of the president's house, police headquarters, the Shilla Hotel, and the Lotte department store. South Korean television programs and radio shows blared from speakers. The center was a "Little Seoul," replete with neon signs for cafés, hotels, nightclubs, restaurants, and boutiques where North Korean spies learned how to act like South Korean consumers. Every week, a spy received five hundred dollars' worth of South Korean won to use for haircuts, checking into hotels, purchasing groceries from supermarkets, and buying drinks at bars. To add verisimilitude, some of the cashiers, porters, and bartenders were South Korean abductees. One student worked in a supermarket; another manned a sporting goods store; Kim Young-nam taught spies to speak with a southern accent.

In February 1986, Kim was introduced to a young woman who was going to teach him Japanese. Barely thirteen when she was abducted, Megumi had been having emotional problems since she got to North Korea. She hadn't yet completed junior high school in Niigata, so she was assigned a Japanese teacher to get her through high school. When she had difficulty learning Korean, she was placed in a remedial class with Yasushi and Fukie Chimura, the Japanese couple who lived in the Invitation-Only Zone. Fukie became something of a mother figure and taught Megumi how to sew.[4] Before that, Megumi had lived for eighteen months with Hitomi Soga, another Japanese abductee. Megumi had been promised that if she studied hard she would eventually be released, and

Kim Young-nam, Megumi, and their daughter (Associated Press)

was devastated when she discovered this was merely a lie to placate her. Her minders hoped she would calm down if they found her a husband. Kim proposed six months after they met, and they were married in August. Megumi gave birth to a daughter on September 13, 1987, which Kim says brightened her mood. "When Eungyong was born, Megumi was delighted and put her heart and soul into raising her," he said. She became a new woman, he says, cooking Japanese food and sharing a few details about her family with him, though not about her abduction.[5]

In June 1994, Megumi and Kim moved into a house in the same Invitation-Only Zone where the Hasuikes and Chimuras lived. Fukie was delighted to see Megumi again but says that she was very depressed. According to Kim, Megumi was in and out of a mental hospital for several years, and the regime reports she committed suicide during one of her stays. Sakie and Shigeru believe their daughter is still alive. "I will never lose hope and believe there will be a day when we are reunited with Megumi. I will wait for that day," says Sakie.

The northwest coast of Japan is a place of violent beauty. Volcanic cliffs plunge into craggy beaches punctuated by jetties and peninsulas where flows of molten lava are cooled by the sea. As I wander up and down the coast, visiting the sites where people were abducted, I am struck by the contrast between the coast's physical beauty and the pain suffered by the families of the missing. Does anyone ever truly recover from the violence of sudden loss? For many, such as Sakie and Shigeru Yokota, time stopped the day their loved ones disappeared.

On May 11, 1963, Tomoe Terakoshi's thirteen-year-old son, Takeshi, disappeared while on a fishing trip with his two uncles.[6]

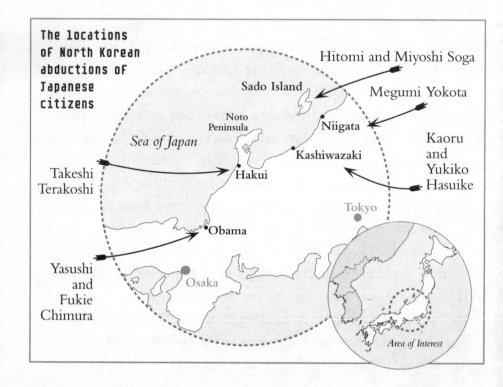

The locations of North Korean abductions of Japanese citizens

Hitomi and Miyoshi Soga
Megumi Yokota
Sado Island
Noto Peninsula
Sea of Japan
Niigata
Kashiwazaki
Kaoru and Yukiko Hasuike
Takeshi Terakoshi
Hakui
Tokyo
Obama
Yasushi and Fukie Chimura
Osaka
Area of Interest

Their small boat was last seen at four in the afternoon, as they set out nets to catch rockfish a quarter mile off the coast of Shikamachi, a fishing village one hundred forty miles southwest of Niigata. The plan was to fish all afternoon and evening, and return that night. The next morning, the boat was found floating four miles offshore. Its motor was intact, but the left side of the bow was damaged, marked with traces of green paint. The fishing net and Takeshi's school uniform washed up nearby. The town's fishermen suspended work and searched the sea and coastline, and the police checked every boat in the harbor for traces of a collision. With no clues, the search was suspended after a week. The Terakoshi family held a funeral, using photos of the missing in lieu of their remains. Takeshi's father couldn't bear to continue fishing in the same sea that had swallowed up his son and two brothers, and found work in a quarry. But even with the funeral, Tomoe couldn't move on. Every morning, she'd burn incense where Takeshi's uniform was found and make an offering of flowers and bean buns, Takeshi's favorite. She visited a fortune-teller who told her that Takeshi was dead, "wrapped in a fishing net, which is why his body can't be found." Years passed, and the Terakoshis moved to nearby Kanazawa, where there were fewer memories of Takeshi. Then, in January 1987, the family received a letter:

> Sister, I cannot express myself well trying to write how lonely I have been for twenty-five years, and how much I want to see my parents. Shoji, Takeshi and I suddenly wound up living in North Korea in May 1963. Please don't worry, since I married here, have two children and am happy with my family.

The letter was signed Kim Chul-ho, the Korean name the uncle had taken, and the address was in a northern province in North Korea. Could Takeshi be alive? A few weeks later, a letter from Takeshi to his mother arrived, written mostly in Korean and sprinkled with bits of Japanese. "Mother, I hope you can use this to confirm it's me. There was a bus stop at the cooperative office, I got off the bus and climbed a hill. In front of a house, there was Grandma's rice field. There were four persimmon trees, two of them were sweet persimmons, and there was a loquat tree," he wrote. The description matched the area around Tomoe's mother's house, where Takeshi had played as a child. He was alive! She'd finally found her son! But what should she do now?

She brought the letter to the local police, who were skeptical about her story and told her that North Korea wasn't within their jurisdiction. She visited the Red Cross, hoping that an international aid organization might help her. "Ma'am, what do you think the Red Cross *does*?" a clerk asked her. "We help those who are in danger. But this letter says your son is alive and happy." She met with members of the local government and went to Tokyo to meet with her national representatives. But every time she mentioned North Korea, their facial expressions changed and a hardness set in. No one was willing to get involved—until she met a Socialist politician who was also a member of the Japan–North Korea Friendship Association. The Socialists then had friendly relations with the North, and he told Tomoe he would help her arrange a trip to see her son.

That August, Tomoe and her husband spent three days in Pyongyang touring the sites. They visited the Juche Tower, the Arch of Triumph (thirty-three feet taller than the one in Paris), and the USS *Pueblo*, and they took an overnight trip to the DMZ. "By the end of the third day, I thought I had been fooled and Takeshi was dead after all. I feared they were going to bring in someone who looked like him. I was too sad even to cry," she tells me. The next morning, her interpreter arrived at her hotel, brought her downstairs, and asked if she wanted to see her son. "My legs froze. They opened the door and I saw a crowd of party officials. "I didn't recognize anyone and thought, 'Oh, this is a big lie!'" Finally, Takeshi emerged from the crowd. He hugged his father but not his mother. "I cried and cried, but he didn't," she says. "He had been instructed not to show too many emotions."

Takeshi worked in a steel mill in a remote industrial area three hours north of Pyongyang, near the Chinese border. His wife was a singer and a member of the corps of beautiful young women charged with entertaining Kim Il-sung. They'd met when Takeshi was in his twenties, having spent his formative years in the North, successfully passing as a full-fledged North Korean citizen. Ethnic purity is taken very seriously in North Korea, so Takeshi's Japanese heritage would have diminished his social standing and made him a much less desirable mate. He hid his past from his wife and in-laws, but in the back of his mind he feared that one day the truth would come out. In preparation for Tomoe's visit, the regime shipped Takeshi's whole family to Pyongyang for a month so that they could eat well and acquire the veneer of urban sophistication. The day before Tomoe arrived, Takeshi finally confessed to them that his mother, and therefore he, was from Japan. With the realization that she had unwittingly married an enemy foreigner, a match that would surely diminish her family's status, Takeshi's wife fainted.

Determined to make up for the lost years, Tomoe began visiting Takeshi once or twice a year, bringing as many clothes and electric appliances as her small budget allowed. In between visits, she would send money, concealing Japanese yen in pickled plum jars or sewing bills into neckties and overcoats to keep them from being stolen. When she received a letter thanking her for the delicious plums, she knew Takeshi had received the money.

What Takeshi's wife didn't anticipate was that her husband's new status as a Japanese-born North Korean who claimed he was living happily in his adopted home would overnight make him more valuable to the regime and thereby elevate his place in society. He was promoted to a position as the assistant director of the steel-workers' union, and the family moved to Pyongyang permanently, living in a floor-through apartment in a modern, twenty-six-story building. With eight rooms and two bathrooms (one Western and one Japanese), it was located in fashionable central Pyongyang.

Tomoe's emotions wavered over the years, and at one point she was persuaded to add Takeshi's name to the official list of abductees. "Mother, is it your intention to cut relations with me forever?" he wrote. Takeshi insisted he had been rescued, not abducted, and explained that her saying otherwise would have unpleasant consequences for him. She quickly begged the Japanese government to remove his name, which it did.

I ask Tomoe what she thinks really happened that night in 1963, and she looks away. "Well, he certainly didn't *walk* to North Korea; I know that much," she says with a sigh. "There are many complaints I want to make to North Korea. There also are many complaints I want to make to the Japanese government. But I never speak up. This is not a matter between two countries. This is a matter between a mother and her son." I ask whether she feels a connection between herself and Sakie Yokota. Their stories of loss are similar, but Tomoe has been given the opportunity to establish a relationship, strained though it is, with her long-lost child. The two women have met, and Tomoe was for a time a member of the association of families with abducted children that the Yokotas helped found. "I think that in our hearts we support each other as mothers who lost their children at age thirteen," Tomoe replies. "However, the two mothers are now walking separate roads."

# 12

# AN AMERICAN IN PYONGYANG

The one-hundred-sixty-mile-long, two-and-a-half-mile-wide demilitarized zone (DMZ) between North and South Korea is the most heavily fortified border in the world. Thirty-five miles from Seoul (population ten million), it is an untouched stretch of nature, home to several endangered species—the red-crowned crane, the Amur leopard, the Asiatic black bear—and one million land mines. A combination of U.S. and South Korean troops, operating under the aegis of the United Nations, has patrolled the DMZ since an armistice agreement brought fighting to an end on July 27, 1953.

On the evening of January 4, 1965, Sgt. Charles Robert Jenkins drank a six-pack of beer and set out on his nightly patrol of the DMZ. Jenkins had been in the military since dropping out of school at age fifteen and talking his way into the National Guard. Born on February 18, 1940, in the tiny town of Rich Square, North Carolina, he had a simple motivation for joining. "I didn't have nothing else to do, and in the National Guard I got one day's worth of army pay for doing just two hours of work a week," he tells me.[1] He joined the army's First Cavalry Division when he turned eighteen, and served at Fort Dix and Fort Hood before volunteering to go to Korea, which earned him a promotion to sergeant. After easy tours in South Korea and Germany, he was posted to Camp Clinch, right on the DMZ, and assigned to a four-man "hunter-killer" team, tasked with drawing fire from North Korean troops during nightly patrols.

Sergeant Jenkins (Associated Press)

If providing target practice for the enemy wasn't bad enough, there were rumors that his division was going to be sent to Vietnam. Jenkins grew depressed, drank heavily, and came up with a plan. "I would walk north across the DMZ and into North Korea. Once there, I would ask to be handed over to the Russians, and request a diplomatic exchange for passage back to the United

States," he writes in his memoir, *The Reluctant Communist*.[2] At 2:30 a.m., Jenkins informed his squad that he was going to check the road, but instead he tied a white T-shirt to his M-14 rifle and crossed into the DMZ, taking "high, slow, deliberate steps to avoid trip wires that would set off a mine," he writes. "It was the stupidest thing I've ever done," he tells me matter-of-factly. Three weeks later, one of the North's propaganda loudspeakers announced the news of his arrival. "The Republic that is the Eternal Paradise will protect with hospitality the brave Sergeant Jenkins!"

The U.S. military tried to keep Jenkins's defection quiet, for fear that more soldiers might follow. He was not the first. A month earlier, Jerry Wayne Parrish, also of the First Cavalry, had defected, and two other soldiers, Larry Abshier and James Dresnok, had defected three years before. None were motivated by ideological conviction. Abshier was being court-martialed for intoxication and dereliction of duty. Dresnok, described in an army report as "a chronic complainer, lazy . . . belligerent, defiant to authority," was facing court-martial for forging signatures on documents that granted him extra leave.

After being debriefed by the North Koreans, Jenkins was assigned to live with the other three men in a two-room house, where they took turns sleeping on the floor. Compared to the bleak existence for most North Koreans, Jenkins lived well, carousing like a drunken frat boy with the three other Americans. "We were Cold War trophies, which is why we were never treated like POWs. Our pictures were in propaganda pamphlets and movies, so they had to keep us looking healthy," he says.[3]

The American defectors worked primarily as English teachers. In the seventies, Jenkins taught at a military school. "If my students made mistakes, sometimes I corrected them and sometimes I didn't," he tells me. They also worked as actors whenever a North Korean film or television show called for Western villains.

The most popular was *Unsung Heroes*, a twenty-episode series featuring Jenkins as "Dr. Kelton," the head of the U.S. Korean War operations. Among the oddest jobs Jenkins had was translating English-language films for Kim Jong-il. Even this seemingly innocuous assignment was cloaked in secrecy, as Jenkins could listen to, but not view, the films he was working on. In addition, each movie was spliced into segments and mixed up with segments from other movies. "We really were just translating strings of words rather than anything that made sense, not enjoying a story," he writes. Still, he gleaned enough to identify *Kramer vs. Kramer* and *Mary Poppins*. At night, the Americans would watch Western movies, tapes of which Jenkins was able to get from members of Pyongyang's small diplomatic community. The most reliable was an Ethiopian named Sammy, a composition student at the Pyongyang music college. He and Jenkins established a routine in which they'd meet in a downtown Pyongyang restaurant with floor-length drapes in the windows. Sammy would hide the tapes behind the curtains, stroll by Jenkins's table, and tell him things were "in position." At night, the defectors watched the movies with the curtains drawn and the volume low. Jenkins later developed a particular fascination with Michael Jackson after watching his *Thriller* video. In 1972, Jenkins was informed that, thanks to the benevolence of Kim Il-sung, he had been granted North Korean citizenship. "What if we don't take it?" he asked. "Then you won't be here tomorrow," the cadre replied.

In 1978 the regime began pairing the defectors with women who had been abducted from a variety of countries. Parrish married a Lebanese woman named Siham Shrieteh, who had been lured to North Korea with three other women with the promise of secretarial jobs that paid a thousand dollars a month. The parents of one of the women had connections to the Lebanese government, which was able to free all four of them. But when Siham arrived home pregnant, her family sent her back to North Korea to live with her husband, Parrish. Abshier married a Thai woman named Anocha Panjoy, who was working as a masseuse in Macau when she was abducted. Dresnok married Doina Bumbea, a Romanian artist who had been lured from Italy with the promise of an art show.

Hitomi Soga (Kyodo)

In the spring of 1980, Jenkins was told the regime wanted him to teach English to a woman, to whom he would be introduced. He'd previously been assigned a series of cooks, with whom he'd been sexually involved, but this was the first time he was formally introduced to someone. At 10:00 p.m. on June 30, there was a knock at Jenkins's door. He gasped when he opened it, for standing in front of him was a twenty-one-year-old woman wearing a white blouse, a white skirt, and high-heeled shoes. "I had never seen anyone so beautiful in my life," he writes. "It was like she was from a dream, or from an entirely different planet."

The woman's Korean was so good that Jenkins initially suspected she was a spy sent to watch him. Their courtship lasted several months, during which they would smoke, talk, and play cards. When she told him she was Japanese, he assumed she was a student of *juche* who had come to North Korea voluntarily and then not been allowed to leave. One night while playing cards, Jenkins ventured that he had heard of a number of Japanese people who had been brought to the North against their will. The woman looked frightened. She remained silent but pointed to her nose to indicate that she was one of them.

Late on the afternoon of August 12, 1978, the nineteen-year-old Hitomi Soga and her mother, Miyoshi, had gone shopping at the general store near their home on Sado Island. Sado is an isolated isle of rice paddies and verdant, looming mountains twenty-five miles off the coast of Niigata. Hitomi was studying at a nursing college and was looking forward to receiving her degree the following week. It was nearly dusk when mother and daughter bought ice-cream cones to relieve the late-summer heat during their walk home. Suddenly, three men leaped from behind a tree. Bound and gagged, the two women were carried a few hundred feet down the road to the Kono River, where a small skiff was hidden beneath a bridge. When Hitomi Soga arrived in North Korea, her mother was gone.

For her first eighteen months in North Korea, Hitomi shared a Pyongyang apartment with Megumi Yokota. She says that Megumi cried all the time, longing to return home and see her parents. Only a few years older than Megumi, Hitomi became a sister figure. Years later, Megumi gave her daughter a version of Hitomi's Korean name, Hae-gyun. When Hitomi moved in with Jenkins, Megumi gave her the badminton bag she'd been carrying when she was abducted, as a keepsake. Hitomi didn't see Megumi again until 1985. She and Jenkins were shopping in the food section of the Rakwon Dollar Store in Pyongyang when Megumi and her minder entered. The two women recognized each other instantly, and Megumi asked Jenkins if he spoke Japanese. He didn't, so Megumi addressed him in Korean. "Your wife and I are very good friends," she said. "I know that," he replied. "I've heard a lot of nice things about you." Jenkins stepped away to let them talk privately, and never saw Megumi again.

One of the few minders Jenkins was fond of urged him to marry Hitomi. "You and she don't seem alike, but you are actually the same. You both have nothing here. Together, you would each at least have something," he said. After that conversation, Jenkins proposed every day. His entreaties were well intentioned, if clumsy. "I know that you do not love me. How could you so soon? And I must honestly admit that I do not love you, though I think that I could," he said. After several weeks of this, she relented, and they were married on August 8, 1980. They had two daughters, Mika in 1983 and Brinda in 1985.

Jenkins became something of an expert abductee-spotter. One day in 1986, he and Hitomi were shopping with Jerry Parrish, the American soldier who defected two years before Jenkins, and Siham Shrieteh, his Lebanese wife. They spotted a Japanese couple. "Good afternoon. How are you?" the Japanese man greeted them, in perfect English. Siham had met the woman a few months earlier, when they were both in the hospital giving birth, and the woman confided in Siham that she and her husband had been kidnapped from Europe by a Japanese terrorist group. Having spent twenty years in the North, Jenkins was no longer surprised that the regime would resort to such measures. "The rules of logic, order, and cause-and-effect ceased to apply. Things happened all the time that made no sense, and for which we were given no explanation," he writes.[4] He notes that most of what the abductees did was little more than busywork. For instance, during her twenty-four years in captivity, Hitomi, a trained nurse, never worked.

So what, then, *was* the point of the abductions? I ask Jenkins. He perks up. "Everybody says they were abducted for language training, but that's just silly," he says. "Would you like to know the *real* reason?" he asks me, a sly smile coming over his face. As a way of answering, Jenkins tells me about a visit two North Korean cadres paid to his home in 1995. Such visits were unusual, so he was nervous. He became more alarmed when the conversation turned to his daughters. "Thanks to the great benevolence of Kim Jong-il, we want to send them to the Pyongyang University of Foreign Studies," they announced. For Jenkins, this was a mixed blessing. The college was indeed one of the most prestigious in North Korea. But it was also a feeder school for the country's intelligence service. "That's when I knew they were planning to turn Brinda and Mika into spies," he says. Jenkins's fears weren't entirely unfounded. Kim Hyon-hui, a North Korean terrorist who blew up a South Korean airliner in 1987, was trained there.

"Think about it," Jenkins says. "They would be perfect raw material for North Korean spies because they looked nothing like someone would *expect* a North Korean spy to look." Indeed, while mixed-race children are common in South Korea and Japan, they are unheard of in the North. The abduction project, Jenkins explains, was actually a long-term breeding program. That was why most of the Japanese were abducted in pairs, usually a girlfriend and boyfriend out for a romantic evening. It was also why the North Koreans had no use for Hitomi Soga's mother. "The North Koreans wanted Japanese couples who could have children that they would then use as spies," Jenkins says.

But what would the advantage be of using the children of Japanese abductees? After all, they were raised to believe they were North Korean, spoke only Korean, and had none of their parents' familiarity with Japanese culture or language. Jenkins looks at me pityingly and replies, "Because if their parents are

Japanese, then their children will have one hundred percent Japanese DNA! That way, if they get caught spying in Japan, they could take a blood test and prove to the police that they were Japanese, and not North Korean. They'd be the *perfect spies!*"[5]

# 13

## TERROR IN THE AIR

Korean Air Flight 858 departed Baghdad's Saddam International Airport at 11:30 p.m. on November 28, 1987. The Boeing 707 was filled with South Korean laborers returning to Seoul, with stops in Abu Dhabi and Bangkok, after months of working on construction projects throughout the Middle East. Also on the plane were the Korean consul general in Baghdad and his wife. Two Japanese tourists, Shinichi and Mayumi Hachiya, a seventy-year-old father and his stunning twenty-five-year-old daughter, occupied seats 7B and 7C. They checked no luggage, placing their few packages in the overhead locker.

At 2:04 a.m., the pilot radioed Rangoon International Airport. "We expect to arrive in Bangkok on time. Time and location normal." One minute later, as it passed from Burmese to Thai airspace, the plane exploded, killing all 115 passengers and crew, brought down by a Panasonic radio packed with plastic explosives.

A quick check of the passenger list showed that the Japanese father and daughter had disembarked at Abu Dhabi, and on further inspection it was discovered that their passports were fake. In the meantime, the Hachiyas had flown on to Bahrain, where they were awaiting a flight to Rome. The Bahraini police detained them and escorted them to security for questioning. Before entering the office, Mr. Hachiya asked permission for him and his daughter to have a smoke. Immediately after putting the cigarette to his lips, he collapsed and died. Seeing this, a quick-witted police woman knocked Mayumi's cigarette from her mouth and wrestled her to the ground. The cigarettes were laced with cyanide, but Mayumi's only caused her to lose consciousness. "The pitch blackness enveloped me like a comforting blanket. *Everything was over,*" she recalled.[1]

Mayumi awoke in a Bahrain hospital, the inside of her mouth covered with blisters from the poison. She insisted she had had nothing to do with the bombing and was interrogated for two weeks before being taken to South Korea, where the questioning continued. One afternoon, the interrogators took her on a drive through downtown Seoul. "There was a flood of automobiles. Not even in Western Europe had I seen so many cars, jostling in the broad streets. Shocked, I studied the drivers. They were Koreans, not foreigners," she recalled. "The spectacle was so different from what I had expected that I didn't know what to say." She confessed the next day. "Forgive me, I am sorry. I will tell you everything," she said.

Her name was Kim Hyon-hui, and she and her "father" were North Korean agents. The bombing was a direct order from Kim Jong-il, intended to discourage people from attending the upcoming Seoul Olympics. It is only a slight exaggeration to say that Kim Hyon-hui had been training for this mission all her life. At sixteen, she was singled out for her intelligence and beauty, and given special language training. At eighteen, she entered espionage

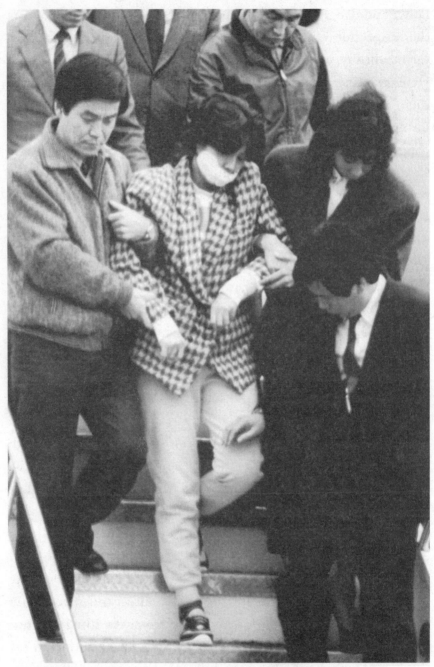

The terrorist Kim Hyon-hui being taken off a plane in South Korea
(Associated Press)

school, where she underwent seven years of grueling training, mastering martial arts, knife combat, shooting, swimming, and code breaking. In one exercise, she infiltrated a mock embassy, cracked the safe, and memorized the message it held. She beat the guards unconscious, for good measure.

Her linguistic training was similarly thorough. After attending the Pyongyang University of Foreign Studies, she received Japanese lessons from a woman who had been abducted from Japan in June 1978. They became close friends, and the Japanese tutor told her about the children she'd left behind. One day, the tutor asked to see how ordinary North Koreans lived, and the next afternoon they snuck out of the military college to visit a nearby village. "We found a decrepit cluster of houses and filthy children running around the streets, some naked. I was ashamed at this and tried to pull [her] away. But she stared at the children with tears in her eyes," recalls Kim. "'So *this* is your brave new world?' she asked. 'I pity you.'" The description of the tutor matched that of a twenty-two-year-old bar hostess and mother of two who had disappeared from Tokyo in 1978. For the first time, the Japanese government had direct evidence of the abductions.

"She is even more gorgeous in person than in her photograph," Hitoshi Tanaka, the Japanese Foreign Ministry's director for Northeast Asian affairs, thought to himself. The man in charge of Japan's relations with the Korean Peninsula, Tanaka was the first Japanese official to meet Kim Hyon-hui. The United States was pushing Japan to impose sanctions on North Korea immediately after the bombing, but Tanaka wanted to be sure that the crime had in fact been committed by North Korea. South Korean intelligence had manufactured cases against the North in the past, and the Americans were being too pushy for his taste. If nothing else,

Tanaka wanted to show them that Japan was an independent state, with its own foreign policy.

South Korean intelligence, fearing the North would assassinate Kim, had secured her at a safe house deep in the mountains. Tanaka's car climbed up the twisting, remote roads for several hours. "I went to meet her, to see her with my own eyes, and understand who she was," he says.[2] For a woman who had just murdered more than a hundred people, she possessed an otherworldly calm he found unsettling. "You've traveled the world and can see through the lies North Korea tells its people. How could you have done such a thing? Didn't you hesitate when you realized all the innocent people you'd kill?" he asked. Her response said as much about her as the regime that had produced her. She admitted she had traveled through the West but claimed she had been told what she saw there was an illusion. "I was taught that it was superficial, and designed to hide the awful capitalist reality that lurked behind it," she said without emotion. It was astounding to behold someone convinced she was floating through a fictional world. She reminded Tanaka of a plastic flower: beautiful but lifeless.[3]

# 14

# KIM'S GOLDEN EGGS

Having sent her husband and four children off for the day, Kayoko Arimoto was enjoying a restorative cup of tea when the telephone rang. It was just after ten on a late September morning in 1988. She didn't recognize the voice on the line, and nearly dropped the phone when she heard whom the woman was looking for. "Is this Miss Keiko Arimoto's residence?" the woman asked.[1]

In April 1982, Kayoko's daughter, Keiko, had moved to London to study English. Keiko's parents hadn't liked the idea of her going so far away, but they gave their permission, on the condition that she return home the next year. She agreed, but as soon as she got to London, she began looking for a job. In March 1983 the Arimotos received

Keiko Arimoto
(Asger Rojle Christensen)

a brief letter from Keiko: "I will be home later than the original schedule because I found a job here. I am not going to stay in one place, as this is marketing research. I'll write to you from wherever I go." They never heard from her again.

The caller that September morning in 1988 explained that she was in a similar position. Her son, Toru Ishioka, had disappeared while traveling through Spain eight years before, and she had just received a letter from him, in which he asked her to contact Keiko's family. "I can't be more explicit, but during our travels in Europe we ended up here in North Korea," the letter began. He and Keiko were living in Pyongyang with another Japanese man. "We basically support ourselves here, but we do receive a small daily stipend for living expenses from the North Korean government. However, the economy is bad, and I have to say it is a hardship to be living here for so long. It's especially difficult to get clothes and educational books, and the three of us are having a hard time. Anyway, I wanted to at least let you know that we are all right, and I am going to entrust this letter to a foreign visitor."

Written on a single piece of paper, the letter had been folded down to the size of a postage stamp. On the back was written, "Please send this letter to Japan (our address is in this letter)." The envelope bore a Polish postmark and stamp, and had presumably been mailed by a Polish tourist. In it were two photographs: one of Toru, Keiko, and a baby; and the other of an unidentified Asian man. Keiko looked thin, her normally plump face sallow. Still, Kayoko was grateful to receive news that her daughter was alive. But how had Keiko gotten to North Korea? And who, she wondered, was that baby?

One might say that Keiko Arimoto's journey to North Korea began in November 1969, when the Japanese National Police raided a paramilitary training camp deep in the woods of rural Yamanashi prefecture, where a radical group called the Red Army Faction was preparing to attack the prime minister. The Red Army Faction advocated "simultaneous, worldwide revolution" through violent tactics, in the name of Third World and other oppressed minorities, and had developed links to Germany's Red Army Faction and to New Left groups in Italy and the United States. The Red Army Faction had its roots in the student protests against the 1952 Japan-U.S. mutual security treaty, which gave the U.S. military the right to keep soldiers, aircraft, and other weapons in Japan. The Japanese left believed that the treaty turned Japan into a de facto military base from which the United States could support the wars in Korea and Vietnam. Initially under the auspices of the Japanese Communist Party, the Red Army broke away in order to refashion itself as a more youthful, New Left vanguard, mobilizing the students of Japan's expanding post-war universities. In 1969 the protests grew so disruptive that academic activity across Japan came to a standstill. Tokyo University simply canceled that year's incoming class.

Only a few Red Army Faction members escaped the police raid on their training camp. With most of his comrades in jail, Takamaro Tamiya, the group's leader, decided to move operations abroad. Charismatic and imaginative, Tamiya planned to hijack an airplane to North Korea and then get military training in Cuba, whose leader, Fidel Castro, was reputed to be on good terms with Kim Il-sung. "We are going to North Korea, determined to do everything necessary to receive military training and remake ourselves into great revolutionary heroes," Tamiya wrote in a document called "Declaration of Departure." "No matter what hardships we must endure, we will return across the sea to Japan to stand at the head of the armed revolution."

Nobody had ever hijacked a Japanese plane before 1970, so

Japanese airports had no metal detectors and little security. The concept of a hijacking was so foreign that, when arrest warrants were issued, the only charge against the Red Army Faction allowed by Japanese law was for the "theft of a plane." The plan was for each of the men, separately, to board the morning flight to the western Japanese city of Fukuoka carrying pipe bombs, traditional swords, and a toy gun. They rehearsed the action in Tokyo University classrooms, with chairs and desks arranged to approximate an airplane's layout. Once airborne, Tamiya would stand and signal the others to rush the cockpit. Tamiya boarded the plane that morning, and all seemed to be unfolding according to plan until he glanced around and realized that only four of his eight comrades were on the plane with him. Never having flown before, the missing members of the group hadn't anticipated the logistics of reservations, tickets, and assigned seats. Tamiya called off the action, and the five disembarked in Fukuoka, only to find they hadn't enough money for a return flight. Deflated, they took the overnight train back to Tokyo.

Four days later, on March 31, 1970, at 7:30 a.m., Japan Airlines Flight 351, nicknamed "Yodogo," departed from Tokyo. This time, all nine hijackers sprang into action when the Fasten Seatbelts sign went off. "We are the Red Army Faction! You will fly us to Pyongyang!" Tamiya shouted. "If you don't, we will detonate a bomb!" he said, waving a stick of dynamite. The pilot explained that the plane needed to refuel if it was to reach North Korea, and at Fukuoka, the hijackers released twenty-three passengers while the ground crew pumped gas. North Korea wasn't on the pilot's route, so he requested an additional map. After a frantic search, one was located and brought to the plane. The pilot gasped when he saw that the "map" was little more than a faded illustration photocopied from a grade school textbook. A note scrawled at the top read "No aviation map available; tune radio to 121.5 MC."

"Have you contacted the North Koreans yet?" the pilot asked Tamiya once the plane was aloft. "No. We won't know whether they will take us until we get there," Tamiya replied. The pilot was alarmed. According to the 1953 Armistice Agreement, any aircraft flying over the DMZ separating North from South Korea without permission could be shot down. The pilot's radio calls to Pyongyang grew frantic. Finally, he got a faint response: "This is Pyongyang. Tune your radio to contact frequency 134.1 MC."

The voice on the radio fed the pilot instructions, and two hours later the plane landed. Everyone on the plane could hear the sound of Korean-language announcements blaring over the airport's loudspeakers: "This is the Democratic People's Republic of Korea! Please disembark from the aircraft. We welcome all of you who are against Japanese imperialism!" Rows of women wearing traditional Korean *hanbok* lined up along the tarmac cheering. But as airport workers wheeled stairs toward the plane, Tamiya sensed that something was amiss. If this was Pyongyang, why did he not see any North Korean flags or portraits of Kim Il-sung? Peering out of the cockpit window, he spotted a tanker with a Shell Oil emblem on it, and a plane with a Northwest Airlines logo on its tail—not the kinds of things one expects in North Korea. "This is Seoul, isn't it?" Tamiya shouted out the window to a nearby soldier. Startled by the direct question, the soldier instinctively told the truth. The hijackers had been tricked into landing in *South* Korea.

Surrounded by military vehicles, the plane sat on the tarmac for four days, the standoff broadcast live on Japanese television. The hijackers kept the plane's doors and air vents locked to prevent soldiers from storming the aircraft or injecting it with sleeping gas. The stifling heat and the odor from the overflowing toilet were unbearable. The South Korean government wouldn't agree to Tamiya's demands because a South Korean flight had been hijacked to the North three months before, and while most of the passengers and crew were returned, eleven had been abducted. Finally, it was agreed that the Japanese vice minister of transportation could trade places with the passengers and accompany the hijackers to Pyongyang. On the final evening of the standoff, the passengers and hijackers celebrated with the plane's remaining rice balls and juice. "We will fight to the end on behalf of the world's oppressed proletariat," Tamiya promised in a farewell speech. "We have caused you unhappiness, but we hope you will understand that we did it because we love Japan." Despite the hardship, the passengers had grown fond of their captors. "If those nine hijackers ever get back, I'm going to recommend them to Japan Airlines," said one passenger. "They cleaned up the ashtrays, picked up paper from the floor, and even brought me a magazine to read." Others were concerned that the serious young men didn't know what they were getting into. "Take care of yourselves," said the last passenger to leave.

The "Japanese Village of the Revolution," the Red Army Faction's North Korean home, is twelve miles outside Pyongyang, bordered on three sides by forests and on the fourth by the Daedong River. Set apart from nearby farms and shielded from the road, it is patrolled by soldiers. The village consists of a dozen buildings, including living quarters, offices, classrooms, and a tennis court. Each apartment has three bedrooms, a dining room, and a kitchen, and is equipped with Japanese washing machines and televisions. The compound is fully staffed, with an on-site doctor and nurse, a chef who presides over a well-stocked kitchen, and a fleet of chauffeured cars. The compound's radios can pick up any signal, and bundles of Japanese newspapers and magazines arrive weekly. Every morning the residents awake at dawn to exercise and

raise the Red Army flag. In the mornings they take classes on ideology and Korean language from a professor at Pyongyang's social
sciences institute, and in the afternoons they hold review sessions.

After a year of this routine, Tamiya grew restless. While the
North Koreans had made it clear that Tamiya and his comrades
weren't going to be allowed to continue on to Cuba, they promised to provide some military training. But when? Every time
Tamiya asked, his minder told him that the Red Army Faction
first needed to acquire a deeper knowledge of North Korean ideology and language. This didn't make any sense to Tamiya, as he
and his comrades intended to return to Japan once they were
trained. So why learn Korean? And as for ideology, they'd already
spent four years fashioning their theory of "simultaneous world
revolution" as students at Japan's most prestigious universities.
What more did they need to know? They started to pose questions about *juche*, going so far as to criticize it, using the kind of
free-ranging inquiry that is unheard of in North Korea.

What Tamiya and his comrades failed to understand was that
in North Korea, technical and ideological training were parts of a
perfect whole, and that whole was Kim Il-sung's philosophy of
*juche*. Because the Red Army's theory of "simultaneous world
revolution" hadn't emerged from Kim Il-sung's mind, it was by
definition ideologically impure. The fact that the group clung to
its idiosyncratic ideas was a problem. Fortunately, Kim Il-sung's
philosophy provided guidance for how to deal with those who
resisted it.

A new routine developed. As before, their professor arrived
every morning to lecture on the thoughts of Kim Il-sung. But
when Tamiya and the others bombarded him with questions, he
would ignore them, smile, and simply repeat the lecture. The next
day, the process would begin all over again. It wasn't long before

the group's defenses began to crumble, leaving them in a state of depression and self-doubt. Disoriented, they finally reached out and grabbed the sturdy rope their teacher dangled in front of them.

In April 1972, when Kim Il-sung judged that the group had been successfully reeducated, he called an impromptu press conference with a group of Japanese journalists who were already in Pyongyang to interview him. "When they arrived [the Red Army Faction members] were anarchists who made fanatical statements about world revolution," Kim announced. "But now their ideological state seems to have improved." The members of the Red Army Faction, wearing black suits with Kim Il-sung badges, sat stiffly at a conference table. "Under the generous and revolutionary leadership of our comrade, the supreme leader, we have finally reached the point where we understand the relationship between the leader, the party, and the masses, who are the source of authority," announced Tamiya.[2] It was a perfect description of *juche* thought.

Why did Kim take such a keen interest in the Red Army Faction? Seventeen years after the Korean War, the two Koreas were competing fiercely to prove that theirs was the superior system. As with the "return" from Japan of ninety-three thousand ethnic Koreans in the 1960s, the arrival, and conversion, of a group of elite Japanese students was a coup for the North. Kim took to referring to them as his "golden eggs," and planned to use them to spread the gospel of *juche*. The only problem was that there simply weren't enough of them. "A revolution must grow to survive" is one of *juche*'s principles. But how could Kim increase the number of Japanese in North Korea?

In 1975, Takako Fukui, the girlfriend whom Red Army Faction member Takahiro Konishi was dating before the hijacking, arrived in Pyongyang. Her presence immediately altered the chemistry of the all-male group as she became the group's Yoko Ono, the woman who comes along and upends the band. She and

Konishi took romantic walks and kept the others awake at night with their lovemaking. With Konishi alone able to satisfy his sexual appetite, the group's frustration boiled over. The only other women in the Revolutionary Village were North Korean staff, and there had always been some tension between them and the men. Soon after Takako arrived, several of the Yodogo men forced themselves on female staffers. One of the women filed rape charges.

Given the vexed history of Japanese-Korean relations, the image of Japanese men forcing themselves on Korean women was intolerable. Tamiya called a group meeting to announce a change in the group's plans. "Men preparing for revolution should have wives and children," he explained. "We all must find women. It is our revolutionary mission to do so." It was a subtle but significant shift in tactics. The plan up to that point had been for the Red Army Faction to return to Japan and spread the gospel of Kim Il-sung. But if they got married and had children in North Korea, the members of the group would have to stay there for the foreseeable future. Because North Korean law forbids marriage between its citizens and foreigners, the wives would have to come from somewhere else.

Ever the romantic, Tamiya proposed that he and the six remaining bachelors crisscross Europe, wooing Japanese tourists and students with the prospect of joining the revolution. His North Korean overseers rejected the plan as too complicated, and made a countersuggestion. What if North Korean spies recruited suitable Japanese women and brought them to North Korea to get married? Tamiya was doubly disappointed: not only did this undercut his self-image as a romantic revolutionary, but it also made it clear that his fate lay firmly in North Korean hands.

Megumi Yao grew up in the city of Kobe, in the Kansai region of central Japan, home to the majority of its ethnic Koreans. As a child, she was outraged by the discrimination she witnessed against them. It wasn't unusual for Koreans to "pass" as Japanese in order to avoid being treated badly, but she was stunned to learn that even her best friend was an ethnic Korean who had taken a Japanese name and was pretending to be Japanese. The revelation brought the injustice closer to home and inclined Megumi to be even more sympathetic toward Koreans. She knew almost nothing about North Korea when she saw *The Story of a Troop Leader*, a propaganda film about a North Korean soldier during the colonial era whose girlfriend is tortured to death by Japanese soldiers when she refuses to betray him. A few days later a member of a local *juche* study group invited her to come to a meeting.

North Korea had cultivated ties with "nonaligned" developing nations since the mid-1950s, offering *juche* as a model to emulate. For many postcolonial countries, the idea of self-reliance, and North Korea's economic record, held a powerful allure. The regime funded a global network of study groups and research institutes, with a large concentration in Japan, which even today hosts the International Institute of the Juche Idea. By 1977 every prefecture in Japan had at least one *juche* study group. When Megumi moved to Osaka to study nursing, she joined a group filled with students, office workers, and teachers. They viewed North Korea as a socialist "Paradise on Earth," where everyone was treated equally and the state provided for all its peoples' needs—the mirror opposite of the capitalist Japanese society. The members of the group seemed so pure and kindhearted that she felt immediately accepted.

When Megumi told the group's leader she wanted to study *juche* in Korean, he offered to arrange for her to go to North Korea and asked only that she keep the trip secret. She told her parents she was taking a trip to Europe. The day before she left, the group's leader presented her with half a dozen postcards, prestamped and addressed to her parents, and asked her to fill them with the kinds of banalities one often finds on postcards ("The weather here is beautiful"). He told her they would be mailed from European countries over the next few months so that her parents wouldn't worry about her.

Megumi Yao arrived in Pyongyang in March 1977 and spent the first six weeks studying Korean. In April a North Korean official stopped by her dorm to check on her progress. Did she like Pyongyang? Was she lonely? If so, would she be interested in making friends or even meeting a man? "After all, no one can make a revolution by oneself," he reminded her cheerfully. She declined his initial offer, but he was persistent, calling on her every few weeks. In fact, he said he had a particular young man in mind. It soon became clear it was more than a suggestion, and she reluctantly agreed to meet him.

Yasuhiro Shibata, the youngest member of the Red Army Faction, only sixteen at the time of the hijacking, hadn't matured much during his seven years in North Korea. Still, Megumi liked him at first. Boyish, if a bit impulsive, he was less stern than his comrades. Anyway, it didn't seem she had much say in the matter. It was rumored that Kim Il-sung himself had decided who was to marry whom. While the circumstances of the matches were un-usual, the practice was not. Arranged marriages were common in Japan at the time, as they still are in North Korea.

The Marriage Project, as it came to be known, culminated in May 1977, when the entire Red Army Faction group got mar-ried, one by one, over the course of a week. On May 14, Kim Il-sung visited the Revolutionary Village to celebrate the occasion. Now that they were married, he said, they must "continue the revolution by giving birth to the next generation." The first child was born within a year, and nurseries, kindergartens, and single-family homes began popping up all over the village. Kim's visit was thereafter referred to as the "5.14 Enlightenment."

Takako Fukui came to North Korea with the intention of marrying her boyfriend. It is unclear how the other wives got there, or whether they were aware that they were being recruited as brides for the Japanese hijackers. Like Megumi Yao, most were members of *juche* clubs back in Japan and were drawn to North Korea for ideological reasons. To this day, the Red Army Faction's Japan-based supporters argue that the women went of their own free will and that neither they nor anyone else was misled or "abducted."

Takako returned to Japan in 2002, served a year and a half in prison for passport violations, and is now part of the defense team lobbying the government to allow the four remaining members of the Red Army Faction still in Pyongyang to return home. She agrees to talk with me in the hope that I will be sympathetic to her plight, but she clams up when I ask how the other women who were married that week in May 1977 got to North Korea. "Every few months another one would just show up in North Korea," she tells me, looking me in the eye. And did they ever discuss how they got there? "No, we never discussed it," she says. I try to compose myself in the face of this obvious lie. So you are telling me that the subject didn't come up during the entire twenty-three years you lived together? I ask. "No, we never discussed it. Not once during that entire time," she says.[3]

The Red Army Faction wives were in many respects more useful operatives than their husbands. They were women without pasts, having led fairly uneventful lives. They hadn't broken any laws, weren't on any international Most Wanted lists, and could move around the world freely. According to Japanese intelligence, in the next decade, the wives passed through fifteen European

countries, traveling between North Korea and Europe more than
fifty times. Most missions were launched from Zagreb, where
they kept an apartment they referred to as the "front office." The
Yugoslavian government gave North Korean spies and their Japanese affiliates safe passage to and from Western Europe, refrain-
ing from stamping their passports and thus making it more
difficult to track their movements. The wives' most important
possessions were their Japanese passports, which they each renewed
several times. One might think of them as traveling agitators,
spreading the word of Kim Il-sung's revolution. They worked
with antinuclear groups in Europe and made multiple recruiting
trips to Japan. While abroad, they communicated with their minders by tuning into a shortwave radio frequency at an appointed
time every evening, receiving coded instructions.

In the winter of 1979 the wives spread out across Europe on
the "Consent Mission," their most ambitious project yet, the goal
of which was to recruit young Japanese who, once properly reeducated, would join the Red Army Faction and, in turn, recruit
more members. Using a Japanese equivalent of the Lonely Planet
guide, they prowled through hostels and cheap hotels, striking up
friendships with Japanese students, sharing meals, sightseeing,
and even going on dates. They would quiz potential recruits about
their hopes and dreams, their education and background. (Did
any of their family members work for the police?) If a recruit was
judged acceptable, he or she would be offered a free trip to North
Korea, the assumption being that, once there, he or she would be
turned into a true believer by the power of Kim Il-sung's *juche*
philosophy. Megumi Yao later confessed that she believed even
those whom she deceived would thank her once they compre-
hended the glory of Kim Il-sung.

In March 1980, Toru Ishioka flew from Niigata to Russia and

Red Army Faction wives and Toru Ishioka in
Barcelona (Jiji Press)

took the Trans-Siberian Railway to Moscow. An agriculture student, he wanted to study Spain's dairy industry, so he traveled to Barcelona, where he met another male Japanese student, who was there working on his Spanish. One afternoon, the men met two attractive Japanese women, and the foursome spent several enjoyable days sightseeing and flirting. One of the women said she knew someone who could arrange a free trip to North Korea. Were the boys up for an adventure? The only evidence of their stay in Barcelona is a photograph of Toru that emerged many years later. In it, he is smiling, sitting on a bench in the city's zoo beside two women—Yoriko Mori and Sakiko Kuroda, wives of Red Army Faction members. The two men never returned.

Still, the logic of the Consent Mission had a fatal flaw—a flaw impossible for a loyal follower of Kim Il-sung even to imagine. It turned out that not everyone exposed to *juche* was won over by its truth. The two Japanese students from Barcelona, furious at being seduced and tricked, resisted it fiercely after they arrived in Pyongyang. To make matters worse, one of them fell in love with the wife who'd tricked him into coming to North Korea, which only fueled his rage. One day, he leaped up and grabbed her. "You bitch! You deceived me! You led me on, and then you tricked me!" he screamed. The two Japanese students were immediately transferred to a more rigorous educational institution, run by the North Korean Workers' Party.

The episode posed a serious problem. The Yodogo group's members could have as many children as they liked, but if they didn't recruit more adult comrades, there was no way the revolution could succeed. The group mulled over their failure at several meetings. Because questioning the transformational potential of *juche* was forbidden, they restricted their scrutiny to operational matters. Maybe they were targeting the wrong people? Perhaps their techniques were too subtle? One wife suggested that perhaps the two men were lonely and would be easier to work with if they had girlfriends. "Well, if it's going badly because it's just the two of them," replied another wife, "let's bring in some women for them."

Growing up in Kobe, Japan, Keiko Arimoto was a shy, quiet girl with a passion for the English language. As a teenager, she moved from her parents' to her aunt's home in downtown Kobe, to be closer to an English school. She received a degree from Kobe University of Foreign Studies in 1981, and arrived in London to continue her studies in the spring of 1982. She didn't have much money, so worked mornings as an au pair, taking care of a six-year-old girl and her eight-year-old brother, and took English classes at International House in the afternoon.

Keiko was lonely in London and wanted to make foreign friends. A plain girl who wore no makeup and had never visited a nightclub or attended a rock concert, she had trouble socializing with non-Japanese people. That fall, Megumi Yao had leased a furnished room in West Kensington, where she entertained the Japanese students she met at International House as part of the

Consent Mission. It was natural that Keiko Arimoto and Megumi Yao would become friends. Only a few years apart in age, they'd both grown up in Kobe, their homes barely a thirty-minute drive from each other. Megumi made Keiko feel less lonely by cooking her favorite Japanese meals and talking about home. One evening, Keiko complained to Megumi that her year in Britain was almost up and she hadn't found a job. She wanted to see more of the world, but would soon have to return home. Megumi mentioned that she knew of a position at a trading company in market research that would entail traveling the world comparing the prices of various goods. The job sounded like a fairy tale to Keiko, and although she knew her parents would be upset, she couldn't pass up the opportunity. "This could be my first step into grown-up life," she wrote to a friend in a June 13, 1983, letter.

> I will leave London at the end of this month. I feel a little sad, but I have so many things to do now. London has been so much fun! And I'll come back again someday. I already bought a ticket home, but what do you know, suddenly I have found a job. The job is in "market research," and involves doing research into the prices, demand, and supply of foreign products. If I take this job, I will be able to see all different parts of the world. I really want to give it a try! . . . I feel pretty lucky!

Megumi and Keiko went to Copenhagen to meet Keiko's future employer. Denmark at the time was one of the few European countries that recognized North Korea, which repaid the compliment by using its Copenhagen embassy to oversee its Western European intelligence network. The two young women spent the day exploring the city, taking rides in Tivoli Gardens, and laughing. That evening they met a man over dinner at a Chinese restaurant. Keiko was nervous, but he spoke perfect Japanese and was

so kind and funny that she soon felt at ease. It was a skill Kim
Yu-chol had perfected during his career as a North Korean agent.
He explained that the job was based in North Korea, and assured
Keiko she would be well cared for. He showed her catalogues
with pictures of the kinds of goods she'd be doing research on,
and Keiko accepted on the spot. Keiko and Kim Yu-chol would
leave the next day, but first he suggested she write a few letters to
her parents in advance, so that they wouldn't worry about her.

And that was the last her parents heard of Keiko Arimoto until
the day in the fall of 1988 when her mother received a copy of
Toru Ishioka's letter, along with a photograph of Keiko and the
infant grandchild she didn't know she had.

# 15

# A STORY TOO STRANGE
# TO BELIEVE

In December 1991, Japanese television producer Kenji Ishidaka was in Seoul interviewing a former North Korean diplomat about the North's nuclear weapons program for *Sunday Project*, the Japanese equivalent of *60 Minutes*. Over dinner that night, the South Korean intelligence agent who had set up the interview asked if Ishidaka was interested in meeting an Osaka-born Korean who'd immigrated to the North in 1973 and later defected to Seoul. "He was one of the repatriates," the agent said.[1]

Despite the fact that a quarter of Japan's ethnic Koreans lived in Ishidaka's hometown, Osaka, he knew almost nothing about the repatriation project that had transported ninety-three thousand of them to North Korea. Ishidaka was only eight years old when the program began in 1959, and the news of Japan's postwar economic success had pushed memories of the project aside. Ishidaka met with the defector, and his ears pricked up when he told him that half the repatriates had disappeared after they arrived in North Korea. What had happened to them? Ishidaka wondered.

Back in Japan, Ishidaka tracked down a former Chosen Soren official whose book, *Paradise Betrayed,* criticized the repatriation project. Most of the author's family had moved to the North in 1962, and he was unprepared for what he'd found when he visited them for the first time in 1980. His family was in tatters, with several in North Korea's gulag and the rest living in poverty. "Why didn't you grab my leg and hold me back when I was getting on the boat?" his eighty-year-old mother screamed at him.

Ishidaka began interviewing dozens of Koreans throughout Japan, all of whom asked for anonymity to protect their families in the North. He learned of relatives whose minor infractions had sent them to labor camps, where they either starved or were executed. The brother of an Osaka native named Grace Park had a successful career as a radio announcer after repatriating. She listened to him every night via shortwave radio, until the fall of 1980, when he was replaced, with no explanation. Grace Park never heard her brother's voice again. Ishidaka's documentary, *People Who Went Missing in Paradise,* aired in May 1994, and the reaction of the Japanese public was one of disbelief. Ishidaka received threatening phone calls, and Chosen Soren complained to his employer. It was a sad story, of course, but he had to move on. He assumed it was the last North Korea story he'd produce.

Kenji Ishidaka originally wanted to become a novelist. Born in Osaka in 1951, the youngest of three children, he attended Tokyo's prestigious Chuo University, where he was two

Kenji Ishidaka
(Kenji Ishidaka)

years ahead of Kaoru Hasuike, the Japanese man who was abducted from a beach with his girlfriend in 1978. In the summer of 1972, Ishidaka hitchhiked through Europe and the Middle East. He had never been abroad and was thrilled to encounter foreign people and places. He initially held the common Japanese prejudices against Africans and Arabs, but these were soon washed away by the fraternal feelings that emerge among young people, of all races, traveling the world on a budget. Where were the safe places to sleep? Which restaurants had the cheapest food? He picked up bits of French, Arabic, and English, and funneled his newfound cosmopolitanism into his poetry. He published a book of poetry when he returned to Japan, but felt the pull of journalism. So he completed his undergraduate degree and took the entrance exam at the Asahi Broadcasting Company.

Japanese television news until the late sixties was a fairly primitive affair, consisting of little more than print journalists reading their articles on air. In order to draw a larger audience, the Tokyo Broadcasting System began requiring journalists to study film techniques, and TV Asahi, its competitor, soon followed suit. Ishidaka was among the first of its journalists to undergo the training, although he considered himself first and foremost a writer and wasn't sure how he felt about this emphasis on the visual. He had never so much as touched a video camera when his boss put a 16 mm camera in his hand and told him to "figure it out."

Large Japanese corporations employ a strictly hierarchical apprentice system, and Asahi was no different. During his first two years, Ishidaka carried heavy equipment—lenses, lighting, tripods—for more senior cameramen. In his third year, he was allowed to shoot some footage of his own. Those in the senior ranks were loath to share their secrets, so when he'd ask a veteran cameraman how he got a particular shot, the man would just stare back at him silently. But Ishidaka was crafty, and he learned the techniques he needed by, essentially, spying on his colleagues. His natural talent was soon recognized, and he was sent for advanced training sessions at a Tokyo film school, where he learned the basics of directing and producing. He immersed himself in the work of iconoclasts such as Eisenstein, Fellini, and Godard. He identified with the rebellious themes that ran through their movies and was particularly taken with Godard's *Pierrot le Fou*, in which unhappily married Jean-Paul Belmondo is fired from his job at a TV company and runs off with his girlfriend. Handsome, with tousled hair and a booming voice, Ishidaka developed a Belmondoesque swagger, and began wearing monogrammed collarless shirts. His documentaries were thoroughly researched and stylishly edited. He was never one to follow the crowd, and after a stint in Tokyo he returned to Osaka, where he could be a big fish in a somewhat smaller pond. He married and had two daughters, but he was hungry, always on the lookout for a big story.

In the summer of 1996, Ishidaka received a call from Grace Park, one of the Osaka-based ethnic Koreans he had interviewed for his repatriation documentary. She and her family were loyal members of Chosen Soren, and most of the family, including her brother, had moved to North Korea in 1964. Park, who had stayed behind in Tokyo to run the family's barbecue restaurant, asked about her brother's disappearance in 1987, when she visited her family in North Korea. They were too scared to discuss him, but her sister-in-law later pulled Grace aside and told her that he had been charged with espionage and executed in 1985.

In 1992, when Grace Park first shared the story of her brother with Ishidaka for his documentary, she claimed she had no idea why her brother had been executed. But she was racked with guilt and in 1996 she confessed the truth. "I lied to you in our interview because I was so ashamed. I *do* know the reason my brother was arrested and executed," she said. "It was all my fault. He was killed because I fell in love with a North Korean spy!"

Grace Park met a North Korean spy named Shin Kwang-soo in 1973. She was separated from her husband and having difficulty supporting herself and her son and two daughters. Shin was handsome, charming, and generous. He swept Grace off her feet and moved in, supporting the family and treating her children as if they were his own. Grace was so happy, she didn't mind that he was so often away on "business" or that he wouldn't tell her anything about his work. Soon after he moved in, he gave her four million yen (thirteen thousand dollars), and told her to "take care of it." She knew better than to ask any questions.

In the fall of 1976, Shin told Grace he had to go abroad on a long trip and didn't know when he'd return. A month later, she received a letter from him postmarked Pyongyang. With no pleasantries or explanations for his absence, Shin got right to the point. "Do you remember the four million yen I loaned you? I need it back now. Go to Yokohama and give it to a business associate of mine," he instructed. With no indication of when, or whether, Shin was returning, Grace was devastated. What's more, the money was gone. She'd used it to supplement her meager income. She thought it would be rude to deliver the bad news to him by letter, so she wrote to her brother in Pyongyang and asked him to visit Shin and explain the awkward situation she found herself in.

When Park's brother visited the Pyongyang address his sister gave him, the man who answered the door was clearly not pleased a stranger was asking after Mr. Shin. He warned the brother never to return, and within days, he noticed he was being followed to and from his job at the radio station. Soon after, he was under twenty-four-hour-a-day surveillance, with one car parked outside his apartment and another outside his office. "What kind of trouble have you got me into!?" he wrote to his sister. And that's when he disappeared.

It turns out that Shin was in the "business" of abducting Japanese people to North Korea. An ethnic Korean born in Japan in 1929, Shin immigrated to North Korea at the end of the Second World War and trained to be a spy. He infiltrated Japan in 1973, and in 1980 he was ordered to abduct a Japanese man whose identity he would assume. One of Shin's contacts, the owner of an Osaka restaurant, had the perfect candidate: Tadaaki Hara, a forty-three-year-old chef. Hara had such a minimal public profile (deceased parents; no wife or children; no passport, criminal record, or bank account) he'd never be missed.

The North Korean intelligence agency communicates with its spies through coded messages broadcast via shortwave. What to the average listener sounds like a jumble of numbers holds instructions for its spies. In June 1980, Radio Pyongyang broadcast a five-digit number (29627) over and over again. It was the signal for Shin—June 27, 1929, was his birthday—to abduct Hara, to whom Shin had offered a job in a fictitious Beijing-based trading company a few weeks earlier. Hara had already accepted the position when Shin told him the company needed him immediately. The two men celebrated over dinner at an elegant restaurant near Osaka station, and the next day the unsuspecting Hara boarded a ship that took him not to China but to North Korea.

Shin spared no details in assuming Hara's identity. He took a cooking course so he could pass as a chef. He used Hara's name to obtain a driver's license and passport, with which he traveled through France, Switzerland, and Thailand. His ruse wasn't good enough to fool South Korean intelligence, however, and he was arrested in April 1985 when he tried to enter the country using Hara's passport. Back in Pyongyang, North Korean intelligence suspected that Grace Park's brother had blown Shin's cover. After all, he had made that odd visit to Shin's home and was already a dubious character, being a member of the group that had repatriated from Japan. Grace Park's brother was executed two months after Shin's arrest. Shin was found guilty of espionage and sentenced to death but was granted amnesty by South Korean president Kim Dae-jung in 1999, as part of the conciliatory "Sunshine Policy" designed to coax North Korea to the negotiating table. In September 2000, Shin returned to North Korea, where he received a hero's welcome and was awarded the National Reunification Prize for his service. He is thought to be living in Pyongyang today.

The story was so full of skulduggery and intrigue that Ishidaka had trouble believing it was true. It sounded more like the plot of a James Bond movie than anything the news division of *Asahi* would air. He found a June 1985 newspaper article about Shin's arrest that mentioned that Shin was wanted in Japan concerning the disappearance of Tadaaki Hara. But Ishidaka was still skeptical. The article's main source was a South Korean intelligence agent, and Ishidaka knew that South Korea's national intelligence service often fabricated stories to make the North look bad. Ishidaka needed more proof. He got the transcript of Shin's trial, but too much had been redacted by the South Korean government to be of use. He asked to interview Shin in jail, but his request was denied. As a consolation prize, a South Korean agent Ishidaka was friendly with gave him a list of Shin's associates in Japan. It turned out that Shin had been arrested along with a man named Ahn Young Kyu, who had confessed to helping Shin abduct Hara. Ahn Young Kyu had been released from jail in 1990. If Ishidaka could get him to confirm that he and Shin had abducted Hara, he would have enough evidence to run the story.

In February 1995, Ishidaka got a lucky break. With the aid of one of his sources, Jung Yon, a Chosen Soren member, Ishidaka learned that Ahn Young Kyu was living on Jeju Island, South Korea. Jung Yon had been friends with Ahn and offered to visit him with Ishidaka. The day after Ishidaka and Jung Yon got to Jeju, Jung invited his old friend to meet at their hotel's coffee shop at seven that evening. Ishidaka prepared for the meeting with military precision, hiding a microphone in a flower vase and positioning a video camera behind some curtains. He even convinced the proprietor to turn the music down to improve the sound quality.

At 6:50 the proprietor told Jung that there was a call for him. It was Ahn. "You are with someone I don't know," he said. "So I'm not going to meet you." The North Koreans had trained him well. A friend from his past appears out of nowhere, accompanied by a stranger? Too suspicious. That night, Ishidaka went to Ahn's house and explained that he wanted to know what had happened to Hara. The two spoke through the intercom. "I don't know, either. I only worked for Shin Kwang-soo. He is the only one who knows what happened to Hara," he replied. With that statement, Ahn had unwittingly confirmed to Ishidaka the fact that he knew, and had collaborated with, Shin Kwang-soo. One piece of the puzzle fell into place.

Still, if he wanted to be absolutely certain, Ishidaka had to confront Ahn face-to-face. At 5:00 a.m. the next day, Ishidaka and a camera crew staked out Ahn's house, hiding in a park across the street. It was Ishidaka's forty-fifth birthday, and as he waited in the freezing morning air, he wondered if this was the best way to celebrate it. Ahn left his house at 7:00 a.m., checked the street, and, confident the coast was clear, started toward the bus stop. Ishidaka waited until Ahn was past the point where he could easily return to the house, then ambushed him, microphone in hand. The scene was captured on film, and resembles a prolonged mugging more than an act of investigative journalism. For twenty minutes, Ishidaka shouts questions at Ahn, chasing him up and down the block in the early morning light. "I know nothing! I know nothing!" Ahn screams, before collapsing to his knees and weeping. Ahn's confession tumbles out between sobs. He was used by Shin to trick Hara, but he had never meant to hurt anyone. He confirmed everything. "I did a *terrible, terrible* thing to Hara," Ahn moaned. Finally, Ishidaka had proof that the crazy abduction stories were true.

*Between the Dark Waves: North Korea's Espionage Project* was broadcast at 8:00 p.m. on May 24, 1995. Ishidaka steeled himself for the criticism he was sure to receive from North Korea sympathizers. What he wasn't prepared for, however, was the complete silence that followed the broadcast. The story was simply too far-out for the average viewer to believe. The idea of a chef being abducted by North Korean spies was just too bizarre. And the sources for the story—a motley crew of convicted criminals, spies, and intelligence agents—didn't help. Why would *anyone* believe them? Ishidaka was devastated.

It isn't quite true that the documentary got *no* response. The next day, Ishidaka received a call from an editor at Asahi's book publishing division. "That documentary you showed last night was interesting. Did all that stuff really happen?" the editor asked. Ishidaka didn't know whether to laugh or cry. He had produced a documentary whose plot was so bizarre that someone inside his own company was skeptical. Annoyed, he assured the editor that it was journalism, not fiction. "Okay, then how about writing a book about it so that future generations will know what happened?" Ishidaka had always fancied himself a writer, so the idea of a book no one could doubt appealed to him. Finishing the book took two more years of reporting, but he was determined to prove to the world, once and for all, that the abductions had taken place.

Finances were a problem. Japanese book publishers don't generally give authors an advance, and the disastrous television show had already aired, so there would be no further funds from his TV company. Japanese wives traditionally handle the family's finances, so Ishidaka begged his for enough money to continue the reporting. She reluctantly agreed, and put him on an allowance. Ishidaka adopted a strict routine. Every day at 2:00 p.m., after the morning show he produced had wrapped and the next day's program was set, Ishidaka turned his attention to his abduction research. Every Friday, he caught a 5:00 p.m. flight from Osaka to Seoul to interview North Korean defectors, South Korean intelligence agents, and assorted spies.

Back in Japan, he met with anyone who suspected that a family member had been abducted. He was flooded with calls and letters from families who had spent years asking the Japanese police and government for help. Other families, who felt they had been mistreated by the media, didn't respond to Ishidaka. Kaoru Hasuike's father had posted a sign, "Interview Requests Not Accepted," on his front door. He told Ishidaka, "No matter how much we ask for help for Kaoru, the government refuses to do anything. I don't think we can get him back. It's painful even to think about it." Ishidaka learned of the 1988 letter that Toru Ishioka had written from Pyongyang about himself and Keiko Arimoto. Ishidaka accompanied Mr. and Mrs. Arimoto to the Ministry of Foreign Affairs, where an exasperated official warned them that their persistence might endanger their daughter. "If we ask the North Koreans about her, she'll be in danger. That country is capable of anything. We can't do anything," the official said.[2]

Myeongdong is central Seoul's busiest shopping district, crowded with boutiques, restaurants, and bars, and where the fragrance of barbecued beef lingers twenty-four hours a day. It is the perfect place for meeting people who don't want to be noticed. On June 23, 1995, Ishidaka met with a South Korean intelligence agent who had information he was eager to share. He had twice tried to relay it to the Japanese police, but they didn't seem to be interested. Perhaps Ishidaka would bite? "A child was abducted from Japan. She was thirteen years old and was on her way home from badminton practice at school. It happened in either 1976 or '77," the agent said.[3] The agent didn't know the girl's name or where in Japan she was from. The information had come from a North Korean defector who had met the girl in a Pyongyang hospital, where she was being treated for depression. She was suicidal, and it was her second extended stay there. "I was abducted and told that if I studied hard and mastered Korean within five years, I'd be sent back to my parents," she told him. She had done as she was told, but when she turned eighteen her handlers refused to release her.

Ishidaka had already completed his reporting for the book and didn't know what to do with this information. He had checked every case meticulously, confirming the dates and circumstances for each abduction. Haunted by the humiliation of the documentary, he was determined not to take any chances. The idea that North Korea was abducting Japanese people was bizarre enough. Who would believe they had targeted a thirteen-year-old girl? "It was just too crazy," Ishidaka tells me. "If I included her story, people might think that the stories I told of the other abduction victims were also unreliable. I couldn't risk that."[4]

In September 1996, advertisements for *Kim Jong-il's Kidnapping Command* appeared in the *Asahi Daily*. At the offices of *Modern Korea* magazine, run by Katsumi Sato, the activist who had once worked on the repatriation project, saw the ads and contacted Ishidaka with an idea. Perhaps he would write an article for *Modern Korea* telling the story behind the book? Ishidaka agreed, and his article "Why I Wrote *Kim Jong-il's Kidnapping Command*" appeared in *Modern Korea*'s October issue. Sato asked whether Ishidaka would include some material that hadn't made it into the book. Ishidaka immediately thought of the thirteen-year-old girl, and added a brief summary to the piece.

A few weeks later, Sato was in his hometown of Niigata, lecturing on North Korea to an audience of about eighty people. He described his youthful infatuation with communism and North Korea, his subsequent loss of faith, and the terrible suffering the regime inflicted on its people. He plugged Ishidaka's book and, as an afterthought, mentioned the story of the thirteen-year-old girl. Afterward, an older gentleman approached Sato. "That girl with the badminton racket. That just *has to be* Megumi Yokota. She disappeared from Niigata in 1977."[5]

# 16

# THE GREAT LEADER DIES,
# A NATION STARVES

On the morning of July 9, 1994, Kaoru Hasuike was awakened by the announcement that a broadcast of great importance was scheduled for noon that day. With prolonged negotiations over North Korea's nuclear weapons, tensions were high and there had been several such announcements over the past few months. The United States had accused the regime of diverting plutonium from the Yongbyon nuclear reactor to make warheads and had demanded that the United Nations be allowed to inspect the site. North Korea refused, and threatened to withdraw from the nonproliferation treaty. By June, the situation had grown so dire that President Clinton approved plans to send cruise missiles and F-117 fighters to destroy the reactor—an act of aggression he knew was likely to lead to all-out war.

Kaoru had heard a disturbing rumor that was going around Pyongyang. During a meeting about the nuclear crisis, Kim Il-sung allegedly asked his son what he would do if war came and the North lost. The famously hawkish Kim Jong-il replied, "If that happens, I will blow up the earth. Because without the DPRK, the earth need not exist!" As military drills increased and the tone of the North Korean media grew more belligerent, Kaoru feared war was inevitable, and he devised a plan to keep his family together.

With his children about to return to school, he brought his daughter to a remote graveyard nestled in a pine forest, where he occasionally retreated to think. Ten million Koreans had been displaced during the Korean War, many settling on opposing sides of the divided nation, never to see each other again. What if war broke out and he and Yukiko were separated from their children? "If war comes, Mom and I won't be able to stay here," he explained to his daughter. "Before we leave, I'll put a letter in a bottle and bury it next to that grave," he said, gesturing at a small plot. The letter would specify a place to meet at five o'clock in the evening on the first and fifteenth of every month. She was to wait thirty minutes and then repeat the process until he showed. "This is a secret between you and me. Don't tell anyone, not even your brother," he instructed the twelve-year-old girl.[1]

The last five years had been extremely unsettling for North Korea. In 1989 the Berlin Wall fell and the people of Eastern Europe overthrew their oppressive governments. Closer to home, Chinese students gathered in Tiananmen Square to demand freedom and an end to state corruption. In 1991 the Soviet Union, the first Communist nation in history, collapsed. China, under Deng Xiaoping, welcomed capitalism into its economy. In just three years, North Korea went from being a member of a global Communist movement to one of the last holdouts. Adding insult to injury, Russia and China normalized relations with South Korea, whose economy had grown too large to ignore. Meanwhile, annual trade between North Korea and the Soviet Union dropped from $2.6 billion to $140 million between 1990 and 1994. The North Korean media blamed the Soviet Union's demise on its leaders' lack of revolutionary commitment, and in a stroke of genius it used the failure of Eastern European communism to bolster the case for North Korea's stark brand of totalitarianism: North Korea alone had stayed true to communism's ideals! "The collapse of the Soviet Bloc was attributed not to the failure of socialism, but to the degenerative effect of capitalism, and the penetration of imperialist ideology and culture" says Kaoru.[2]

Kim Il-sung's funeral (Associated Press)

On July 8, at the stroke of noon, Kaoru switched on the radio and heard a trembling, mournful voice announcing news that was literally unimaginable to most North Koreans: Kim Il-sung, the nation's founder and only leader, had died. Although North Korea was officially an atheist state, the regime had never shied away from attributing divine powers to Kim: the messiah who liberated his people from the Japanese in 1945, the benevolent father who lifted them up from poverty, the guardian who protected them from American imperialism. Nobody knew about his heart troubles, and North Koreans had expected his doctors at the Research Center for the Longevity of the Leader to keep him alive indefinitely. For North Koreans, slogans such as "The Great Leader is forever with us!" were taken literally.

The nation descended into a ten-day period of mourning, during which dancing and amusement of all kinds were forbidden. While the people of North Korea pondered the frightening prospect of a future without the Great Leader, Kaoru faced a different dilemma. How would he, a Japanese prisoner, mourn Kim's death? "Citizens were expected to wail and cry, but I couldn't grieve over the death of the man who had abducted me. I didn't think my heart or pride would allow me to," he says. The stakes were high. If his minder suspected that Kaoru's grief was fake, his family might be in jeopardy. He decided to watch how others acted and imitate them. That afternoon, he and his minder brought flowers to a nearby statue of Kim Il-sung, where Kaoru noticed some people sobbing, while others merely wiped tears from their eyes and bowed their heads, a style of mourning he felt he could mimic. During a service held at the Invitation-Only Zone the next day, several people threw themselves to the ground. Kaoru couldn't risk standing out, and quickly fell to his knees, wiping fake tears from his face. The real test came on July 19, when one million people lined the streets of Pyongyang for Kim's state funeral. A car from the Invitation-Only Zone deposited Kaoru in downtown Pyongyang early that morning, and he waited several hours in the sweltering summer heat before he heard faint chords from "The Song of the Supreme General Kim Il-sung." As the limousine bearing Kim's body came into sight, the crowds of people who had stood silently for hours spontaneously began stamping their feet and tearing at their clothes, swept up in a moment of religious fervor that Kaoru found frightening. He stood on tiptoe to glimpse the hearse, which had a huge flower-ringed portrait of a smiling Kim Il-sung perched on top. Amazed by the intensity of emotion around him, Kaoru forgot to cry. Fortunately, his minders were too overcome with emotion to notice.

North Korea is often described as a country where history has stopped, and now as the official period of mourning was extended to three full years, it became a funereal state, led forever by Kim Il-sung, who was designated its "Eternal President." His son, Kim Jong-il, refrained from replacing his father for the duration of the mourning period. The list of forbidden activities grew to include weddings and funerals. When an officer whom Kaoru knew built a tombstone for his recently deceased mother, the man was punished with compulsory labor and a demotion. Fearing they'd get in trouble, farmers refrained from cultivating their fields that summer, further reducing a yield that had been declining since 1990.

In the best of times, North Korea is capable of producing roughly half its food. Traditionally focused on heavy industry and mining, it is so mountainous that only 20 percent of the land can be cultivated, and its cold climate means growing seasons are short.[3] In the past, the shortfall was made up by the Soviet Union and other socialist countries, which, until the fall of communism, offered food, coal, oil, and steel at discounted "friendship" prices. As resources either disappeared or became more expensive, the regime, desperate to negotiate with anyone who could help it survive, initiated a decade-long effort to normalize relations with Japan. South Korea had received billions of dollars in aid when it normalized relations with Japan in 1965. Perhaps the North could one day profit as well?

With fewer outside sources of food, farmers maximized output by using more pesticides and fertilizers, which further depleted the soil. As existing fields fell barren, farmers, encouraged by the party's "Let's Find New Land!" campaign, cleared hillsides of brush. With fewer trees and shrubs holding the soil in place, the annual summer rains caused severe flooding, destroying fields and already harvested grain stored for future use. It is estimated that 20 percent of the country's total forest cover was lost between 1990 and 2000.[4] Coal was in short supply, so people cut down trees for firewood, which cleared more land.

During his trips into Pyongyang it seemed to Kaoru that fields were popping up everywhere. "It reminded me of the stories my mother told me about wartime Japan, when people used every square inch of land, and even schoolyards were filled with rows of sweet potatoes," he says.

Born twelve years after the end of the Second World War, Kaoru had never experienced hunger. He had heard stories from his mother and grandmother about the harsh food situation during the war, but these were little more than fairy tales to him. "In the early nineties, we began hearing stories about the amount of food decreasing, distribution days being delayed and finally not taking place at all," he recalls. The most faithful party stalwarts simply couldn't imagine a world in which the Kim family didn't take care of them, and were among the first to starve. Like the proverbial frog in the heating pot of water, they didn't realize the extent of the famine until it was too late. City dwellers were hurt because they had no land to grow their own food and were completely dependent on the public distribution system. "I saw families living in high-rise apartments raising chickens and pigs on their balconies, feeding them kitchen scraps and cooked corn flour," says Kaoru. As people learned they couldn't rely on the government, alternative foods appeared in markets. There was "synthetic meat," made from soybean oil, which neither looked nor tasted like meat but achieved a comparable texture when cooked. Porridge and noodles produced by grinding the roots of rice plants into a paste left people feeling full, if undernourished. Recipes circulated for reviving rotten pork by boiling it with baking soda. Pine tree bark was ground down and baked into cakes, with the side effect of severe constipation. The very young and the very old died first, and students were mobilized to form body brigades to remove corpses from the streets. Rumors of cannibalism spread, and the number of those who crossed illegally into China for food soared. Border guards were so hungry a small bribe was all it took for them to look the other way.

The ongoing conflict with the United States made the regime reluctant to request food aid, for fear of showing any signs of weakness. "If the U.S. imperialists know that we do not have rice for the military," said Kim Jong-il in a secret December 1996 speech, "they would immediately invade us."[5] The regime's distrust of the outside world hampered aid efforts when it refused to allow nongovernmental organizations to oversee food distributions. Of the food that was allowed in, it is estimated that one-third was claimed by the military and political elite.[6] Most disturbing is that as the humanitarian aid gradually increased, the regime *decreased* the amount of food it imported through commercial channels, effectively using the donations to improve the country's balance of trade.[7] Military spending increased during the famine, with the regime purchasing forty MiG-21 fighters and eight military helicopters from Kazakhstan in 1999.[8] The closest the regime came to economic reform was loosening restrictions on the size and number of the farmers' markets, which had by then become a crucial source of food. Although the real figures may never be known, it is estimated that from 1995 to 2000, between one and three million North Koreans (5 to 10 percent of the population) starved to death. In addition, others were felled by out-breaks of tuberculosis and cholera, along with hepatitis, malaria, dysentery, and other ailments that come from vitamin deficiency.[9] By 2001 the average life expectancy in North Korea had dropped to sixty.

The elite in Pyongyang were largely insulated from the hardship, as were the Japanese abductees. The size of the rations the abductees received held fairly steady, although the quality varied and some items disappeared entirely. Kaoru feared most for the welfare of his children, whose school was in the remote northwestern region, where the famine was most severe. Twice a year, Kaoru's son and daughter would return home skinny and drawn, bringing stories of death and starvation. One by one, their classmates grew listless and stopped coming to school, leaving row after row of empty desks. Those who managed to survive stopped growing, their hair turning brittle and falling out. During one break, the Chimuras' children returned home with fiery red rashes on their faces, the result of eating little other than corn-based porridge.[10] Whereas students were once fed white rice, fish, and even bits of meat, by the late 1990s a typical meal consisted of sour radish soup flavored with salt. And if rice was served, it was mixed with so many pebbles and other grains that people had to roll it around in their mouths before swallowing. "You guys aren't tough enough to make it out there," Kaoru's son told him. "You're too used to eating rice every day."[11]

Even if his children were unlikely to starve to death, Kaoru feared their growth would be stunted by prolonged malnutrition. So in the weeks leading up to their visits, he and Yukiko set aside a portion of their food allotment. Once home, the children would stuff themselves with as much rice, meat, and vegetables as they could manage. In order to make sure they got enough protein at school, Kaoru sent them back with a five-kilo sackful of soybeans he'd roasted for them. (He'd calculated that if they ate five beans a day, they'd receive the minimum requirement.) Kaoru and Yukiko prayed the children would grow even a little by the next time they came home. In the interim they sent food packages, most of which were intercepted by hungry postmen.

The Invitation-Only Zone wasn't entirely untouched by the famine, as Kaoru heard about staff who were having difficulty supporting themselves and their families in the provinces. The wife of one of the drivers had recently given birth to a baby boy, but she was so starved for food that she couldn't produce milk. Kaoru, whose life revolved around his children, felt so sorry for the man that he gave him a few kilos of rice. The driver then cooked the rice, adding salt, water, and sugar to create a paste the infant could swallow in lieu of breast milk.

Vegetables from the small garden Kaoru had tended since coming to the Invitation-Only Zone began disappearing, most likely stolen by neighbors or guards. As the famine intensified, intruders from outside the zone scaled the fences to steal produce and household goods. Kaoru got a dog to deter thieves, but he had trouble feeding it. He began hunting small birds and pheasants, using a slingshot and a clumsily fashioned bow and arrow. Neither yielded more than a few stunned pigeons. He had more success when a neighbor taught him how to catch pheasant using soybeans laced with cyanide (the trick was to disembowel the bird before the poison spread).

The desperation induced by the threat of famine took forms that were by turns savage and absurd. One afternoon, while fishing at his favorite pond, Kaoru spotted a neatly dressed man wading hip-deep in the water. Lacking a rod, the man was trying to catch fish with the kind of net one uses with fish tanks. "One by one he would catch these tiny fish in the net and put them into his jacket pocket," says Kaoru. It was a scene that in better times would have made him smile, but the knowledge that this was the best the man could do to support his starving family made Kaoru look away with shame and sadness.[12]

# 17

# NEGOTIATING WITH MR. X

When the terrorist Kim Hyon-hui confessed to bombing Korean
Air Flight 858, she set into motion a series of events that would
eventually unravel the entire abduction project. Once the Japanese government learned that she had received language training
from a Japanese, it was forced to raise the abduction issue with the
North. The problem was that whenever Japanese diplomats uttered the word *abduction*, their North Korean counterparts would
stand up and leave the room in protest. What's more, the North
Koreans turned the tables on them. Hadn't the *Japanese* abducted
hundreds of thousands of *Koreans* during the colonial and wartime
era, using the men as slave labor and the women as sex slaves? When
former Japanese prime minister Murayama raised the issue during
a visit to North Korea, his host exploded: "Why do you Japanese
always talk to us of abductions!? What about the case of the political leader kidnapped by the South? Do you use the word
'abduction' in that case, too?"[1]

Of the many oddities regarding the abduction issue, the case the North Korean diplomat referred to was perhaps the oddest. The fact is that the only verified case of abduction in Japan at the time was of a leftist South Korean politician kidnapped by the South Korean Central Intelligence Agency (KCIA). On August 8, 1973, the South Korean dissident (later president) Kim Dae-jung was having lunch with supporters in his room at Tokyo's Hotel Grand Palace. Shortly after they left, Kim was jumped by KCIA agents, who knocked him out with chloroform. By the time the American ambassador to South Korea learned of the abduction, Kim was at sea, bound to a plank of wood with weights attached to it. Only a last-minute intervention by the CIA station chief in Seoul saved him. North Korea was not involved in any way. After this incident, most members of the Japanese government and media suspected that the stories about North Korean abductions were KCIA-generated disinformation designed to discredit the North.

It was not until a 1997 meeting, when Japanese negotiators substituted the phrase "missing people" for "abductees," that the North agreed to investigate their whereabouts. In 1998, soon-to-become prime minister Yoshiro Mori made an ingenious, face-saving proposal while visiting Pyongyang with a government delegation. What if North Korea moved any "missing persons" to cities such as Beijing, Paris, or Bangkok? Then they could come forward and claim they had been living there all along.[2] The North Koreans were intrigued. This was a man they could do business with.

Mori became prime minister in April 2000 and sent Kim Jong-il a personal letter that initiated the secret negotiations. However, Mori's low popularity level forced him to resign in April 2001. Soon after Junichiro Koizumi replaced him as prime minister, the North repeated Mori's offer, and Hitoshi Tanaka was given the greatest challenge of his diplomatic career.

Hitoshi Tanaka (Associated Press)

Tanaka had been groomed to achieve great things. His father had twice nearly been killed during World War II, and later grew wealthy as chairman of a major trading company. His travels through New Delhi, London, and Lima had given him a cosmopolitan perspective, and he hoped his son would become a diplomat. Tanaka led a privileged childhood, followed by law school at elite Kyoto University.[3]

The Ministry of Foreign Affairs sent the junior diplomat to Oxford for language training, where he became an Anglophile, pleased to learn the British version of English, rather than the American variant taught in Japan. He discovered that the socially reticent Japanese and British had much in common. Both were former world powers living in the shadow of the United States. Tanaka admired the way Britain had learned to navigate this new terrain, leveraging its remaining strengths through diplomatic prowess, while remaining aloof from its continental neighbors. Tanaka concluded that Japan, too, should rely more on its wits than its power.[4]

Tanaka's most significant experience at Oxford had little to do with academics. During his second year, he fell in love with a Polish student from Warsaw. They spent weekends in the Sussex countryside and traveled throughout Europe. He was moved when their train passed through Germany and she began shaking uncontrollably, a response to her country's wartime victimization. She told him she feared returning to Poland, where family members and friends spied on one another. They planned to marry, but when Tanaka consulted with the Japanese ambassador, he was told that doing so might hurt his career, as some would think his wife was a Communist spy. Offended, he considered quitting the foreign service. His first post after Oxford was Jakarta, which he suspects was part of the Japanese government's plan to thwart his relationship by putting as much distance as possible between him and his girlfriend. Indonesia refused to grant her a visa to join him, and she eventually returned to Poland.

The 1950s and '60s were the years Japan proved to the world that its wartime behavior had been an aberration. It joined the United Nations in 1956, hosted the 1964 Olympics, and normalized relations with South Korea in 1965. Tanaka was a rising star when he returned to Japan in 1974, moving swiftly through the ranks of the Ministry of Foreign Affairs, helping Japan craft a new role for itself on the world stage. He developed a reputation as a lone wolf in a culture that prizes consensus and cooperation. He was handsome, fiercely intelligent, and wore exquisitely tailored English suits. These qualities served him well during the decade he worked in the United States overseeing Japan's North

American affairs, and during the fraught trade negotiations of the 1980s. Tanaka valued Japan's strong alliance with the United States, but lamented its unintended effects, especially the way it enabled Japan to avoid uncomfortable facts. "Japan has lived in a rather peaceful world since the end of the war. The United States guaranteed Japanese security, so anything to do with military action was quite remote. Although there was a clear threat from a country like North Korea, we tried not to see it, because of Japan's history," he tells me.[5]

Having excelled in the United States, Tanaka was given his choice of jobs. The head of the Bureau for Northeast Asian Affairs wasn't a particularly coveted position. With a military regime in the South, a Stalinist autarky in the North, and Japan's hands tied by the limitations of the Cold War, it was considered a career-ender. But Tanaka chose it because the Korean Peninsula was central to his worldview. Given Japan's long and intimate history with Korea, he believed the peninsula was the route through which Japan could mend its relations with the rest of Asia. He thought it was disgraceful Japan had taken so long to normalize relations with the South, and that a similar resolution with the North was long overdue. "We colonized Korea, so the least we can do is help create a peaceful peninsula. Peace in Japan is threatened by instability on the Korean Peninsula," he says. As head of the bureau, Tanaka was determined to address the two countries' unequal relationship. "Korean diplomats speak excellent Japanese, so we normally worked in our language. I didn't think that was fair, and insisted that we do business in a third language, English," he explains. In addition, Tanaka challenged the cultural assumption that Japan's northeast neighbors were too "emotional" to negotiate with rationally. "One of my senior colleagues, a China specialist, advised me to use *heart* when dealing with Korea, because they are so emotional." The colleague believed that the only way to get diplomatic work done was for officials to visit the sauna together, and then to drink and sing. "I told him I had no intention of doing that. I want to conduct crisp business in English, and thought it was a mistake to appeal too much to emotions. I wanted our negotiations to be rational."[6]

Junichiro Koizumi became Japan's prime minister in April 2001 with an 85 percent approval rating, based largely on his vow to reverse Japan's decade-long economic decline. To do so, he proposed the kind of privatization and market reforms that, though conventional wisdom in the West, were anathema to the Japanese public. The immediate result of the reforms was more economic pain, and one year later his approval rating had plummeted.

Koizumi needed to make a bold move to take people's minds off the economy, and normalizing relations with North Korea seemed ideal. However, his plan for engaging with that country was complicated when President George W. Bush included North Korea (along with Iran and Iraq) in his 2002 "Axis of Evil" speech. Could Japan normalize relations with a country on which its closest ally had all but declared war? Tanaka saw an opportunity to show the United States that Japan was capable of making its own foreign policy. "We are not a protectorate of the United States!" he protested when a U.S. diplomat cautioned him. Such sentiments earned Tanaka the nickname Kokutai-san, or "Mr. National Interest," among U.S. diplomats. Koizumi instructed Tanaka to keep the negotiations secret, limiting information to a small group. Even the minister of foreign affairs was kept in the dark. If the talks succeeded, Koizumi would notify the United States and the rest of the Japanese government before signing an agreement.

Tanaka took the early morning commercial airline flight from Tokyo to the coastal Chinese city of Dalian so that he'd have time to explore the city before the first meeting with his North Korean counterpart. The Japanese colonists had designed Dalian's wide roads and elegant circular plazas to create an Asian version of Paris. "Dalian was the ideal city the Japanese saw in their dreams," architectural historian Yasuhiko Nishizawa writes. It was showcased as an example of how Japanese rule would bring modernity to its colonies. The city also provides a palimpsest of Asia's contested history. The Han dynasty staged its invasion of Korea from here in the second century AD. Between 1850 and 1950, Dalian was controlled by Britain, Russia, Japan, and finally the Soviet Union, before being returned to China in 1950. Tanaka visited the elegant Yamato Hotel, built in 1914 by Japan's South Manchuria Railway Company, whose company logo even today adorns the city's manhole covers.

The ritual of exchanging business cards is a crucial element of East Asian culture, and the fact that the North Korean negotiator didn't offer one at the first meeting was a cause for suspicion. "Kim Chul," as he called himself, claimed to be a high-ranking member of the National Defense Commission, the division from which Kim Jong-il ruled. Tanaka assumed that the name was a pseudonym (Kim Chul being the Korean equivalent of John Smith) and noted that the other members of the North Korean delegation referred to him simply as Mr. General Manager. Tanaka took to referring to him as Mr. X.[7]

The troubled relations between Japan and Korea hung heavily over the negotiations. "Tanaka-san. My grandmother was forced to take a Japanese name," Mr. X said, as a way of introduction. "Japan colonized the Korean Peninsula, and abducted millions of Koreans to work for slave wages in Japan. I want to know how you will compensate us for these acts." Tanaka tried to bring the conversation closer to the present day. Schooled in the British art of understatement, he was not the sort of person given to sharing personal experiences. In this case, however, he sensed that doing so might ease the tension. He recounted the efforts he'd made over the past fifteen years to heal the wounds Japan had inflicted on Korea, and he mentioned the agreements he'd worked on, including Prime Minister Murayama's 1995 apology. "My desire has always been for peace on the Korean Peninsula. I don't consider making peace to be easy work. Why don't we put our misgivings aside and talk straight to each other, with open minds," he said.[8]

A plan for the clandestine negotiations emerged. The meetings took place mainly in Dalian and other Chinese cities. Because using a conference room might cause suspicion, the sessions were held in ordinary hotel suites, the beds and dressers pushed to the side. The North Koreans always sat with their backs to the windows and asked that the shades be drawn, no matter how high up the room. They would arrive one by one, with Mr. X entering last. The Koreans never presented a proposal, letting the Japanese side produce draft after draft, which they would edit.

It mattered less *who* Mr. X was than whether he was the right person for Tanaka to be negotiating with—a crucial question in an authoritarian state where only one opinion, Kim Jong-il's, ultimately carries any weight. Could Mr. X bring his promises to fruition? Tanaka wondered. In order to find out, he devised a series of tests to gauge his influence in Pyongyang. In 1999 a retired reporter for the Japanese financial daily *Nihon Keizai Shimbun* was arrested in North Korea and accused of spying. He had been in jail for two years when Tanaka asked Mr. X to show good faith by getting him released. On February 12, 2002, with no explanation, the reporter was put on a flight from Pyongyang to Beijing. Tanaka knew he was talking to the right man.

Meanwhile, in Japan, the abduction issue was heating up. Word of the negotiations leaked, forcing Koizumi to meet with the family members and promise not to normalize relations unless the

abduction issue was settled satisfactorily. But after twenty meetings, negotiations stalled. Tanaka knew that the possibility of a
Koizumi visit to North Korea was the most important card he
could play and was ultimately more important to the North than
a monetary settlement. So every time Mr. X tried to get him to
commit to Koizumi's visit, Tanaka held firm and repeated Japan's
basic requirements. The negotiations wouldn't progress until the
North agreed to acknowledge and apologize for the abductions,
provide information on the victims' whereabouts, and release any
survivors. Tanaka made it clear that anything less would cause
him to leave the table. Mr. X was visibly unnerved by the ultima-
tum. "What you must understand is that, while the worst that
could happen to you is dismissal, my situation is much more serious. My *life* might be at stake," he said.

Koizumi met with Tanaka in early June to take stock of the
negotiations. He and Mr. X were going around in circles, Tanaka
explained: the North Koreans demanded a specific amount of
money and a guaranteed visit before they would provide information about the abductees. With his popularity sinking, Koizumi needed a grand gesture more than ever. He hadn't come this
far simply to walk away. "I am prepared to visit North Korea, even
though they haven't provided us with satisfactory information about
the abductees," he told Tanaka. "If they will provide that information only if I visit them, then I can go along with that."

How many Japanese had been abducted? How many were still
alive? Tanaka wouldn't find out until after he and Koizumi arrived in Pyongyang.

# 18

# KIM AND KOIZUMI IN PYONGYANG

The prime minister's plane departed at 6:46 a.m. on September 17, 2002, headed west from Tokyo, and continued due north, across the demilitarized zone.[1] The plane was full, with fifty journalists from twenty-five Japanese news organizations. Among them was *Asahi* reporter Tsutomu Watanabe, who had been covering Koizumi for the past two years.[2] Watanabe was the perfect person to chronicle this trip. It was his third time in the North, and he spoke Korean, which he'd learned while working in the paper's Seoul bureau. Koizumi was something new in Japanese politics: a maverick who promised to jolt the country out of its complacency by opening up markets to competition, privatizing state operations, and weakening the power of the bureaucrats who had run Japan for the past fifty years. He was more conservative and promilitary than his predecessors, and his regular visits to the Yasukuni Shrine, whose dead included more than a thousand Japanese convicted of war crimes, had offended China and both Koreas. He was a gambler who took large risks for large rewards, and nothing was riskier than being the first sitting Japanese prime minister to visit the North since the end of the the Second World War. As the plane crossed the DMZ, Watanabe noted that the landscape faded from green to brown. The rivers that South Korean industrialists had straightened to ease navigation became twisted and haphazard.

Watanabe had been surprised when Koizumi had announced the trip two weeks earlier. The history of negotiations between Japan and North Korea wasn't pretty. Over the years, several Japanese politicians had made unofficial trips to Pyongyang, with dreams of signing mining or construction contracts, only to return empty-handed. All the press attaché told Watanabe was that Koizumi intended to sign an agreement—a prelude to normalization— and clear up the mystery of the Japanese allegedly abducted by the North. This might be too big a bet, Watanabe thought, even for a gambler as good as Koizumi.

The plane touched down at Pyongyang's Sunan International Airport at 9:14 a.m. and Watanabe craned his neck, peering through the window to see who would greet the prime minister. Two years before, Kim Jong-il himself had greeted South Korean president Kim Dae-jung, who won the Nobel Peace Prize for his efforts. But this morning Koizumi was met by the president of the Supreme People's Assembly, the second-highest-ranking official in North Korea, a calculated slight. The journalists were bused to the Koryo Hotel, where a pressroom was waiting for them. After checking into his room, Watanabe tried to sneak out a side door to wander the streets of Pyongyang on his own. It was an old reporter's trick, but the North Koreans had anticipated it and positioned minders at every exit. To learn what was going on, Watanabe would have to wait for the afternoon press conference like all the other reporters.

Koizumi was whisked by limousine to the Hundred Flowers Guesthouse, near the Kumsusan Memorial Palace, where Kim Il-sung lay in state. Designed for honored foreign guests, the guest-house had been used by former U.S. president Jimmy Carter when he brokered a nuclear deal in 1994, and Secretary of State Madeleine Albright in 2000. While Koizumi settled in, Tanaka was taken to a distant building for a last-minute briefing. He was nervous. Would Kim Jong-il apologize for the abductions, as Mr. X had promised? Would enough of the victims be alive to justify Koizumi's trip in the eyes of the Japanese public? North Korea's normalization wish list was virtually identical to the South's in 1965: it wanted the money and investment that normalization would bring, and it wanted Japan to apologize for colonizing Korea. The knotty question was precisely how North Korea would apologize for the abductions, given its past attempts to avoid the word *apology*. As they drafted the Pyongyang Declaration in the weeks leading up to the summit, Mr. X had begged Tanaka to exclude such language from the historical document, which would provide a road map for the new era in Japan–North Korea relations. The compromise left both sides unhappy. The Koreans translated the Japanese word for "apology" into the Korean word for "atonement," and the text referred to the abductions as "regrettable incidents, which took place under the abnormal bilateral relationship, and would never happen in the future." In return for allowing the Koreans to employ diplomatic euphemisms, Tanaka had insisted that Kim Jong-il apologize for the abductions to Koizumi in person.

It wasn't until Tanaka's last-minute meeting that the North's calculations suddenly became clear. North Korea had deliberately waited until the very last second to hand over the list of surviving and deceased abductees, which Tanaka had spent months trying to wrangle from Mr. X. As Tanaka scanned the document, the reason for the North's deceptiveness became apparent. On it were the names of thirteen Japanese whom the North admitted kidnapping, eight of whom the regime claimed were dead, including Megumi Yokota and Keiko Arimoto. The circumstances of their deaths— suicide, swimming accidents, asphyxiation, heart attack, and a car crash in a country with few cars—were suspicious, and the evidence the regime presented was questionable. All the death certificates had been issued by the same hospital, and it was said that no remains existed for any of the abductees, the graves having been washed away by floods. The North claimed that only five of the abductees—two couples and a single woman—were alive. Tanaka had been trapped. By agreeing to a Koizumi visit without first learning the fate of the abductees, he had lost his leverage. Although he and Koizumi had assumed that some of the abductees might have died, the fact that the deceased outnumbered the living, and that the evidence of death was so flimsy, wasn't something they had anticipated. How would the Japanese public react when it learned that the prime minister was normalizing relations with a regime that had kidnapped and perhaps killed or was still holding so many fellow citizens?

With barely thirty minutes to go, Tanaka ran several hundred yards to the guesthouse. Had the Koreans intended to deliver the news in a place where he would have difficulty reaching the prime minister? he wondered. Koizumi was shocked by the news Tanaka brought him. But what had he expected? Diplomats must be coldly realistic in their calculations in ways the public can't be expected to be. He knew that some of the abductees must be alive—otherwise Kim Jong-il wouldn't have invited him to Pyongyang in the first place. But the North had been so unforthcoming that he'd suspected some were dead. It was common knowledge that the regime seldom admitted its mistakes. Its na-

Koizumi and Kim (Associated Press)

tional pride depended on everything going according to plan, or at least seeming to, despite evidence to the contrary. The Japanese had assumed the North would announce the names of the surviving abductees and report the others as "missing," the euphemism the two sides had used in previous negotiations. But they departed from the text and delivered the bad news with unseemly directness. North Korea's definitive, if not honest account—since nobody knew if *all* the abductees were accounted for—made it all but impossible for the Japanese to save face.

Kim Jong-il entered the room at eleven in the morning wearing his signature khaki-colored military jacket. Koizumi was careful to avoid the bonhomie that ordinarily occurs when two heads of state greet each other for the first time. The Ministry of Foreign Affairs had advised him to keep it simple: no smiles, use only one hand to shake, make sure not to bow. "As the host, I regret that we had to make the prime minister of Japan come to Pyongyang so early in the morning in order to open a new chapter in the DPRK-Japan relationship," Kim said. Reading from note cards, Kim explained he wanted to become "true neighbors" and establish new relations with Japan. "I, too, hope that the opportunity that this meeting presents will greatly advance bilateral relations between our two countries," Koizumi responded.

After a few minutes of pleasantries, Koizumi had had enough and departed from his script. "I was utterly distressed by the information that was provided" about the abductees, he began. His tone was angry. "I ask that you arrange a meeting for us with the surviving abductees. And I would like you to make an outright apology." Kim listened in silence, looking uncomfortable. Tanaka wondered if Mr. X had ever actually told Kim that Koizumi would require him to make a public apology. Kim neither acknowledged Koizumi's remarks nor offered an apology. "Shall we take a break now?" he suggested, after a long pause.

The meeting had lasted barely an hour. Discouraged, Koizumi and the delegation retreated to an anteroom to consider their options. The North had wanted to host a state visit, with banquets and performances, but the Japanese insisted it be an all-business one-day affair, and even brought along their own bento boxes for lunch. Koizumi didn't want to be photographed toasting a dictator. In the anteroom, they watched the Japanese television news coverage of the talks, keeping the volume high on the assumption that the room was bugged. "If the North Koreans won't acknowledge their wrongdoings, you have to push them," Tanaka said. It pained him to think that a year of diplomacy might be for naught, but what else could they do? And if Kim refused to address the abductions and apologize? "You should not sign the joint statement," said Cabinet Undersecretary Shinzo Abe.

Koizumi's bento went untouched, and he wondered if he had made a mistake.

The afternoon session began at two sharp, and Kim, having eavesdropped on his guests' lunchtime conversation, got right to the point.[3] "We have thoroughly investigated this matter," Kim read from a memo. "Decades of adversarial relations between our two countries provided the background of this incident. It was, nevertheless, an appalling incident." Kim continued: "It is my understanding that this incident was initiated by special mission organizations in the 1970s and 1980s driven by blindly motivated patriotism and misguided heroism." He explained that the purposes of the abductions were to find people to teach its agents Japanese and to steal identities with which to infiltrate the South. "As soon as their scheme and deeds were brought to my attention, those who were responsible were punished." He claimed that the two people responsible for Megumi Yokota's abduction had been tried and found guilty in 1998. Both were now dead: one was executed and the other died while serving a fifteen-year sentence. "I would like to take this opportunity to apologize straightforwardly for the regrettable conduct of those people. I will not allow that to happen again," Kim promised.[4]

The explanation was implausible on several levels. It was inconceivable to Koizumi that a covert program like this could have existed without Kim's knowledge, especially as he was in charge of espionage operations during the years most of the abductions occurred. Despite his misgivings, Koizumi signed the Pyongyang Declaration at a 5:30 ceremony, an event immortalized on a North Korean postage stamp. What choice did he have? Kim had apologized for the abductions, even if his account was unsatisfactory. And what might happen to the remaining abductees if Koizumi refused to sign? After the ceremony, the Japanese delegation returned to the Koryo Hotel to announce the news to the world.

Tsutomu Watanabe's heart sank as Koizumi and the others stepped up to the lectern. The officials looked nervous, their faces pale. Abe, the Cabinet undersecretary, spoke first. He described the Pyongyang Declaration as an important step toward normalization and quickly moved on to the only subject anyone wanted to hear about. As he began reading the names of the abductees, noting who was alive and who was dead, Watanabe was overcome with grief. When big news is announced at press conferences, reporters immediately run to their phones, but he and his fellow reporters just stood in shocked silence. "The Japanese people are going to be very angry," thought Watanabe. "Koizumi, the gambler, has failed after all."

"Did you confirm that the eight abductees were dead?" asked the first reporter. Abe replied that the information came from North Korea's investigation. "Well, why did *you* not confirm it?" asked Watanabe. He was surprised by how emotional he was. After a few more questions, the reporters finally ran to the pressroom to phone in their stories. "Five people alive, eight people dead," Watanabe told his editor. The editor didn't believe him. "Really? *Eight* people dead!?" he responded, incredulous.

The next day, every newspaper in Japan ran similar headlines: "Eight Dead, Five Alive." News of the Pyongyang Declaration was relegated to the second line, if it was mentioned all. The missing abductees, especially Megumi Yokota, were all anyone talked about.

# 19

## RETURNING HOME: FROM NORTH KOREA TO JAPAN

In the summer of 2000, Kaoru Hasuike received a visit from a high party official. With the attention the abductions had been receiving in Japan, such visits were rare, and seldom brought good news. Were they being moved to a new Invitation-Only Zone or, worse, away from Pyongyang altogether? No, the official had a question: Would he and Yukiko be willing to appear at a press conference and tell the world they were living happily in North Korea, of their own free will? Kaoru and Yukiko were confused. Was this a trick to test their loyalty to the regime? After twenty years of hiding their identities, trying to fit in as normal North Koreans, were they now really being asked to step out from the shadows?

Kaoru could barely breathe, his heart beating so fast he feared it would burst from his chest. He tried masking his panic with the calm, deadpan façade he'd cultivated over the years. "If this is an order, we will do it," he replied, choosing his words carefully.[1] It was essential that he come across as dutiful above all, and he certainly couldn't show any enthusiasm. But all he could think about was the possibility of seeing his family again. Kaoru had long ago given up the hope of returning to Japan, resigning himself to life in the North with his wife and children. Of course, it wasn't the life he'd planned, but it was a life nonetheless, and after twenty years he'd gotten used to it. It was painful to again feel the longing for home and family, but he couldn't pass up this opportunity.

What Kaoru didn't know was that this was the regime's first step in the long process of normalizing diplomatic relations with Japan. Still reeling from the damage done by the famine, North Korea was desperate for the aid that was once provided by the Soviet Union. Japan seemed a promising source, but the abduction issue was a stumbling block. In negotiations, no matter how many times the regime denied the existence of the abductees, the Japanese would bring them up again. Kaoru didn't learn anything more until a year and a half later, when he read an article in the regime's official newspaper, *Rodong Sinmun*, that reported a search for "missing people" from Japan, a woman named Keiko Arimoto among them. Kaoru didn't recognize her name, but he assumed that she, too, had been abducted. Although the regime still denied the abductions, the article suggested to Kaoru that its position was changing.

In April 2001, Kaoru received another visit from the official, who told him that the regime had concocted a cover story to explain his presence in the North. They wanted him to say that he had fallen in love with the idea of *juche* philosophy while a student at Chuo University and fled to the North with his girlfriend to live in the socialist paradise. Kaoru countered that he'd been such an apolitical student that nobody would believe the story. And how would he and Yukiko even have managed to get to North Korea in 1978? Undeterred, the official came up with another story: On the July evening in 1978 when he and Yukiko were strolling on Kashiwazaki's main beach, Kaoru jumped into a motorboat bobbing offshore and zipped around for a few hours. The boat ran out of fuel and drifted all night, until a North Korean spy boat rescued them. Once in North Korea, the couple was grateful to be free of Japan's "brutal capitalism." Now married with children, they lived happily in Pyongyang. Even with minor adjustments, Kaoru said he would never be able to tell the story convincingly. "We don't need to *convince* them," the official replied angrily. "All you have to do is stick to the story. In the end, Japan will *have* to accept it." Resigned, Kaoru rehearsed the ludicrous tale until he almost believed it.

In June 2002, Kaoru Hasuike's family moved from the Invitation-Only Zone into a modern thirty-story high-rise on Tongil ("Unification") Street, a massive boulevard in one of Pyongyang's most exclusive neighborhoods, full of shops and restaurants. With three bedrooms, a living room, dining room, kitchen, color television, refrigerator, fish tank, and telephone, it was the kind of dwelling reserved for the North Korean elite. The apartment afforded a clear view of downtown Pyongyang, across the Taedong River. The relocation wasn't an act of kindness or generosity on the part of the regime as much as a shrewd calculation that Kaoru and Yukiko needed some practice living freely in order to convince their families they were thriving. The plan was for the abductees' relatives to come to North Korea for the reunion so they could see the splendor in which they were living. Like most of the staged experiences visitors to North Korea are allowed to have, the reality was less appealing. The Hasuikes' fourth-floor apartment was prized because there often wasn't enough electricity to power the elevators. The stairs leading to the apartment were dirty and dimly lit, even during the day. Most of the building's windows were broken and had been patched with sheets of plastic. The streets behind the grand boulevard were unpaved and lacked proper drainage, leaving enormous puddles when it rained. Kaoru knew his parents would be dismayed by his family's circumstances, which even the most impoverished Japanese wouldn't put up with. "They shouldn't judge it by Japanese standards," the official replied. "Tell them that this is a very high-class apartment in our country."

The four months he and his family lived in the apartment was the only period during Kaoru's twenty-four years in the North when they were not under surveillance. With no friends or relatives, Kaoru and Yukiko wandered through Pyongyang, the capital city of two million people, for hours. It was thrilling to be free from the watchful eyes of minders, although Kaoru noted how dingy even the nicest neighborhoods were. Hidden behind rows of imposing high-rise apartments lay decrepit three-story buildings built in the fifties and sixties, with cracked façades covered in black soot from coal and wood stoves. Even in central Pyongyang, vacant lots were planted with corn, a reminder of the famine. The prices of goods and services were higher than Kaoru was used to, with basics such as rice and public transportation more than he could afford. With the children home for summer vacation, he took them to a nearby restaurant for Naengmyeon, the local specialty of cold noodles and beef broth. The meal cost 480 won for the four of them, a quarter of Kaoru's monthly wage. Everywhere he turned, Kaoru was struck by a fact he hadn't had to deal with in decades: freedom is expensive.

At the end of September, Kaoru and his fellow abductee Yasushi Chimura were summoned to a meeting with their minder. They knew that Kim Jong-il had confessed to Koizumi about the abductions (which made Kaoru's implausible cover story unnecessary) and that the two countries had embarked on the path to normalization. While the original plan was for the abductees' families to visit them in the North, the diplomat Hitoshi Tanaka had insisted the abductees go to Japan instead. Kaoru and Yasushi were informed that they and their wives were to visit Japan for ten days, two weeks at the most, and return to the North, where their Japanese families could visit them at a later date. Their children would remain in the North. Because no loyal North Korean citizen is supposed to want to leave his beloved country, Kaoru and Yasushi struggled to mask their reactions. They feared the whole scheme was an elaborate loyalty test, and responded accordingly. "Do we *have* to go? Can we come back quickly?" they asked. Finally, grudgingly, Kaoru told the minders that he and Yasushi would agree to visit Japan, as much as it pained them to do so, and then return "home" to the North.

After the meeting, Kaoru and Yasushi went over what had transpired, wondering what else they should have said or asked. It was the first time in years they had been consulted about their future, and it made them anxious. "We didn't know what our lives would be like somewhere else. All we knew is North Korea," Yasushi tells me. "We would go to Japan for our country, and then come back and see our children again. That is all we knew."[2] In particular, Kaoru worried about the effect their visit to Japan might have on his children. If the fact that they were Japanese was known in the North, his children's reputation would suffer. And how would they feel learning that they had grandparents and relatives in Japan? Or that everything their parents had told them was false?

Kaoru had no choice but to lie to his children one more time. He explained that he and their mother were taking an extended educational tour through the North's important historical sites and would be gone for two weeks. The children returned to school on the day before their parents left for Japan. Whereas Kaoru usually saw them off with a few parting words, this time he found himself delivering a lecture urging them to work hard and take care of themselves—hardly the words of a parent leaving for a short trip. The children, twenty-one and seventeen, waved back warily, aware that something wasn't quite right.

# 20

## AN EXTENDED VISIT

The government-chartered Boeing 767 landed at Tokyo's Haneda Airport at 2:20 p.m. on a clear October day, one month after Koizumi's trip to Pyongyang. Kaoru Hasuike and Yasushi Chimura wore dark suits, while their wives wore beige skirts with matching jackets. Hitomi Soga, in a demure blue jacket and skirt, was alone, her husband, Charles Jenkins, having stayed in North Korea, afraid he'd be arrested for desertion if he set foot in Japan. Each of the abductees wore two pins: a small image of Kim Il-sung, and a small blue flag, the symbol of Japan's abductee rescue movement. The two symbols provided a visual snapshot of their predicament: from one perspective they were loyal North Korean citizens visiting their families in Japan; from the other, they were Japanese abductees escaping from their North Korean kidnappers.

The looks on their faces alternated between relief and terror: relief at seeing their relatives again and terror that the army of

Abductees descending from plane: Hitomi Soga (top left); Yukiko and Kaoru Hasuike (center); special adviser on the abduction issue, Kyoko Nakayama, and Fukie and Yasushi Chimura (bottom). (Associated Press)

waiting reporters would ask questions that might imperil their children in the North. They had been told by their minders that their every move would be monitored from Pyongyang, and that two members of the North Korean Red Cross had been assigned to keep track of them in Japan. They were instructed to check in at the end of every day, and given special cell phones with which to call the North. The surveillance aside, at the bottom of the steps the abductees fell, sobbing, into the arms of their relatives awaiting them on the tarmac.

The major television stations ran specials and live coverage all day, devoting thirty hours to the homecoming.[1] The story became a national obsession, dominating newspapers and magazines. A poll found that 80 percent of the Japanese believed they were on the brink of war with the North. The sudden return of the abductees left the public feeling simultaneously aghast at North Korea's treachery and patronized by the Japanese government's incompetence. In the following weeks, every major political party included the abduction issue in its official election agenda.

The fanfare around the five abductees' homecoming was in stark contrast to the subdued welcome Takeshi Terakoshi had received two weeks earlier when he visited Japan for the first time in thirty-nine years. Since disappearing at sea with his uncles when he was thirteen, Takeshi had made a life for himself in the North and rejected the abductee label. He'd taken the name Kim Yeong-heo, and was visiting Japan in his capacity as a North Korean union official. The only extraordinary aspect of the visit was its timing, with Takeshi returning to North Korea only days before the other abductees arrived in Japan. By sending *two* groups of Japanese-born North Koreans to visit their original home, the North sent a message. North Korea and Japan were now "true neighbors," the phrase Kim Jong-il had used with Koizumi in Pyongyang, and these visits exemplified the new relationship.

Kaoru Hasuike, before and after (Kyodo)

Everyone attributed Kaoru's gaunt appearance to malnutrition, but the truth was he'd been too tense to eat in the weeks leading up to the trip. Despite the immense joy he felt at reuniting with his family, he was racked by anxiety. "I've just got to get through these ten days, and then I'll be back with my kids," he thought to himself.[2] With his children serving as de facto hostages, he had to avoid saying anything that might upset the North Korean regime. The first challenge came not from the media, but from his brother, Toru, who had become a leader of the Abductee Family Group and took a particularly hard line against the North. Toru hadn't been particularly political and knew nothing about North Korea before meeting the communist-turned–North Korea expert Katsumi Sato. Over the years, Sato had become an eloquent critic of the North, using his perch as director of the Modern Korea Institute to attack the pro-North Korean sentiments he had himself once held.

Toru was spellbound by Sato, who became his mentor at a time when the Japanese establishment either ignored Toru and the other abductee activists or dismissed them as delusional. "He spoke with so much authority, as if he had just returned from North Korea. He would hold forth for hours, on every aspect of the country, providing more and more information, answering any questions we had. We drank it in," he tells me.[3] Toru had been granted a leave of absence from his job as a nuclear engineer at

Tokyo Electric Power Company to dedicate his time to rescuing his brother and the other abductees. Now that this seemingly impossible goal had been attained, he was intoxicated by the triumph. The first thing he wanted to do was hold a press conference at a downtown Tokyo hotel for the five abductees to denounce the North Korean regime.

Kaoru, who had become the informal leader of the group of visiting abductees, at first refused. Making public statements of the sort his brother envisioned would expose them and their families to risks Toru couldn't conceive of. Had they so much as thanked the "Great Leader" or spouted the requisite patriotic pabulum, it would horrify the millions of Japanese who had rallied to the cause in the month since Koizumi met with Kim Jong-il. On the other hand, if they neglected to acknowledge Kim Jong-il or dared criticize the regime, they might never see their children again. "You have to say *something*, even if it is only a few words. If you don't, the media will never leave you alone," Toru begged his brother. The five finally agreed to address the press but looked terrified as they stared at the microphones in front of them. Kaoru spoke first, choosing his words carefully. "I apologize for the inconvenience I have caused my family," he said. "I apologize for any grief I've brought to my loved ones," followed Yasushi Chimura. When it was her turn to speak, Hitomi Soga could barely get a word out. "I look forward to, to . . ." she whispered, before trailing off.

A rift emerged between the families of those who had returned and the families of those whom the North said had died. It had started the day Koizumi returned from Pyongyang, when all the families were ushered into the Ministry of Foreign Affairs and informed, one by one, whether their son or daughter was either alive or dead. The encounters were curt and unemotional, and the families were furious that the Japanese government was uncritically conveying information from the North Koreans. How could anyone believe a country that had lied about the abductions for twenty-five years? Katsumi Sato, in his capacity as head of the abduction support group, drew a line in the sand: until the North proved that the other abductees were dead, he would proceed on the assumption that they were alive. "The information about the fate of the abductees is utterly ungrounded," he said, accusing Koizumi and Tanaka of bungling the operation and imperiling the unaccounted-for abductees' lives. "Because the Japanese government has informed their families that those eight are dead, there has emerged the danger that they actually will be disposed of."

After the news conference, the families of the missing begged Kaoru and the others for information about their sisters, brothers, sons, and daughters. The brother of the woman who had taught Japanese to the terrorist Kim Hyon-hui asked about his sister. "They were looking down, and wouldn't make eye contact. I think they were forced to say that they knew nothing about other abducted people," he said. "I felt like I was listening to a tape recorder." The only abductee the five were willing to discuss was Megumi Yokota, whom they had met. However, they wouldn't say much other than that she was a quiet girl who had suffered from depression. They were careful neither to confirm nor to deny the North's claim that she'd hanged herself in 1993 while a patient in a psychiatric hospital. Many found the similarities in their accounts odd. "They all tell us that my daughter was so quiet, but she was really a very active girl, always loud, and almost never got sick," said Sakie Yokota. When asked whether he thought it likely that Keiko Arimoto could have been accidentally asphyxiated by a malfunctioning coal heater, as the North alleged, Kaoru launched into a detailed explanation of heating problems in the North. "It sounded like he was justifying the information provided by North Korea," said Toru.[4] Some of the most right-wing members of the activist group started wondering if Kaoru was a North Korean "sleeper" spy.

It wasn't until the entire Hasuike family retreated to the hotel suite in the evening that the two brothers had an opportunity to talk. After twenty-four years apart, they were bound to find things awkward, but Kaoru appeared even stranger than Toru had feared he'd be. For one thing, he kept referring to himself as a "citizen of North Korea" and "a member of the North Korea delegation," whose purpose in visiting Japan was to help normalize relations between the two countries. "We're going back, so next time you must come visit me in North Korea," Kaoru said, as if doing so were as easy as taking a trip to Hawaii.[5] Again and again, Toru tried to draw his brother out with provocative questions, practically begging him to criticize the North. In response, Kaoru explained to Toru that North Korea, while a small country, was a great nation and would never be defeated by the Japanese or American imperialists. He not only avoided speaking ill of the North but also used the honorific title "Great Leader" or "Great Marshal" whenever he mentioned Kim Jong-il. "He's been brainwashed and isn't able to think for himself," Toru thought to himself.

That evening there was a second press conference so that the abductees' family members could answer questions. Toru had been brooding over his brother's strange behavior all day and could no longer keep silent. "Something is not right here. All he talks about is North Korea, as though he were a North Korean," he announced to the assembled crowd of journalists and television cameras. Toru said he was repulsed by Kaoru's behavior and didn't recognize him anymore. "I want the little brother I lost twenty-four years ago. But he studied North Korea's ideology for twenty-four years. I think this mind-set is ingrained in him."[6]

Kaoru sat in the suite a few floors above watching the press conference on television. He leaped from his chair the minute Toru entered the room. "What kind of *bullshit* is this? All I've been doing is telling you the truth! Who do you think you are to say things like that about me?" Kaoru yelled. Witnessing the argument, their mother started to cry. "Here you haven't seen each other in twenty-four years, and you are already fighting!? I'm going to jump out the window and kill myself!" A panicked look came over Kaoru's face and he immediately tried to console her, addressing her as *Okaasan*, "Mother." Toru was aghast. "Obviously, as part of the mission, Kaoru was sent to Japan to honor his parents and convince them to visit him in North Korea. He wasn't upset that he'd made her cry. He was upset because her crying threatened the success of his mission," Toru tells me. The next evening, Toru invited a few of Kaoru's childhood friends to visit them. Perhaps seeing faces from Kaoru's past would bring him back? After chatting about old times for a while, one of the friends grew tired of Kaoru's cautious statements and urged him to express his hatred of North Korea. "Look, I tried hard during the past twenty-four years," Kaoru yelled at him. "You're not telling me they were wasted, are you? Are you guys trying to brainwash me?"

The terms Hitoshi Tanaka had negotiated required the abductees to return to the North after two weeks. But from the moment they arrived at Haneda, Toru tried to convince his brother to stay in Japan permanently. He was relentless, as if failing to convince him would be a personal and professional defeat. After all, how would it look for the brother of the leader of the abductee family association to return to the North? "Please consider living in Japan," he begged. "Don't you have feelings for this country?" After two days at the hotel, Toru saw small signs of the Kaoru he had once known. "I realized that Kaoru hadn't been brainwashed; he was just wearing the psychological body armor he needed in order to survive for all these years," he says. Toru concluded that the only way to get Kaoru to remove the armor was to bring him to his home town of Kashiwazaki and immerse him in the world he'd lost. Once there, Toru did everything he could think of to reconnect his brother to Japan. They went to city hall to add his marriage and the birth of his two children to their family registry. They got him a new driver's license. At first Kaoru went through the motions, if only to avoid conflict. But he was bitter that his brother wasn't taking his dilemma seriously. "How come you're so cold to me?" he thought to himself. "Here I am trying to hold everything together. Don't mess up my head. I have to return to North Korea for my kids. What about that do you not understand?"

With only days to go before the abductees were scheduled to return to North Korea, Toru booked rooms for the whole family at a resort one hour inland from Kashiwazaki, where they used to ski as children. After a day on the mountain, the brothers soaked in the naturally heated therapeutic waters. Toru took another tack, concentrating not on why Kaoru should stay in Japan but on why he *couldn't* return to the North. The political situation had intensified in recent weeks. On October 16, the day after Kaoru and the others returned to Japan, North Korea had admitted it had secretly restarted its nuclear weapons program. "Now it's no longer just about the abductions. The nuclear issue is back, and relations are going to get really complicated," Toru explained. Kaoru had to understand that the army of photographers at Haneda two weeks earlier had beamed the story of his abduction all over the world. Even ordinary North Koreans had learned the truth, so the life Kaoru intended to return to was impossible. By now, everyone would know that he, his wife, and his children were Japanese. The conversation evidently made an impression on Kaoru, who crept into his brother's room the next morning and woke him up. "I've decided to stay in Japan," he said. "But you must promise to get my children back." Toru couldn't believe what he was hearing, and he made Kaoru repeat it, just to make sure. Toru immediately called his contact at Japan's Ministry of Foreign Affairs before Kaoru could change his mind.

Yukiko became frantic when Kaoru told her he wanted to remain in Japan. "What the hell are you talking about? What about the kids?" she cried. Kaoru had never seen such a pained expression on her face. "Listen, this is for the children's sake. There is no other option but to live in Japan. They'll never have a normal life in the North now that everyone knows about the abductions," he said "The Japanese government said they will get them back to us. We have to trust them." Yukiko was not the only one desperate to return to the North. For days, Hitomi Soga had been begging the government to allow her to go back, convinced that it was the only way she'd see her husband and daughters again.

The members of Koizumi's Cabinet were divided over whether to return the abductees to North Korea, as the Japanese government had agreed to do. Both options held risks. If the Japanese government sent the five back and no progress was made, or the abductees weren't allowed to leave the North with their children, Koizumi's government would fall and the public would never forgive him. However, keeping them in Japan violated the agreement Tanaka had negotiated with Mr. X, which stipulated that their stay in Japan be a "temporary return." Finally, Cabinet Undersecretary Shinzo Abe broke the logjam, insisting that the abductees decide for themselves. Two days before they were scheduled to return, the Japanese government announced that the visit was being "extended," which for all intents and purposes meant they would remain. In addition, it requested that the North allow their children and other family members to join them. It would take eighteen months of negotiation, a second Koizumi visit to Pyong-yang, and 250,000 tons of rice to release the children, who finally joined their parents in May 2004.[7] The Japanese media described the children as "returning" to Japan, no matter that they had spent their entire lives in North Korea and spoke little or no Japanese.

# 21

# ABDUCTION, INC.

Abductee activist Katsumi Sato divided the day of September 17, 2002, between watching the televised coverage of the Pyongyang summit and answering questions from the reporters lined up outside the offices of *Modern Korea*. "Where the hell have you been for the past twenty years?" he thought to himself.[1] At seventy-three, he'd traveled a long road, in thrall first to the emperor of Japan and then to North Korea's Communist experiment. The message that he'd preached during the last half of his life, that the North was a tyranny, capable of anything, had been ignored by the liberal Japanese media and government. Until now, the notion that North Korea had been kidnapping Japanese since the 1970s received only slightly more credulity than reports of alien abductions.

Yet this afternoon, none other than Kim Jong-il himself had confessed. From the comfort of his office, Sato sensed Japanese public opinion turning a full 180 degrees. Not only had the Japanese government failed to protect its people, but it emerged that

Katsumi Sato and Sakie Yokota (Associated Press)

it had been aware of the abduction project almost from the start, and that the government and media had dismissed reports of abductions publicly long after they suspected they were true.[2] And now Koizumi had the nerve to normalize relations with the rogue regime? Within a week, public support of Koizumi's government plunged from 81 percent to 44 percent. "You've heard of the eye of a hurricane? Well, it was very still where we were sitting. But the whole world was spinning out of control around us," Sato tells me. Japan became obsessed over Kim Jong-il and North Korea, much as the United States had fixated on Osama bin Laden and Al Qaeda one year before. A nation that had cared little about North Korea could now think of hardly anything else.[3] And nobody had more and better stories than Sato. "Mr. Sato, you have defeated the entire Japanese communications industry," one reporter told him. "Everything is precisely as you said. The win goes to you." All eyes were on Sato, the man proved right—morally and politically, on national television—when everyone else had been wrong.

An ex-Communist with an elementary school education, Sato was promoted to the level of "statesman." His small magazine, *Modern Korea*, had given him a small audience of North Korea–watchers, but his leadership role in the abductee movement increased his visibility. But now his every utterance was noted, and politicians and industrialists scrambled to kiss his ring. "We'd make a statement in the morning and receive an official government response by the end of the day," he says.[4] After years of indifference, the abductees' families became sacrosanct objects of sympathy and compassion. Even the North Koreans understood who was actually running Japan's foreign policy. "The ones wielding power in Japan are not the government or the Ministry of Foreign Affairs," a North Korean negotiator confided to a Japanese politician. "They're always overturned if the abductees' family organization voices opposition."[5]

The abductee activists had been working on a shoestring for years, always in debt, surviving on small donations collected at demonstrations and events. With the entire nation reeling from the revelations, money started to pour in. Kazuhiro Araki, Sato's right-hand man, took responsibility for keeping track of it.[6] A Korea specialist, Araki had begun writing articles for *Modern Korea* in the 1980s and was soon after hired as an editor. Sato became his mentor, introducing Araki to the woman who would become Araki's wife. In Japan, when one sends money via a wire transfer, it is confirmed by a receipt, delivered by mail, Araki explains to me. "Every day, we would get dozens of receipts, stacked two or three inches thick," he says, spreading his thumb and forefinger in an imaginary wedge. "Our financial problems disappeared in three months. It was a full-time job just keeping track of the money. Some of the donations were for ten dollars, but others were for several thousand."[7]

To atone for their sins of omission, the media threw dozens of reporters at the story, every paper creating a permanent "abduction beat," a position that still exists today, despite the lack of news to report. (News organizations fear that eliminating the position would offend the abductees.) The *Niigata Nippo*'s abduction correspondent, Shito Yokoyama, was the first reporter assigned to the beat. Her reporting has taken her to North Korea, and won the praise of the abductees' families, but in eight years on the beat, she has never interviewed any of the abductees themselves. "We aren't allowed to interview the abductees," she tells me.[8]

Two days before the abductees returned to Japan, the heads of twenty-one major news organizations agreed to "exercise restraint" in reporting the story in their papers and magazines and on television programs.[9] The agreement was an act of self-censorship, by which they abrogated their news judgment and deferred to a coalition of activists, abductees, and their families. Similar arrangements are common in Japan, where news organizations operate restrictive "*kisha* clubs" for their reporters, who in return for access, agree not to scoop one another or cover various ministries and corporations too aggressively. The abduction *kisha* club took its instructions from Sato, whose years as a Communist organizer had trained him in the art of manipulating the narrative. The rules were as simple as they were strictly enforced: all requests for information or interviews had to go through Sato. The abductees could be interviewed only in groups, and the stories that emerged were required to be positive in tone and substance. To ensure that the club's reporters were too busy to snoop around on their own, Sato held several press conferences a week, whether or not there was any actual news. The smallest development would require the reporters to assemble at Sato's feet. He was unforgiving and much feared by the press. "Given the choice, I'd rather negotiate with North Korea than with Sato," one reporter told me. Any publication that ran a negative or unapproved story lost access, as happened when a reporter for the *Asahi Weekly* magazine conducted an impromptu interview with Fukie and Yasushi Chimura after they returned home to Obama. The morning the article appeared, Sato charged into the magazine's headquarters and demanded a meeting with the editor in chief. The magazine soon ran an apology for breaking the rules.

It isn't until I get a copy of the article that I understand the reason Sato was so enraged. Worse than violating the self-censorship agreement, the article threatened to undermine his carefully constructed narrative of Japanese victims imprisoned by an evil regime by providing an unscripted glimpse of the Chimuras' pedestrian life in North Korea. When asked about their relationship with their North Korean minder, Fukie replied simply, "He wasn't really someone who watched us as much as he was a tutor who took care of us whenever we went out." Yasushi added, "Sure, he watched us, but from our point of view, he was someone who would take us shopping. They were not bad people." After this article, nobody was allowed to speak directly with the abductees.

While the Japanese were angry with North Korea, the most vicious attacks were reserved for the "enemies within," the allegedly pro-North Korea Japanese intelligentsia. "I call for a reexamination of what remarks have been made by whom, when, and in what newspapers, magazines and other media," critic and novelist Ayoko Sono wrote in the conservative *Sankei Shimbun* two days after the Kim-Koizumi summit. "To glorify North Korea has been the trendy demeanor of the progressive cultural elite and the progressive media, but this attitude has also disrupted" the lives of the abductees.[10] Other conservative magazines encouraged the witch hunt. "The Death Throes of the North Korea Clique: Rip Out Their Double-Talking Tongues!"[11] read one headline; "The

Politicians, Bureaucrats, and Debaters Who Have Stood By and Watched Eight Abductees Die: Apologize for Your Great Sins Through Death," read another.[12] Shinzo Abe rode the abduction issue into the prime minister's office, accusing anyone who opposed him on the subject of "siding with North Korea." Hitoshi Tanaka, the diplomat who negotiated the abductees' freedom, was labeled a "Class-A war criminal" and accused of being "soft" on North Korea by the magazine *Shukan Bunshun*. One morning, a bomb was discovered in front of his home, accompanied by an envelope addressed to "Hitoshi Tanaka, traitor." When asked what he thought of the attack, the conservative Tokyo governor Shintaro Ishihara said Tanaka "got what he deserved." When asked whether the statement meant that he supported terrorism, Ishihara replied that he didn't, but that Tanaka still "deserved to die ten thousand deaths." Even Shinzo Abe's own party, the Liberal Democrats (LDP), was criticized. "What country are our government and our ruling party working for? Why doesn't the LDP just put up a sign reading 'The Korean Workers' Party—Japan Branch Office'?" remarked one leading activist.

One of the first actions Shinzo Abe took upon becoming prime minister in 2006 was to establish the Headquarters for the Abduction Issue, a Cabinet-level office with an enormous budget to coordinate the government's abduction-related efforts.[13] It broadened the public's awareness of the abductions through films, comic books, and cartoons, publishing a two-volume graphic manga comic book about Megumi Yokota, which it translated into Korean, Chinese, Arabic, and English. It also commissioned an animated cartoon version of Megumi's story, which it put online.[14] Abe ordered NHK, the government-funded broadcaster, to increase its coverage of the abduction issue, even though it had already devoted one-third of its roughly two thousand North Korea–related broadcasts to it in the first nine months of 2006.[15] Abe used the abductions to advance the nationalist and militarist sentiments that had been growing since the early 1980s. "I began to notice that the events I attended were no longer just about abductions. They were also about teaching the 'proper version of history' in schools, how the Rape of Nanking was a 'gross exaggeration,' and other standard, right wing causes," says Eric Johnston, a *Japan Times* reporter who covered the issue.[16] Until recently, it was taboo to question whether Japan's U.S.-authored constitution should be revised to allow the Self-Defense Force to be used more widely. Under Abe, an argument raged over whether Japan should become a so-called normal nation, allowed to defend itself, and even take proactive measures, rather than depending on the United States. Japan's legislature loosened restrictions on the military, allowing it to support the U.S. invasion of Afghanistan and combat "potential or actual" terrorist attacks at home. The Ministry of Defense was upgraded to a full Cabinet position for the first time since the end of the Second World War.

The Japanese government wasn't the only organization considering a more robust international role. Since the government was plainly incapable of doing anything about the plight of the abductees, Sato hatched a plan. Ahn Myung-jin was a North Korean spy who defected to the South in 1993. A graduate of the Wonsan Foreign Language Institute and the Kim Jong-il Military Academy (where the terrorist Kim Hyon-hui trained), Ahn had worked at the center of the regime's intelligence operations. He claimed to have information about Japanese abductees, such as Megumi Yokota, and had been meeting with Katsumi Sato and other abductee activists since the late 1990s. "He was a very important source of information to us," says Toru Hasuike, who at one point went to Seoul to meet with Ahn. "I took a photograph of Kaoru with me and asked him whether he'd seen him in North Korea." (He hadn't.)[17]

It became an article of faith among the activists that Kim Jong-il had lied to Koizumi and was holding on to the other abductees because they knew too many secrets. To prove that they were alive, Sato needed someone to infiltrate the North and locate them. Perhaps he could even help them escape! "We paid Ahn one hundred thousand dollars to, at a minimum, provide photographic evidence that other abductees were alive," Toru tells me. Half the money came from the family and support organizations, and the other half from several Japanese politicians. The mission barely got off the ground. "Ahn was spotted when he got close to the North Korean coast," says Toru. "I don't think he even made it onto land. He wasn't arrested, but he thought that he was about to be apprehended, so he headed back to South Korea." Ahn didn't return the money, according to Toru.

While Sato was busy with press conferences and reconnaissance missions, Kazuhiro Araki was manning the phones at *Modern Korea*.[18] He was troubled that so much attention was being directed at the returned abductees when there was mounting evidence that there were many abductees who were still unaccounted for. Since September 17 he had fielded dozens of calls from families whose relatives had gone missing. "I'd answer the phone, and an old woman would say, 'My child vanished years ago, and I've looked and looked for him, and can't find a reason why he left. Is it possible he, too, was abducted and taken to North Korea?'"[19]

Their suspicions found substance in the troubling case of Hitomi Soga. Her name had never appeared on any of the lists of missing Japanese, official or otherwise. Had the North Koreans not included hers with the names of the Hasuikes and Chimuras, Soga might very well still be in the North. If this one woman who had disappeared without anyone's knowledge had shown up in North Korea, perhaps others were there as well? Araki asked each caller to draft a statement detailing the circumstances of his or her loved one's disappearance. As the statements began to arrive, Araki noticed patterns emerging. "Soga was a nurse, and it turns out there were a bunch of other nurses who vanished. Also, there were a lot of engravers, who would have been useful when the North printed fake U.S. currency. I noticed that people are more likely to be taken from certain parts of Japan than others, and people tended to be abducted at certain times of day, and under certain weather conditions," he says. Once Araki compared the factors, he was convinced that some of those he was receiving calls about had been abducted. "At a certain point, you have to admit that these can't be accidental or coincidences, that these patterns are meaningful," he says.[20] With hundreds of names in hand, Araki decided that the officially recognized abductees needed him less than those still languishing in North Korea, and he left Sato's group to found the Investigation Commission on Missing Japanese Probably Related to North Korea.

Today Araki's organization is on the third floor of a threadbare apartment building a few blocks from Tokyo's bustling Iidabashi railway station. When I enter the office, I spot him in a makeshift plywood sound studio, conveying the news of recent nuclear arms negotiations into a microphone. Posters with photos of the hundreds of Japanese whom Araki believes were abducted are plastered all over the office. Leaning against one wall is a contraption that looks like a torpedo, on top of which someone has affixed handlebars and a seat. It is a replica of one of the military Jet Skis North Korean spies used to infiltrate Japan's waters. Seated beside it is a mannequin wearing a wet suit and swim goggles. An identification card hanging from its neck identifies him as a "Shiokaze Staff" member.

*Shiokaze* is the twice-a-day shortwave broadcast Araki began beaming into North Korea in 2005. The broadcast begins with a message telling the abductees to keep the faith, because "it will not be long until we rescue you." Soothing piano music plays in the background. Each segment includes some international news items and messages to individual abductees, often read by friends and relatives. The broadcasts are in Japanese, English, Chinese, and Korean, due to the international nature of the abduction phenomenon.

Araki finishes up the Korean-language portion of the broadcast, exits the studio, and joins me for tea at a worn conference table. He says he believes the North has kidnapped more than two hundred fifty Japanese and that the kidnappings continue to this day. "At first, we only read the names of the missing Japanese, along with their dates of birth and the places they were taken," he says. North Korea didn't jam the signal until he included news about the outside world. Since then, *Shiokaze* has switched frequencies regularly, but the North Korean regime quickly locates and jams the new one. The project is a pure act of faith: a show whose broadcast signal is jammed, directed at a country where radios are illegal and electricity scarce, to be heard by abductees who may not exist. Is there any evidence that anyone in North Korea has ever heard the broadcast? Araki and his producer consult with each other. They cite a passage from Charles Jenkins's memoir in which he says he listened to shortwave radio, but they concede that this took place years before *Shiokaze* began. "Well, we once heard about a junior high school student who was able to pick up the program in Pyongyang, but we're not sure about that," he says. After more tea, Araki excuses himself and returns to the sound booth. It is almost twelve, and he needs to finish a segment before the program is beamed into North Korea that afternoon.

# KAORU HASUIKE AT HOME

It is an uncommonly warm April afternoon when I meet Kaoru Hasuike. In 2002 he and his wife returned to Kashiwazaki, where they were joined by their son and daughter in 2004 after Prime Minister Koizumi made a second trip to Pyongyang. Kaoru's shaggy haircut and taut, angular face make him appear a decade younger than he is. The only evidence of his time in North Korea are his discolored, uneven teeth. In 2010 Kaoru completed his undergraduate degree at Chuo University via a correspondence course, and he is now working toward a graduate degree in Korean Studies at Niigata University. He recently informed the Japanese government that he no longer needs the stipend awarded the abductees to compensate them for their ordeal. He and Yukiko worked part-time at city hall during the year and a half it took for their children to be freed, and Kaoru now makes a living translating from Korean and writing his own books. Yukiko is a cook in a local kindergarten; their daughter, Shigeyo, is a graduate student; and their son,

Katsuya, earned a degree in computer science from Waseda University and is working at a bank in Seoul, South Korea.

Kaoru Hasuike today

I ask Kaoru how his children reacted upon learning their family secret. "For years we had to lie to our kids in order to protect them. If they were known to be different from other North Koreans, they would be in danger," he tells me.[1] They learned half the truth during the eighteen months it took for the Japanese government to negotiate their release. "Once the North Korean authorities came to the conclusion that they would have to return the kids, they told them that they were Japanese and that their mother and father were in Japan, although they didn't mention the abduction part. My children were cards in this game, and the regime couldn't send them home upset or traumatized, or else they would lose their promotional value, and have hurt the North's reputation," he tells me. After a night in Tokyo, the whole family went to Kashiwazaki. "They didn't say much during the first few days we were home, but we just let time pass," he says. Knowing that their Japanese was poor, Kaoru had purchased a few Korean

DVDs for them to watch. "They looked sad and troubled, and were worried about their future in Japan." Once they learned about the abductions, they knew the lives they'd imagined for themselves in North Korea were impossible. "Anyone who is born and raised in the North knows that your identity within the society determines your fate. It doesn't matter how smart you are or how hard you work. If your identity or public image or presentation isn't correct, you'll never marry well, you'll never get the job you want, you will never succeed. They'd seen this all their lives, they knew it in their bones," he says. The fact that their parents had come to the North involuntarily didn't upset them as much as Kaoru had feared it might. "You have to understand that in North Korea you are taught that the *result* is all that matters— whether it is winning the revolution or defeating the United States—and it doesn't matter whether it is won through violence or treachery. So I think it was fairly easy for them to understand that their parents had been stolen." Now that the whole family is together in Japan, there are no more secrets. "Today, when I speak with my children, I never lie about anything. That is the rule. Once you open that door, you have to continue to speak truthfully and be completely open."

Kaoru is polite but wary. The Japanese press has sensationalized the story, he tells me, and he fears the abductees who remain in the North may be suffering the consequences. Among the conditions for our interview is that we not discuss the abductions. In addition, he asks for compensation, which is a common practice in Japanese journalism. The request makes me scrutinize my ethics. After all, if *anyone* deserves to be paid for his story it is a man who spent half his life in North Korea. However, I explain, American journalists look askance at the practice. To my surprise, he agrees to talk anyway.

While Kaoru is reluctant to speak about the abduction, he has hardly kept a vow of silence since his return. Now a professional translator, he has published a dozen books in six years. The first trip he took abroad was to South Korea. He blogged about his visit to Seoul—"The Seoul Tower has a toilet from which you can enjoy the view while doing your business," he writes—and published a small book about the trip titled *Back to the Peninsula*. How did it feel to be around people so different from, yet so similar to, those who had abducted him? "I felt a sense of closeness to them. Five or ten minutes after I'd meet someone, they'd be telling me their problems, bragging about their kids," he says, smiling broadly at the memory. "I don't know how to say this, but I had this amazing sense of family. I didn't feel out of place. In fact, I felt strangely *not* out of place."

I'm struck by the depth with which Kaoru alone among the returned abductees seems to have rooted himself in Korean culture. Throughout our conversation, he notes how certain Korean characteristics augment Japanese deficiencies (and vice versa). "Japanese relationships are never black and white. They begin from the most neutral possible gray, and then dance around until we eventually agree on some common point," he says. Korean culture is more direct. "In Korea, one guy is 'white' and one guy is 'black.' And from these opposite views they work toward a compromise. And then, when they're done, they shake hands and that's that."

Kaoru is evenhanded to a fault and seems determined not to offend either culture. Although our interview is officially restricted to the topic of translation, I decide to test the boundaries. It seems to me, I begin, that the best translators have deep connections to both the languages in which they work. Every language is rooted in a culture, and every culture contains both good and bad elements, I continue. "So, how has your experience of all aspects of North Korean culture, both good and bad, helped you as a translator?" I ask. At this, he explodes. The *positive* side of North Korea?

"I want to make sure you know that I was in *North*, not South Korea," he lectures, dividing an invisible map with sharp hand gestures. "I was *abducted* from Japan and *taken* to North Korea. You understand this, right?" My interpreter apologizes for the rudeness of my question. The conversation soon returns to normal. Kaoru's outburst seems to free him up, and our conversation becomes less cautious.

Having spent fully half his life as a Korean among Koreans, it would be odd if he were able to shed his experience as easily as one gets rid of a winter coat at the first sign of spring. Critics have portrayed him as a kind of "tragic mulatto"—a man caught between two cultures, unable to choose—or, worse, as a "sleeper" spy waiting for instructions from Pyongyang. Japanese culture has difficulty with elements that don't fit precise categories. The suspicion that Kaoru was ambivalent about returning to Japan, that he was somehow Korean *and* Japanese, drove people crazy. But Kaoru strikes me more as a man who survived his ordeal by living as normally as possible—a life with more than its share of oppression, fear, and misery, of course, but a life nonetheless. He married, had children and, one presumes, friends. What was the alternative? He could have raged about his predicament for twenty-four years, I guess. But this surely is the way of madness, perhaps even suicide.

The fact that "translation" is the official topic of our interview turns out to be a blessing in disguise. As we talk, I begin to understand the degree to which it has become a metaphor for his life. Mediating between two different cultures is an act of perpetual translation. So how *does* one translate between such different sensibilities? I ask. Japanese and Korean literary aesthetics are completely different, Kaoru explains, and when translating, he must take those differences into consideration. Expressing emotion in Japanese literature, for example, is an exercise in withholding. "The whole point is the *suppression* of emotion, of not showing it on the outside. Rather, for the Japanese, emotion is conveyed through the subtle gesture, the passing comment. The Japanese interpret this as beautiful and profound," he says.

He must keep his readers' sensibilities in mind. He cites a common Korean expression of fondness that he had trouble translating in a novel. "A Korean who loves someone might say, 'I'll wait for you for ten years, for a hundred years, for *a thousand years!*' And to a Korean reader this would be absolutely normal." But translating the phrase literally would perplex the Japanese reader. "'A *hundred years?*' he'd wonder. 'But I'll be *dead* by then!'"

So where does he fit in? "Right in the middle," he says with a sigh. "When I was in North Korea, I was told a lot of unpleasant things about Japan. 'Your grandfather killed our ancestors, they took them off to labor camps'—I heard that every day," he says. Despite the fact that he was a victim of North Korea, he felt awful about Japan's past. "Of course I wasn't ignorant of the history. But how could I live bearing the sins of all my ancestors? I was right in the middle of the gears grinding between Japan and Korea."

In the spring of 2011, over dinner with Kaoru, I asked him the question I'd hesitated to pose earlier. "Why, *really,* do you think you were abducted?" I ask. He flashes me an odd smile. "I've thought about that a lot," he says. It wasn't until the last second that he and his girlfriend decided to visit the beach that fateful July evening, and he has since been told that the tide that night was unusually high, making it one of the rare occasions when a midsize North Korean boat could get so close to the shore. What he seems to be telling me is that a dozen unrelated circumstances lined up that night in such a way that he was sucked into a cosmic wormhole. "The whole thing is still a paradox to me," he says. "There was no real reason for our abductions, or at least no reason that makes any sense. We were taken in order to be used as a chit in some future negotiations. That is the only conclusion I have come to," he says.

# EPILOGUE

On the morning of October 16, 2002, I came across a photograph on page A-3 of the *New York Times*. In it, five middle-aged Japanese—two couples and a single woman, all wearing boxy 1950s-era suits, ties, and skirts—descend from a Boeing 767 at Tokyo's Haneda Airport. "Tears and Hugs as 5 Abducted Japanese Go Home to Visit," read the headline.

As I stared at the photograph, my mind reeled with questions. Who were these people who had spent half their lives in the least-accessible nation on earth? Why had they been abducted? What could they tell us about that secretive nation? Having divided their lives between Japan and North Korea, with which country did they identify? Had they been brainwashed? How many others had been abducted? Were any of *them* still alive?

One year before, the events of September 11, 2001, had shaken me. Standing on the roof of my Brooklyn brownstone, I saw the twin towers fall. Although lucky enough not to have lost anyone close to me in the disaster, I recoiled at the nationalistic feelings that swept through the country afterward. I watched in dismay as many of my colleagues transformed themselves into de facto "war correspondents" in an attempt to remain relevant by covering the story that was "changing everything." The next decade produced some extraordinary journalism and gave many reporters a new sense of purpose. I was not one of them. I didn't want to write about the war or about radical Islam, and I was appalled by the way the terrorist attacks had tricked America into curtailing the very freedoms that made it a great nation. In an odd way, my fascination with Japan's abductions helped me deal with America's nervous breakdown.

The abductions came to light in 2002, when Japan was struggling to define its postwar national character. Its economy in decline, its birthrate in free fall, it was experiencing a crisis of faith. Was it the militarist aggressor that had colonized Asia and attacked the United States, or the pacifist nation victimized by the atomic bomb and, now, the abduction of its citizens? My Japanese friends sometimes referred to the abductions as Japan's 9/11, much as the Al Qaeda bombings in Madrid (2004) and London (2005) that scarred Spain and the United Kingdom were memorialized there. This puzzled me at first, as Japan is one of the safest places on earth. But as I witnessed the country redoubling its counterterrorism strategy and immigration controls, I began to understand that "Japan's 9/11" was less an event than a state of mind. Like the United States, Japan was traumatized by the sudden realization that the world was more dangerous than it had thought, a place where even the most prosperous and powerful nations are ultimately incapable of protecting themselves, whether from Al Qaeda or North Korea. "The Japanese people have been living in a greenhouse since the American occupation ended in 1952," Tsutomu Watanabe, the *Asahi*'s political editor, tells me over coffee one afternoon. "And in 2002 they realized that the outside world was actually cold and hostile."[1] And with trauma, of course, came the seduction of victimhood, a status neither Japan nor the United States heretofore had much claim to. The 2011 earthquake and subsequent meltdown at the Fukushima nuclear power plant only deepened Japan's sense of distress.

The dominant story in Asia today is the rise of Japan's erstwhile colonies. Compared with Korea's surge of wealth and China's dramatic military and economic rise, the Japanese feel diminished and are mystified when accused of bullying their neighbors. "Many Japanese, and particularly younger ones, feel that in today's Asia, they are more victims than victimizers," explains the writer and editor Yoichi Funabashi. For them news of the abductions had a strangely cathartic effect. "They are tired of the way South Korea and China have played the history card. So in 2002, when they got proof that Japanese were being abducted by North Korea, they felt that finally they, too, were victims!"[2]

From the day I saw the photograph, I was obsessed—with the abductions, with the window they gave me into North Korea, and with the perspective they gave me on the vexed politics of Northeast Asia. Every year from 2008 to 2015, I spent between three weeks to three months reporting in Japan and South Korea. Having written about race and ethnicity in the American context, I was especially curious about the way these concepts had been used throughout history to alternately unite and divide Japan, Korea, and China. Though "race" is a biological fiction, its power comes from the stories it enables us to tell about the differences between those over whom we feel superior and those to whom we feel inferior. Asia didn't possess anything like the West's version of "race" until the late nineteenth century, when Meiji Japan imported it as part of its modernization process. Looking at the outside world, the Japanese of that period had a dilemma: how could they manage to employ a concept used principally to rank peoples of different colors (white, black, yellow) in order to differentiate among similarly hued peoples (Koreans, Chinese) with whom Japan shared deep historical roots?

I had thought I was working on two separate reporting projects during my first visit to Japan. One was the abductions. The other was a story about how Japan was dealing with its coming demographic crisis. I had noticed a small body of scholarship on the steps homogeneous Japan was taking to open itself up to foreigners—not by choice, but out of necessity. With one of the lowest birthrates in Asia, and the world's most rapidly aging population, by 2050 Japan is projected to see its population fall from 130 million to 90 million—the same as it was in 1952, when the U.S. occupation ended. Something has to give, and experts I surveyed suggested that a more open immigration policy was inevitable. Recently, Japan had been experimenting by creating a special class of visas to bring in Brazilians with Japanese ethnicity and small groups of carefully selected foreign professionals, such as nurses from the Philippines. I was interested in how a country that is so protective of its ethnic purity might deal with these challenges.

I decided to focus on Japan's largest ethnic minority as a test case of Japan's potential as a multicultural country. Facing discrimination similar to that once suffered by American blacks and Jews, Japan's six hundred thousand Korean permanent residents (known as Zainichi) had found their way to professions—sports, entertainment, financial speculation—where their ethnicity hindered them less. Several generations on, most Zainichi families have so thoroughly assimilated that they are, for all intents and purposes, Japanese. Many neither speak nor read Korean, and have taken Japanese names. Yet they are still disenfranchised, unable to vote or hold political office because they are "permanent resident foreigners," not Japanese citizens. In order to travel abroad, they must obtain a passport from either South or North Korea, their official "home countries," despite the fact that they may never have set foot in either. Japan's Koreans are in a state of permanent limbo, in but not of the only home most of them have ever known. Is this what's in store, I wondered, for the immigrants Japan so desperately needs in order to save itself from extinction?

I'd barely started my work when something odd began to happen. About halfway through an interview for the abduction article, my subjects, unbidden by me, would start to talk about Japan's "Korean problem." When I guided them back to the topic of the abductions, some postulated that the abductees had been tarnished in North Korea, even "brainwashed," and might now be "too Korean" to qualify as "proper Japanese." "If they are *really* Japanese," one asked me, her voice dripping with suspicion, "why won't they denounce Kim Jong-il?" Others suggested that one or more of the abductees were North Korean "sleeper" spies awaiting coded instructions from Pyongyang.

Similarly, many of my interviews for the multiculturalism article would at some point swerve toward the subject of the abductions. One interviewee suggested to me that the Zainichi minority's pro-North Korea sentiments (and alleged role in aiding the abductions) had exposed the fallacy of multiculturalism, and undermined their protected status as ethnically defined "permanent residents." I gradually came to understand that the subterranean link between Japan and Korea—whether by way of immigration, colonialism, or abduction—*was* the story. Understood in their proper historical context, the abductees were anything but unique. Rather, they were only the most recent reminder of the intimate connection between Japan and the rest of Asia. From the sixth century to the tenth, the young state of Japan exchanged emissaries with the independent Koguryo, Paekche, and Silla kingdoms on the Korean Peninsula. Japan traded with Korea's ancient empires and, through them, with China, absorbing the fruits of its more advanced civilization. Contact thrived through Japan's period of self-imposed isolation, up until the end of World War II.

Like the millions of people who in previous centuries moved back and forth between the peninsula and the archipelago (voluntarily or not), the abductees were living proof of the region's deep, and deeply denied, connectedness. Japan's colonial empire was a rare example in modern history of one ethnic group annexing a similar, neighboring ethnic group, as opposed to distant "natives." As the historian Tessa Morris-Suzuki writes, Japan "colonized the regions with which it had the deepest and most ancient cultural ties," which led to an "almost obsessive concern with similarity and difference: a passion both for detailing the links that bound the colonizer to the colonized and for assiduously tending the frontiers that kept them apart."[3]

Despite their aesthetic appreciation of ambiguity, the Japanese have difficulty conceiving of identities that don't fit neatly into categories. Whether they are Japanese abductees in North Korea or Koreans born in Japan, groups that don't fit in make the Japanese anxious. I came to think of the return of the abductees as akin to Freud's "return of the repressed"—the unrecognizable element of Japanese history that haunted the present.

For every nationalist who saw the abductions as a (literal) call to arms against the North, there was a liberal who cited the dispute as a reminder of Japan's guilty conscience, and of how little progress Japan had made mending relations with its neighbors. Many people I talked to were quick to point out that Japan itself had forced (some said abducted) millions of Koreans to work in its mines and factories in the 1930s and '40s. Were their lives worth less than those of a dozen Japanese?

It turned out that the abductions divided the Japanese public as much as they united it. Most people viewed the abductees as innocent victims of North Korean treachery. Others were more suspicious, and pointed to their continued reluctance to talk about their experience as proof that they were not entirely victims, and must have compromised themselves by working against Japan while in North Korea. Still others tried to pretend that the whole episode had never taken place. When I interviewed Yasushi and Fukie Chimura, I was struck by the way their families tried to avoid the fact that the couple spent fully half their lives living as North Koreans. "It's like they never left," Fukie's uncle told me. "Things just went back to normal the moment they got back. Nothing's changed about them."

After some initial awkwardness, Fukie talked for an hour straight. Surely she had gone over this territory before, I asked. "No, none of my friends ask me anything about North Korea. They don't want to be rude," she said.

I often describe this book as an act of "extreme journalism," the reporter's equivalent to the rock climber who leaves behind his ropes. Reporting on a series of events spanning several decades, in three countries, in two languages I don't speak, sometimes struck me as foolish, if not insane. I believe that, done correctly, literary reportage has the power to bridge the gaps between people who hold radically different worldviews, and this book is a test of my convictions.

Throughout the project, I kept returning to something the writer Lawrence Wright told me in my book *The New New Journalism.* "When I'm reporting an international story I do my best to strip away the exotic veneer of the place in order to write about my characters in a fashion that is recognizable in any context," he said. "Then, once I've established their everyday humanity, I can get at the truly exotic dimension of the story." The most exciting part of being a reporter is interacting with people who are different from, and more interesting than, me. I've rarely written a story in which I wasn't, in some sense, the odd man out, and I wouldn't have it any other way. I'd never found my oddness more obvious than in Asia, whether I was reporting in Seoul, Tokyo, Niigata, or Osaka. I know I miss a lot because of my outsider status, but the advantage of not belonging to any of the relevant ethnic groups was that it allowed some of my subjects to speak more freely than they might have otherwise. In cultures as hierarchical as those of Japan and Korea, the low expectations many have of outsiders is a great advantage for a reporter. I hope I have been a worthy receptacle for the stories people were so generous to share with me.

# TIME LINE

July 18, 2004    Charles Robert Jenkins and daughters come
                 to Japan
        2006     Shinzo Abe is elected Japanese prime minister
        2011     Kim Jong-il dies
        2012     Shinzo Abe is elected Japanese prime minister
                 for the second time

# NOTES

## 1. Welcome to the Invitation-Only Zone

1. Interview with the author, Kashiwazaki, Japan, June 19, 2010.
2. Bruce Cumings, *Korea's Place in the Sun: A Modern History* (New York: W. W. Norton, 1997), p. 423.
3. In 1990, North Korea imported 1.2 million tons of rice and grain. S. Kim, "North Korea in 1995: The Crucible of Our Style of Socialism," *Asian Survey* 36, no. 1 (1996): 61.
4. Interview with the author, Tokyo, Japan, June 12, 2009.

## 2. The Meiji Moment: Japan Becomes Modern

1. Kenneth B. Pyle, "The Japanese Self-Image," *Journal of Japanese Studies* 5, no. 1 (Winter 1979): 2.
2. "Characteristics of the International Fair," *Atlantic Monthly*, July 1876, p. 88.
3. Quoted in Carl Dawson, *Lafcadio Hearn and the Vision of Japan* (Baltimore, MD: Johns Hopkins University Press, 1992), p. 16.
4. Christopher Benfey, *The Great Wave: Guilded Age Misfits, Japanese Eccentries, and the Opening of Old Japan* (New York: Random House, 2003), pp. 50–64.

5. L. O. Howard, "Biographical Memoir of Edward Sylvester Morse" (paper presented at the National Academy of Sciences Annual Meeting, Charlottesville, Virginia, 1935), p. 7.
6. Eikoh Shimao, "Darwinism in Japan, 1877–1927," *Annals of Science* 38, no. 1 (1981): 93–102.
7. Hyung Il-pai, *Heritage Management in Korea and Japan: The Politics of Antiquity and Identity* (Seattle: University of Washington Press, 2013), p. 97.
8. Gina L. Barnes, "The 'Idea of Prehistory' in Japan," *Antiquity*, December 1, 1990, p. 929.
9. Edward Morse, "Traces of an Early Race in Japan," *Popular Science Monthly*, January 1879.
10. Edward Burnett Tylor, *Primitive Culture: Researches into the Development of Mythology, Philosophy, Religion, Art, and Custom* (London: John Murray, 1871).
11. Peter Duus, *The Abacus and the Sword: The Japanese Penetration of Korea, 1895–1910* (Berkeley: University of California Press, 1995), p. 414.
12. Tessa Morris-Suzuki, *Re-inventing Japan: Time, Space, Nation* (New York: M.E. Sharpe, 1997), p. 87.
13. Carol Gluck, *Japan's Modern Myths: Ideology in the Late Meiji Period* (Princeton, NJ: Princeton University Press, 1985), p. 159.
14. Hyong Il-pai, *Heritage Management*, p. 99.
15. Urs Matthias Zachmann, "Race and International Law in Japan's New Order in East Asia, 1938–1945," in *Race and Racism in Modern East Asia: Western and Eastern Constructions*, edited by Rotem Kowner and Walter Demel (Leiden, Netherlands: Brill, 2013), pp. 456–57.
16. Tessa Morris-Suzuki, "Becoming Japanese: Imperial Expansion and Identity Crises in the Early Twentieth Century," in *Japan's Competing Modernities: Issues in Culture and Democracy 1900–1930*, edited by Sharon A. Minichiello (Honolulu: University of Hawaii Press, 1998), p. 173.
17. Ryuzo Torii, "Watashi no miru Chosen" [My view of Korea], *Chōsen* 284 (January 1939): 37–39.

### 3. Reunited in North Korea

1. Interview with the author, Kashiwazaki, Japan, May 11, 2008.
2. Andrei Lankov, *The Real North Korea: Life and Politics in the Failed Stalinist Utopia* (New York: Oxford University Press, 2013), p. 49.
3. Kaoru Hasuike, *Rachi to Ketsudan* [Abduction and decision] (Tokyo: Shinchōsha, 2012), p. 110.
4. Ibid., p. 96.
5. Ibid., p. 70.

## 4. Japan and Korea's "Common Origins"

1. Richard Sims, "France 16 December 1872–17 February 1873, 15–20 July 1873," in *The Iwakura Mission in America and Europe: A New Assessment*, edited by Ian Nish (Richmond, England: Japan Library, 2005), p. 45.

2. Eric Hobsbawm, *Age of Empire: 1875–1914* (New York: Pantheon Books, 1987), p. 59.

3. Alexis Dudden, *Japan's Colonization of Korea: Discourse and Power* (Honolulu: University of Hawaii Press, 2006), p. 4.

4. Hyung Il-pai, "Capturing Visions of Japan's Prehistoric Past: Torii Ryuzo's Field Photographs of 'Primitive' Races and Lost Civilizations (1896–1915)," in *Looking Modern: East Asian Visual Culture from Treaty Ports to World War II, Symposium Volume*, edited by Jennifer Purtle and Hans Bjarne Thomsen, The Center for the Art of East Asia (Chicago: Art Media Resources, 2009), p. 269.

5. Akitoshi Shimizu, "Colonialism and the development of modern anthropology in Japan," in *Anthropology and Colonialism in Asia and Oceania*, edited by Jan van Bremen and Akitoshi Shimizu (London: Routledge/Curzon Press, 1999), p. 133.

6. Duus, *The Abacus and the Sword*, p. 422.

7. August 29, 1910.

8. Mark E. Caprio, *Japanese Assimilationist Policies in Colonial Korea, 1910–1945* (Seattle: University of Washington Press, 2009), p. 83.

9. Eiji Oguma, *A Genealogy of Japanese Self-Images* (Melbourne: Trans Pacific Press, 2002), pp. 82–85.

10. E. Taylor Atkins, *Primitive Selves: Koreana in the Japanese Colonial Gaze, 1910–1945* (Berkeley: University of California Press, 2010), p. 101.

11. Hyung Il-pai, *Heritage Management*, p. 150.

12. Hyung Il-pai, "Travel Guides to the Empire: The Production of Tourist Images in Colonial Korea," in *Consuming Korean Tradition in Early and Late Modernity*, edited by Laurel Kendall (Honolulu: University of Hawaii Press, 2011), pp. 67–87.

13. Bruce Cumings, "The Legacy of Japanese Colonialism in Korea," in *The Japanese Colonial Empire, 1895–1945*, edited by Ramon Hawley Myers and Mark R. Peattie (Princeton: Princeton University Press, 1984), p. 482.

14. B. R. Myers, *The Cleanest Race: How North Koreans See Themselves and Why It Matters* (New York: Melville House, 2010), p. 27.

15. Hwaji Shin, "Colonial Legacy of Ethno-Racial Inequality in Japan," *Theory and Society* 39 (2010): 86–87.

16. Mitsuhiko Kimura, "Standards of Living in Colonial Korea: Did the Masses Become Worse Off or Better Off Under Japanese Rule?" *Journal of Economic History* 53 (September 1993): 641.

17. Shin, "Colonial Legacy," p. 331.

18. Voter registration was based on residence. Even native Japanese living in Korea and other colonies could not vote.

19. Brandon Palmer, *Fighting for the Enemy: Koreans in Japan's War, 1937–1945* (Seattle: University of Washington Press, 2013), p. 11.
20. Ibid., p. 19.
21. Ibid., p. 37.
22. Myers, *The Cleanest Race*, p. 32.
23. Palmer, *Fighting for the Enemy*, p. 80.
24. Mark E. Caprio and Yu Jia, "Legacies of Empire and Occupation: The Making of the Korean Diaspora in Japan," *Asia-Pacific Journal* 37, no. 3 (September 14, 2009).
25. Oguma, *A Genealogy of Japanese Self-Images*, p. 305.
26. Arnaud Nanta, "Physical Anthropology and the Reconstruction of Japanese Identity in Postcolonial Japan," *Social Science Japan Journal* 11, no. 1 (2008): 31.
27. Ibid., p. 30.
28. Hyung Il-pai, "The Politics of Korea's Past: The Legacy of Japanese Colonial Archaeology in the Korean Peninsula," *East Asian History* 7 (June 1994): 28.
29. Myers, *The Cleanest Race*, pp. 33–34.

## 5. Adapting to North Korea

1. Interview with the author, Kashiwazaki, Japan, June 19, 2010.
2. Hasuike, *Rachi to Ketsudan*, p. 110.
3. Ibid.
4. Interview with the author, Kashiwazaki, Japan, June 19, 2010.
5. Sonia Ryang, *Reading North Korea: An Ethnological Inquiry* (Cambridge, MA: Harvard University Asia Center, 2012), p. 25.
6. Interview with the author, Kashiwazaki, Japan, June 19, 2010.
7. Lankov, *The Real North Korea*, p. 60.
8. Suh Dae-sook, *Kim Il Sung: The North Korean Leader* (New York: Columbia University Press, 1995), p. 38.
9. Ibid., pp. 30–31.
10. Paul French, *North Korea: State of Paranoia* (London: Zed Books, 2014), p. 79.
11. Haruki Wada, *Kin Nichisei to Manshu konichi senso* [Kim Il Sung and the anti-Japanese war in Manchuria] (Tokyo: Heibonsha, 1992).
12. Myers, *The Cleanest Race*, pp. 108–109.
13. Ryang, *Reading North Korea*, p. 191.
14. Hasuike, *Rachi to Ketsudan*, p. 40.

## 6. Abduction as Statecraft

1. Tessa Morris-Suzuki, "Re-Imagining Japan–North Korea Relations, Part I," The Japan Institute, p. 29.
2. Interview with author, Seoul, South Korea, May 16, 2009.
3. Interview with author, Seoul, South Korea, May 13, 2009.
4. French, *North Korea*, p. 59.
5. Shin Sang-ok and Choi Eun-hee, *Kim Jong Il wangguk* [The kingdom of Kim Jong-Il] (Seoul: Tonga Il-bosa, 1988).
6. Andrei Lankov, *North of the DMZ: Essays on Daily Life in North Korea* (Jefferson, NC: McFarland, 2007), p. 62.
7. Shin and Choi, *Kim Jong Il wangguk*.
8. A pseudonym.
9. Interview with the author, Tokyo, Japan, May 22, 2009.
10. Hwang Jang-yop, "The Problem of Human Rights in North Korea," *Daily NK*, 2002, http://www.dailynk.com/english/keys/2002/9/04.php.

## 7. From Emperor Hirohito to Kim Il-sung

1. Interview with author in Tokyo, Japan, May 25, 2009.
2. United States Central Intelligence Agency, *The Japanese Communist Party, 1955–1963* (Washington, DC: CIA, 1964), p. 6.
3. Robert A. Scalapino, *The Japanese Communist Movement, 1920–1966* (Berkeley: University of California Press, 1966), p. 48.
4. Interview with the author, Tokyo, Japan, July 12, 2010.
5. Interview with the author, Tokyo, Japan, May 18, 2014.

## 8. Developing a Cover Story

1. Hasuike, *Rachi to Ketsudan*, p. 98.
2. Interview with the author, Kashiwazaki, June 3, 2009.

## 9. The Repatriation Project: From Japan to North Korea

1. Twenty-one thousand Koreans are memorialized at Tokyo's Yasukuni shrine. One hundred forty-eight Koreans were found guilty at the Tokyo War Crimes Tribunal. Palmer, *Fighting for the Enemy*, p. 189.
2. The notion that North Korea was their geographic home was incorrect because 97 percent of Koreans in Japan originally came from the southern part of the peninsula.
3. Dewayne J. Creamer, "The Rise and Fall of Chosen Soren: Its Effect on

Japan's Relations on the Korean Peninsula," master's thesis, Naval Post-graduate School, December 2003, p. 24.

4. Tessa Morris-Suzuki, *Exodus to North Korea* (Lanham, MD: Rowman and Littlefield, 2007), p. 199.
5. Interview with the author, Niigata, Japan, June 19, 2010.
6. Interview with the author, Osaka, Japan, June 17, 2010.
7. Interview with the author, Tokyo, Japan, June 1, 2009.
8. Interview with the author, Niigata, Japan, June 20, 2010.
9. Interview with the author, Niigata, Japan, May 15, 2014.
10. Interview with Katsumi Sato, Tokyo, Japan, May 25, 2009.
11. Katsumi Sato, "The Peninsula That Pains Us," *Seiron*, Sept. 1995.


## 10. Neighbors in the Invitation-Only Zone

1. Interview with the author, Obama, Japan, July 13, 2010.
2. Interview with the author, Kashiwazaki, Japan, June 19, 2010.
3. Interview with the author, Kashiwazaki, Japan, May 12, 2008.
4. Hasuike, *Rachi to Ketsudan*, p. 146.


## 11. Stolen Childhoods: Megumi and Takeshi

1. Interview with the author, Tokyo, Japan, May 20, 2009.
2. Sakie Yokota, *North Korea Kidnapped My Daughter* (New York: Vertical Books, 2009), pp. 10–14.
3. Korean Institute for National Unification, White Paper on Human Rights in North Korea, 2007, p. 270.
4. Interview with the author, Obama, Japan, July 13, 2010.
5. *Chosun Ilbo*, "Young-nam 'Never Asked' If Wife Was Kidnapped," June 7, 2006.
6. Interview with the author in Kanazawa, Japan, May 28, 2009.


## 12. An American in Pyongyang

1. Interview with the author, Sado Island, Japan, May 15, 2014.
2. Charles Robert Jenkins and Jim Frederick, *The Reluctant Communist: My Desertion, Court-Martial, and Forty-Year Imprisonment in North Korea* (Berkeley: University of California Press, 2009), p. 72.
3. Interview with the author, Sado Island, Japan, May 11, 2008.
4. Jenkins and Frederick, *Reluctant Communist*, p. 39.
5. Although there is no such thing as Japanese DNA, I've since learned that Jenkins may have been on to something. In his book *Dear Leader*, North Korean defector Jang Jin-sung's describes a program instituted

after it became clear the abductees would never become spies. The "seed-bearing strategy" involved sending attractive North Korean women to seduce foreign diplomats, journalists, and businessmen. The resulting children had a dual purpose. They would give the regime leverage over the fathers, who would be manipulated into aiding North Korea, whether through favorable coverage, business deals, or government aid. Second, these "mixed-race" children would make excellent spies because they looked nothing like the image of a North Korean agent. When I later met Jang, he connected the abduction project to the seed-bearing program. "They were essentially the same project, just using different methods. They went from kidnapping people to kidnapping eggs."

### 13. Terror in the Air

1. Kim Hyon-hui, *The Tears of My Soul* (New York: William Morrow, 1993), p. 114.
2. Interview with the author, Tokyo, Japan, June 22, 2010.
3. Hitoshi Tanaka, *Gaikō no Chikara* [The power of diplomacy] (Tokyo: Nihonkeizai Shinbunsha, 2009), p. 215.

### 14. Kim's Golden Eggs

1. In addition to interviews, this chapter draws from several books and articles. Koji Takazawa, *Shukumei: Yodogō Bōmeishatachi no Himitsu Kōsaku* [Destiny: The secret operations of the Yodo refugees] (Tokyo: Shinchō-sha, 1998); Patricia Steinhoff, "Kidnapped Japanese in North Korea: The New Left Connection," *Journal of Japanese Studies* 30, no. 1 (Winter 2004); *Yodo-go Rachi* [The hijacking of Japan Airlines Flight 351 and the North Korean kidnapping problem] (Tokyo: NHK Publishing, 2004); Asger Rojle Christensen, *Bortført i Københavnion: Japanske skæbner i Nordkorea* [Kidnapped in Copenhagen: Japanese destinies in North Korea] (Copenhagen: Gyldendal, 2011); William R. Farrell, *Blood and Rage: The Story of the Japanese Red Army* (Lanham, MD: Lexington Books, 1990); Eileen MacDonald, *Shoot the Women First* (New York: Random House, 1992); Yao Megumi, *Shimasu* [I apologize] (Tokyo: Bungei-shunju, 2002).
2. Asger Rojle Christensen, *Bortført i Københavnion*, p. 9.
3. Interview with the author, Tokyo, Japan, May 26, 2011.

### 15. A Story Too Strange to Believe

1. Interview with the author, Osaka, Japan, May 27, 2009.
2. Interview with the author, Tokyo, Japan, May 25, 2009.

3. Ibid.
4. Interview with the author, June 17, 2010.
5. Interview with the author, Tokyo, Japan, May 25, 2009.

## 16. The Great Leader Dies, a Nation Starves

1. Hasuike, *Rachi to Ketsudan*, p. 43.
2. Interview with the author, Kashiwazaki, Japan, June 19, 2010.
3. Stephan Haggard and Marcus Noland, *Famine in North Korea: Markets, Aid, and Reform* (New York: Columbia University Press, 2007), p. 25.
4. Robert Winstanley-Chesters, "Landscape as Political Project: The "Greening" of North Korea, Sincerity or Otherwise?" *Yonsei Journal of International Studies* 5, no. 2 (Fall/Winter 2013), p. 263.
5. Haggard and Noland, *Famine in North Korea*, p. 40.
6. Ibid., p. 3.
7. Ibid., p. 10.
8. Ibid., p. 50.
9. French, *North Korea*, p. 41.
10. Interview with the author, Obama, Japan, July 13, 2010.
11. Interview with the author, Kashiwazaki, Japan, May 11, 2008.
12. Hasuike, *Rachi to Ketsudan*, p. 59.

## 17. Negotiating with Mr. X

1. Yoichi Funabashi, *The Peninsula Question: A Chronicle of the Second Korean Nuclear Crisis* (Washington, D.C.: Brookings Institution Press, 2007), p. 31.
2. *Asahi Shimbun* editorial, October 22, 2000, p. 2, and *Yomiuri Shimbun* editorial, October 24, 2000, p. 3.
3. Hitoshi Tanaka, *Gaikō no Chikara*, p. 9.
4. Interview with the author, Tokyo, Japan, June 22, 2010.
5. Interview with the author, Tokyo, Japan, May 20, 2014.
6. Interview with the author, Tokyo, Japan, April 10, 2008.
7. Funabashi, *The Peninsula Question*, p. 8.
8. Interview with the author, Tokyo, Japan, June 22, 2010.

## 18. Kim and Koizumi in Pyongyang

1. Most flights into North Korea originate in either China or Russia.
2. Interview with the author, Tokyo, Japan, July 17, 2010, and May 10, 2012.
3. Jin-sung Jang, *Dear Leader: Poet, Spy, Escapee—A Look Inside North Korea* (New York: Atria, 2014), p. 159.
4. Funabashi, *The Peninsula Question*, p. 5.

## 19. Returning Home: From North Korea to Japan

1. Hasuike, *Rachi to Ketsudan*, p. 213.
2. Interview with the author, Obama, Japan, July 13, 2010.


## 20. An Extended Visit

1. In comparison, the September 11, 2001, attacks on the United States a year earlier received nine hours of coverage. Hyung Gu Lynn, "Vicarious Traumas: Television and Public Opinion in Japan's North Korea Policy," *Pacific Affairs* 79, no. 3 (Fall 2006): 491.
2. Interview with the author, Kashiwazaki, Japan, 2008.
3. Interview with the author, Tokyo, Japan, May 14, 2014.
4. Interview with the author, Tokyo, Japan, June 12, 2009.
5. Interview with the author, Tokyo, Japan, May 14, 2014.
6. Ibid.
7. It took longer for abductee Hitomi Soga's husband, Charles Jenkins, and their two daughters to get to Japan because the U.S. military still considered Jenkins a deserter. He eventually reached an agreement with the U.S. military, served a six-day sentence, and was dishonorably discharged. The family reunited in Indonesia in July 2004 and now live on Sado Island.


## 21. Abduction, Inc.

1. Interview with the author, Tokyo, Japan, July 13, 2010.
2. On December 27, 2002, *Asahi Shimbun* ran a two-page article, "Reviewing North Korea's Abduction-Related Coverage," in which it argued that "since the incident, at that time, was neither official nor confirmed, we felt that reporting based on mere speculations could even result in the endangerment of the abduction victims possibly held in North Korea, and we therefore prioritized confirming the rumor first." The paper apologized for the "misunderstanding."
3. According to an October 2012 Cabinet Office survey, the abduction issue remains the top concern regarding North Korea (87 percent). Fears of Korea's missiles (49 percent) and nuclear weapons (59 percent) are significantly less.
4. The abductee groups remain powerful. Between 2002 and 2014, every new prime minister and U.S. ambassador has met with them immediately after taking office. Secretary of State Hillary Clinton and President Obama met with them as well.
5. Katsuei Hirasawa, *Rachi Mondai: Tai Kitachōsen Gaikō no Arikata wo tou* [The abduction issue: Questioning diplomacy toward North Korea] (Tokyo: PHP, 2004), p. 29.

6. Interview with the author, Tokyo, Japan, June 3, 2009.
7. Interview with the author, Tokyo, Japan, June 22, 2010.
8. Interview with the author, Niigata, Japan, June 18, 2010.
9. Ulv Are Rynning Hanssen, "Changes in Japanese Attitudes Toward North Korea Since '9/17,'" master's thesis, University of Oslo, 2011.
10. "Media to Give Abductees Privacy: News Organizations Agree to Restrain Coverage During Homecomings," *Japan Times*, October 13, 2002.
11. Takeshi Inagaki, *Shokun!*, December 12, 2002, pp. 74–88.
12. *Shukan Bunshun*, August 3, 2002.
13. Between 2006 and 2010, the Abduction Headquarters budget rose from $2 million to $16 million. T. J. Pempel, "Japan and the Two Koreas: The Foreign-Policy Power of Domestic Politics," in *Changing Power Relations in Northeast Asia*, edited by Marie Soderberg, (New York: Routledge, 2011), p. 55.
14. Japanese government Internet TV, March 28, 2008.
15. Trevor Clarke, "Can NHK Keep the Air Free?," *Japan Times*, December 26, 2006.
16. Eric Johnston, "The North Korea Abduction Issue and Its Effect on Japanese Domestic Politics," JPRI Working Paper no. 101, June 2004.
17. Interview with the author, Tokyo, Japan, May 14, 2014.
18. Interview with the author, Tokyo, Japan, April 7, 2008.
19. Interview with the author, Tokyo, Japan, June 22, 2010.
20. Interview with the author, Tokyo, Japan, May 13, 2014.

## 22. Kaoru Hasuike at Home

1. Interview with the author, Kashiwazaki, Japan, May 12, 2008.

## Epilogue

1. Interview with the author, Tokyo, Japan, July 17, 2010.
2. Interview with the author, Tokyo, Japan, April 10, 2008.
3. Morris-Suzuki, "Becoming Japanese," p. 162.

# SELECTED BIBLIOGRAPHY

Armstrong, Charles K. *The North Korean Revolution, 1945–1950*. Ithaca, NY: Cornell University Press, 2004.

———. *The Koreas*. New York: Routledge, 2007.

———. *Tyranny of the Weak: North Korea and the World, 1950–1992*. Ithaca, NY: Cornell University Press, 2013.

Atkins, E. Taylor. *Primitive Selves: Koreana in the Japanese Colonial Gaze*. Berkeley: University of California Press, 2010.

Beasley, W. G. *Japanese Imperialism, 1894–1945*. New York: Oxford University Press, 1987.

Becker, Jasper. *Rogue Regime: Kim Jong Il and the Looming Threat of North Korea*. New York: Oxford University Press, 2005.

Befu, Harumi. *Hegemony of Homogeneity: An Anthropological Analysis of Nihonjinron*. Melbourne: Trans Pacific Press, 2001.

Belke, Thomas Julian. "Juche: The State Religion of North Korea." Ph.D. dissertation. Rutgers University, 1998.

Benfey, Christopher, *The Great Wave: Guilded Age Misfits, Japanese Eccentries, and the Opening of Old Japan*. New York: Random House, 2003.

Bremen, Jan van, and Akitoshi Shimizu, eds. *Anthropology and Colonialism in Asia and Oceania*. Richmond, UK: Curzon Press, 1999.

Buruma, Ian. *The Wages of Guilt: Memories of War in Germany and Japan*. New York: Farrar, Straus and Giroux, 1994.

———. *Inventing Japan*. New York: Modern Library, 2003.

Buzo, Adrian. *The Guerilla Dynasty: Politics and Leadership in North Korea*. Boulder, CO: Westview Press, 1999.

———. *The Making of Modern Korea*. New York: Routledge, 2002.

Caprio, Mark E. *Japanese Assimilationist Policies in Colonial Korea, 1910–1945*. Seattle: University of Washington Press, 2009.

Chinoy, Mike. *Meltdown: The Inside Story of the North Korean Nuclear Crisis*. New York: St. Martin's Press, 2008.

Christensen, Asger Rojle. *Bortført i Københavnion: Japanske skæbner i Nordkorea* [Kidnapped in Copenhagen: Japanese destinies in North Korea]. Copenhagen: Gyldendal, 2011.

Cumings, Bruce. *Korea's Place in the Sun: A Modern History*. New York: W. W. Norton, 1997.

———. *North Korea: Another Country*. New York: The New Press, 2004.

Dale, Peter H. *The Myth of Japanese Uniqueness*. New York: St. Martin's Press, 1986.

Demick, Barbara. *Nothing to Envy: Ordinary Lives in North Korea*. New York: Spiegel and Grau, 2010.

Dower, John. *War Without Mercy: Race and Power in the Pacific War*. New York: Pantheon, 1986.

———. *Embracing Defeat: Japan in the Wake of World War II*. New York: W. W. Norton/The New Press, 1999.

Dudden, Alexis. *Japan's Colonization of Korea: Discourse and Power*. Honolulu: University of Hawaii Press, 2005.

———. *Troubled Apologies Among Japan, Korea, and the United States*. New York: Columbia University Press, 2008.

Duke, Benjamin. *The History of Modern Japanese Education*. New Brunswick, NJ: Rutgers University Press, 2009.

Duus, Peter. *The Abacus and the Sword: The Japanese Penetration of Korea, 1895–1910*. Berkeley: University of California Press, 1995.

Farrell, William R. *Blood and Rage: The Story of the Japanese Red Army*. Lanham, MD: Lexington Books, 1990.

Funabashi, Yoichi. *The Peninsula Question: A Chronicle of the Second Korean Nuclear Crisis*. Washington, D.C.: Brookings Institute Press, 2007.

French, Paul. *North Korea: State of Paranoia*. London: Zed Books, 2014.

Gluck, Carol. *Japan's Modern Myths: Ideology in the Late Meiji Period*. Princeton, NJ: Princeton University Press, 1985.

Haggard, Stephan, and Marcus Noland. *Famine in North Korea: Markets, Aid, and Reform*. New York: Columbia University Press, 2007.

Hanssen, Ulv Are Rynning. "Changes in Japanese Attitudes Toward North Korea Since '9/17,'" master's thesis, University of Oslo, 2011.

Hasuike, Kaoru. *Rachi to Ketsudan* [Abduction and decision]. Tokyo: Shinchōsha, 2012.

Hirasawa, Katsuei. *Rachi Mondai: Tai Kitachōsen Gaikō no Arikata wo tou* [The abduction issue: Questioning diplomacy toward North Korea]. Tokyo: PHP, 2004.

Hobsbawm, Eric. *Age of Empire: 1875–1914*. New York: Pantheon Books, 1987.

Jang, Jin-sung. *Dear Leader: Poet, Spy, Escapee; A Look Inside North Korea*. New York: Atria, 2014.

Jenkins, Charles Robert, and Jim Frederick. *The Reluctant Communist: My Desertion, Court-Martial, and Forty-Year Imprisonment in North Korea*. Berkeley: University of California Press, 2009.

Kim Hyun-hui. *The Tears of My Soul*. New York: William Morrow, 1993.

Kim Jong-il, *On the Art of the Cinema* (trans., 1989). Pyongyang, North Korea: Foreign Languages Publishing House, 1973.

Kim, Mikyoung, and Barry Schwartz, eds. *Northeast Asia's Difficult Past: Essays in Collective Memory*. New York: Palgrave Macmillan, 2010.

Kingston, Jeffrey. *Contemporary Japan: History, Politics, and Social Change Since the 1980s*. Hoboken, NJ: Wiley-Blackwell, 2010.

Kowner, Rotem, and Walter Demel, eds. *Race and Racism in Modern East Asia: Western and Eastern Constructions*. Boston: Brill, 2012.

Kuroki, Maiko. "Nationalism in Japan's Contemporary Foreign Policy: A Consideration of the Cases of China, North Korea, and India." Ph.D. dissertation. London School of Economics, 2013.

Lankov, Andrei. *From Stalin to Kim Il Sung: The Formation of North Korea*. New Brunswick, NJ: Rutgers University Press, 2002.

———. *The Dawn of Modern Korea*. Seoul: EunHaeng NaMu, 2007.

———. *North of the DMZ: Essays on Daily Life in North Korea*. Jefferson, NC: McFarland and Company, 2007.

———. *The Real North Korea: Life and Politics in the Failed Stalinist Utopia*. New York: Oxford University Press, 2013.

Lee, Jaehoon. "The Relatedness Between the Origin of Japanese and Korean Ethnicity," Ph.D. dissertation. Florida State University, 2004.

Lee Seung-hyok. "Missiles, Abductions, and Sanctions: Societal Influences on Japanese Policy Toward North Korea, 1998–2006." Ph.D. dissertation. University of Toronto, 2011.

Lie, John. *Multi-Ethnic Japan*. Cambridge, MA: Harvard University Press, 2001.

———. *Zainichi: Diasporic Nationalism and Postcolonial Identity*. Berkeley: University of California Press, 2008.

Martin, Bradley. *Under the Loving Care of the Fatherly Leader: North Korea and the Kim Dynasty*. New York: St. Martin's Press, 2004.

McCargo, Duncan. *Contemporary Japan*. New York: Palgrave Macmillan, 2004.

Morris-Suzuki, Tessa. *Re-inventing Japan: Time, Space, Nation*. New York: M.E. Sharpe, 1998.

———. *Exodus to North Korea: Shadows from Japan's Cold War*. Lanham, MD: Rowman and Littlefield, 2007.

Morse, Edward S. *Japan Day by Day*. New York: Houghton Mifflin, 1917.

Myers, B. R. *North Korea's Juche Myth*. Busan, South Korea: Sthele Press, 2015.

———. *The Cleanest Race: How North Koreans See Themselves and Why It Matters*. New York: Melville Books, 2010.

Myers, Ramon H., and Mark R. Peattie, eds. *The Japanese Colonial Empire, 1895–1945*. Princeton, NJ: Princeton University Press, 1984.

Nakazono, Eisuke. *Torii Ryūzō den*: (A Life of Torii Ryuzo). Tokyo: Iwanami Shoten, 1995.

NHK News. *Yodo-go Rachi* [The hijacking of Japan Airlines Flight 351 and the North Korean kidnapping problem]. Tokyo: NHK Publishing, 2004.

Oberdorfer, Don. *The Two Koreas: A Contemporary History*. New York: Addison-Wesley, 1997.

Oguma, Eiji. *A Genealogy of Japanese Self-Images*. Melbourne: Trans Pacific Press, 2002.

Orr, James J. *The Victim as Hero: Ideologies of Peace and National Identity in Postwar Japan*. Honolulu: University of Hawaii Press, 2001.

Pai, Hyung-il. *Constructing "Korean" Origins: A Critical Review of Archaeology, Historiography, and Racial Myth in Korean State-Formation Theories*. Cambridge, MA: Harvard East Asian Monographs, 2000.

———. *Heritage Management in Korea and Japan: The Politics of Antiquity and Identity*. Seattle: University of Washington Press, 2013.

Palmer, Brandon. *Fighting for the Enemy: Koreans in Japan's War, 1937–1945*. Seattle: University of Washington Press, 2013.

Robinson, Michael E. *Korea's Twentieth-Century Odyssey: A Short History*. Honolulu: University of Hawaii Press, 2007.

Rozman, Gilbert, Kazuhiko Togo, and Joseph Ferguson. *Japanese Strategic Thought Toward Asia*. New York: Palgrave Macmillan, 2007.

Ryang, Sonia. *North Koreans in Japan: Language, Ideology, and Identity*. Boulder, CO: Westview Press, 1997.

———, ed. *North Korea: Toward a Better Understanding*. Lanham, MD: Lexington Books, 2009.

———. *Reading North Korea: An Ethnological Inquiry*. Cambridge, MA: Harvard University Asia Center, 2012.

Scalapino, Robert A. *The Japanese Communist Movement, 1920–1966*. Berkeley: University of California Press, 1967.

Seiler, Sydney A. *Kim Il-song, 1941–1948: The Creation of a Legend, the Building of a Regime*. Lanham, MD: University Press of America, 1994.

Seth, Michael J. *A Concise History of Modern Korea: From the Late Nineteenth Century to the Present*. Lanham, MD: Rowman and Littlefield, 2009.

Shin Gi-wook. *Ethnic Nationalism in Korea: Genealogy, Politics, and Legacy*. Stanford, CA: Stanford University Press, 2006.

Shin Sang-ok, and Choi Eun-hee. *Kim Jong Il wangguk* [The kingdom of Kim Jong-Il]. Seoul: Tonga Il-bosa, 1988.

Soderberg, Marie, ed. *Changing Power Relations in Northeast Asia: Implications for Relations Between Japan and South Korea*. New York: Routledge, 2013.

Suh Dae-sook. *Kim Il Sung: The North Korean Leader*. New York: Columbia University Press, 2008.

Takazawa, Koji. *Shukumei: Yodogo Bōmeishatachi no Himitsu Kosaku* [Destiny: The secret operations of the Yodo refugees]. Tokyo: Shinchōsha, 1998.

Tanaka, Hitoshi. *Gaikō no Chikara* [The power of diplomacy]. Tokyo: Nihonkeizai Shinbunsha, 2009.

Torii, Ryuzo. *Watashi no miru Chosen* [My view of Korea]. *Chōsen* 284, January 1939.

Wada Haruki. *Kin Nichisei to Manshu konichi senso* [Kim Il-sung and the anti-Japanese war in Manchuria]. Tokyo: Heibonsha, 1992.

Watt, Lori. *When Empire Comes Home: Repatriation and Reintegration in Postwar Japan.* Cambridge, MA: Harvard University Asia Center, 2009.

Wayman, Dorothy G. *Edward Sylvester Morse: A Biography.* Cambridge, MA: Harvard University Press, 1942.

Yamamoto, Yoshi. *Taken! North Korea's Criminal Abduction of Citizens of Other Countries.* Committee for Human Rights in North Korea, 2011.

Yao Megumi. *Shimasu* [I apologize]. Tokyo: Bungei-shunju, 2002.

Yokota, Sakie. *North Korea Kidnapped My Daughter: A Memoir.* New York: Vertical Press, 2009.

# ACKNOWLEDGMENTS

This book is dedicated to my mother, who didn't live long enough to see it published but read and commented on the early drafts. Everyone needs one person who believes in him absolutely, and she was mine. I miss her. My father, who is thankfully still with us, also read early drafts with his usual intelligence.

I am a freelancer by temperament, so it was a new experience for me to have to rely so completely on interpreters. I was extremely lucky to work with David d'Heilly and Shizu Yasua in Japan. More than simply interpreting, they helped me begin to understand the cultural context in which these encounters took place. They and their son, Sai, have become dear friends. I had a similarly productive and pleasurable experience in Seoul with Jisoo Chung, perhaps the foremost expert on South Korea's abductions.

My first trip to Japan, in 2008, was made possible by the Japan Society's United States–Japan Media Fellows Program. In New York, Betty Borden helped my family and me prepare for our stay, and once we arrived in Tokyo Ruri Kawashima provided invaluable support.

I also received funding from the Abe Fellowship Program, administered by the Social Science Research Council, with funds provided by the Japan Foundation Center for Global Partnership. Frank Baldwin and Takuya Toda-Ozaki guided me in Tokyo, and Nicole Restrick Levit and Fernando Rojas helped me in New York.

Throughout the years I spent reporting in Japan, I was assisted by the people at the Foreign Press Center/Japan, then presided over by Terusuke

Terada. I'd like to thank Kazuko Koizumi, Mari Yamauchi, and Kayoko Koga for indulging my American impulsiveness.

The Fulbright Program also supported me, and I would like to thank David Satterwhite, Jinko Brinkman, Mizuho Iwata, and Hilary H. Watts. During my Fulbright, I was hosted by the National Graduate Institute for Policy Studies (GRIPS), and I want to thank my sponsor, Narushige Michishita, and GRIPS president Takashi Shiraishi.

I workshopped a chapter of this book at the Banff Centre, where Ian Brown runs an extraordinary literary journalism program. Ian, Katherine Ashenburg, and Don Gilmour made many helpful suggestions.

Many of the books, documents, and articles I needed were in Japanese or Korean, and I used several different translators. I'd like to thank Mee Christine Chang, Tsuneoka Chieko, Yoona Cho, Jae Won Chung, Sam Holden, Ben Karp, Ryo Kato, Clara Kim, Joel Matthews, Frank Mondelli, Jeesun Park, Hazumu Yamazaki, and Miyako Yoshida.

*The Atlantic* published an article I wrote about North Korea, which helped my thinking on the subject. Thanks to Scott Stossel for assigning it, and to James Gibney for editing it.

A number of people were generous enough to read parts of the book as it progressed. I'd particularly like to thank E. Taylor Atkins, Alexis Dudden, Ulv Are Rynning Hanssen, Hyung Il-pai, Jeffrey Kingston, Tessa Morris-Suzuki, Miwa Murphy, Susanna Sonnenberg, and my New York University colleagues Ted Conover, Brooke Kroeger, Adam Pennenberg, and Charles Seife.

I received advice, recommendations, and assistance from dozens of people over the years. In Japan, I was helped by Kazuhiro Araki, Celeste Arrington, Fukie and Yasushi Chimura, Asger Rojle Christensen, Gregory Clark, Gerald Curtis, Robert Dujarric, Osamu Eya, Yoichi Funabashi, Yoji Gomi, Katsuei Hirasawa, Kenji Ishidaka, Jiro Ishimaru, Hajime Izumi, Kaoru Hasuike, Toru Hasuike, Tatsukichi Hyomoto, Charles Jenkins, Eric Johnston, Miyo Kai, Kang Sang Jung, Chikako Kashiwazaki, Kenichi Kawamoto, Tadashi Kimiya, Donald Kirk, Harunori Kojima, Ko Jong Mi, Hiroshi Koto, Min Jin Lee, Soo Im Lee, Kotaro Miura, Kinya Nakajima, Kyoko Nakayama, Eiji Oguma, Masao Okonogi, Park Jung-jin, Hiroko Saito, Hidenori Sakanaka, Katsumi Sato, Tamiko Sato, Toshimitsu Shigemura, So Chung On, Koji Takazawa, Masaru Tamamoto, Hitoshi Tanaka, Peter Tasker, Haruki Wada, Masahito Watanabe, Takesato Watanabe, Tsutomu Watanabe, Yuki Yakabe, Sakie and Shigeru Yokota, Takeshi Yokota, and Shito Yokoyama.

In South Korea, I was helped by Choi Jini, Choi Sung-yong, Choi Uk-il, Choi Woo-young, Doe Hee-youn, Ha Tae-keung, Ho Jeong-kwong, Kang Cheol-hwan, Kim Dong-choon, Kim Eun-bok, Kim Heung-kwang, Kim Seung-chul, Kim Young-sam, Koo Byoung-sam, Kwon, Eun Kyoung, Andrei Lankov, Lee Chin-cheol, Lee Jae-geun, Lee Keum-soon, Lee Kwang-baek, Lee Sang-ho, B. R. Myers, Park In-ho, Park Myoung-kyu, Kay Seok, and Yi Munyol.

As for those who helped me in the United States, I want to thank Robert

Carlin Mike Chinoy, Steven Chung, John Delury, Paul Fischer, Bon Fleming, Jim Frederick, Donald Gregg, Kei Hiruta, Joscelyn Jurich, Tom Kellogg, Suki Kim, Ellis Krauss, Lynn Lee, John Lie, Hyung-Gu Lynn, Tony Namkung, Steven Noerper, Evans Revere, Rollo Romig, Sonia Ryang, and Patricia Steinhoff. And thank you to those who asked me not to mention them.

NYU is a vast institution, but I have been fortunate to find support from several people in the administration and faculty. Throughout the university. I'd especially like to thank Dalton Conley, Henry Em, Dick Foley, Perri Klass, Michael Laver, Dawn Lawson, and Tom Looser.

I'd like to thank my friend and agent Chris Calhoun for his support, and Ileene Smith and her colleague John Knight at FSG for bringing this book to fruition.

My wife, Helen, and my son, Tyson, have been an essential part of this project from the very start. They've provided optimism when I've been down, and indulged my passion for the subject when it must have been excruciating to listen to me talk. I wouldn't have finished this without their love and support.

# INDEX

Page numbers in *italics* refer to illustrations.